LEICESTER POLYTECHNIC LIBRARY

Private Interest Government

Private Interest Government
Beyond Market and State

Edited by
Wolfgang Streeck
and Philippe C. Schmitter

SAGE Series in Neo-Corporatism
Series Editor: Philippe C. Schmitter
SAGE Publications · London · Beverly Hills · New Delhi

Copyright © 1985 by
Wolfgang Streeck and Philippe C. Schmitter

First published in 1985

All rights reserved. No part of this book may be
reproduced or utilized in any form or by any
means, electronic or mechanical, including
photocopying, recording, or by any information
storage and retrieval system, without permission
in writing from the Publishers.

SAGE Publications Ltd
28 Banner Street
London EC1Y 8QE

SAGE Publications Inc
275 South Beverly Drive
Beverly Hills, California 90212

SAGE Publications India Pvt Ltd
C-236 Defence Colony
New Delhi 110 024

British Library Cataloguing in Publication Data

Private interest government: beyond market and state. — (Sage
studies in neo-corporatism)
1. Industry and state 2. Capitalism
I. Streeck, Wolfgang II. Schmitter, Philippe C.
338.9   HD3611

**Library of Congress Catalog Card
Number 85-062171**

ISBN 0-8039-9722-1
ISBN 0-8039-9723-X Pbk

Printed in Great Britain by J.W. Arrowsmith Ltd, Bristol

Contents

Preface
Wolfgang Streeck and Philippe C. Schmitter   vii

1. Community, market, state — and associations?
   The prospective contribution of interest governance
   to social order
   Wolfgang Streeck and Philippe C. Schmitter   1

2. Advertising self-regulation: organization structures
   in Belgium, Canada, France and the United Kingdom
   J.J. Boddewyn   30

3. Setting accounting standards in the UK: the emergence
   of private accounting bodies and their role in the
   regulation of public accounting practice
   Hugh C. Willmott   44

4. Corporatism in the British voluntary sector
   David C. Wilson and Richard J. Butler   72

5. De-bureaucratization and private interest government:
   the British state and economic development policy
   Michael Hughes   87

6. The politics of the pharmaceutical price regulation scheme
   Jane A. Sargent   105

7. Quality regulation in the Dutch pharmaceutical
   industry: conditions for private regulation by
   business interest associations
   Bert de Vroom   128

8. Prerequisites, problem-solving capacity and limits
   of neo-corporatist regulation: a case study of
   private interest governance and economic performance
   in Austria
   Franz Traxler   150

9. Regulating milk markets: corporatist arrangements
   in the Swiss dairy industry
   Peter Farago   168

10. Private organizations as agents of public policy: the case of milk marketing in Britain
   Wyn Grant — 182

11. Varieties of collective self-regulation of business: the example of the Dutch dairy industry
   Frans van Waarden — 197

12. The governance of the American economy: the role of markets, clans, hierarchies, and associative behaviour
   J. Rogers Hollingsworth and Leon N. Lindberg — 221

Bibliography — 255

Index — 268

Notes on Contributors — 276

Preface

The present collection of papers results from an unusual encounter between two international groups of social scientists. One of them has formed around the international research project on 'The Organization of Business Interests' which the editors have been co-ordinating since 1980. The project covers ten Western industrialized countries: Austria, Canada, Italy, The Netherlands, Spain, Sweden, Switzerland, the United Kingdom, West Germany and — more recently — the United States. Its international co-ordination was at successive stages supported by the Stiftung Volkswagenwerk, the International Institute of Management, Berlin, and the European University Institute, Florence. Research in individual countries was carried out by independently financed, nationally-based working groups following a common research design. At the time of writing, most of the country studies have been completed, and the first systematic cross-national comparisons are in progress.

Originally, the Organization of Business Interests project was designed, more or less exclusively, as a comparative study of the organizational and inter-organizational structure of business interest associations in different economic sectors and national polities. This emphasis resulted in part from the project's close affinity to what has come to be called the 'corporatist paradigm'. Both the selection of the research subject as well as the guiding concepts of the research were inspired by the 'corporatist debate' of the 1970s. By now, the concept of 'corporatism' — or, for that matter, 'neo-corporatism' — has attracted so much attention among social scientists that there is no need to introduce it once more in detail. For present purposes, it suffices to say that 'corporatism' always referred to two different but interrelated dimensions of interest politics (a fact which at times has both confused and enriched the theoretical controversy): the way in which group interests in a society are organized and the way in which they are integrated into the policy process so as to make for better accommodation of interest conflicts. The 'Business Project' focused on the first, organizational structure perspective. Its main theme was, and is, whether and under what conditions business as a collective actor is able to organize itself into comprehensive, encompassing, hierarchically ordered, monopolistic, etc. organizations which are capable of exercising control over their members while at the same time representing their interests *vis-à-vis* other social categories and in the polity at large.

This is not to say, however, that the second dimension of

corporatism — its functional or policy aspect which is often associated with the concept of 'concertation' — went entirely unnoticed. In fact, during the course of the research, there was growing interest among project participants in exploring in more detail the policy implications of the organizational structures that were being studied. This aspect of the research soon came to be called, in the project jargon, 'the structure in action'. While it had been intended from the beginning to carry out a small number of policy case studies as a complement to the 'structural' approach — something that was made possible by a special grant from the Stiftung Volkswagenwerk — sooner or later most of the project's participants began to take an active interest in the social and political forms, functions, and dysfunctions of collective self-government, self-regulation, self-discipline, or self-control by interest groups in specific policy areas. This shift of attention was clearly reinforced by the political controversies emerging in the early 1980s about 'de-regulation' — narrowly, and perhaps too narrowly, defined in the public debate in terms of a reduced role for state interventionism in favour of an enhanced role for market allocation.

The gradual broadening of the focus of the Business Project coincided with a remarkable development in another social-scientific sub-community, that of organization theory and research. Organization theorists have always been interested in the wider societal context in which organizations operate. Indeed, there is a tradition for them to 'emigrate', usually at an advanced stage of their career, to more 'general' social theory. In the late 1970s and the early 1980s, however, and particularly so in Europe, there was quite a different kind of 'emigration' under way, and this was by no means limited to the older generation of scholars. In fact, it was rather among younger theorists and researchers that dissatisfaction with the perceived sterility of contingency theory led to increasing interest not just in the social environment of organizations — a concept which was seen as too abstract and general — but in their political role and status in relation to the domains of public policy and state activity. Indeed, one of the themes around which the growing discontent with traditional organization theory revolved was that it seemed to be essentially and systematically 'non-political'. This led to two related responses by the mid-1970s. One was that the internal politics and the political economy of organization and organizations began to attract much more attention — a tendency which inevitably led to a growing elective affinity between organization theory and the political study of neo-corporatism. Simultaneously, more and more students of organization began to apply the organizational perspective to policy areas and problems of public policy rather than just to organizations in looking, for example, at the labour market, research and development policy, industrial policy, environmental policy and other contemporary political issues.

These developments paved the way for the specific convergence of theoretical and empirical interests from which this book has originated. The participants in the Business Project were mainly political scientists and political sociologists who had found it useful to apply some of the concepts and research instruments of the 'structuralist' strand of organization theory to their field of work. At the same time, a large number of organization researchers and theorists, particularly well-represented among those who had in the early 1970s begun to meet under the auspices of the European Group for Organizational Studies (EGOS), became sufficiently interested in subjects that had been the exclusive patrimony of political scientists and economists. How profoundly this had affected the discipline became obvious when EGOS started to make preparations for its 1983 Colloquium in Florence, under the general title of 'Beyond Bureaucracy'. All three themes that were in the end chosen for Colloquium working groups were more or less remote from the traditional concerns of organization theorists. The first group had as its subject the 'New Social Movements'; the second, 'Who Defines Industrial Strategy?'; and the theme of the third was 'Private Organizations as Agents of Public Policy'. It was in particular this latter group which offered an opportunity to bring together students of organization interested in the 'corporatist paradigm', with political scientists and political sociologists trying to apply an organizational perspective to both the theory of interest associability and the analysis of public policy problems.

The chapters in this volume are the result of this encounter. The introductory chapter by the editors is a revised version of one of the three keynote addresses that were given at the EGOS Colloquium. It represents an attempt to integrate, within a more general social-theoretical framework, central concepts and problems from essentially three disciplinary backgrounds: political inquiry into interest associations, sociological theory of organization, and policy-oriented research on implementation and, more recently, regulation. The other chapters, with the exception of those by Hollingsworth/Lindberg and Sargent, were presented and discussed at the Colloquium working group on 'Private Organizations as Agents of Public Policy'. All of them are empirical studies that, in one way or another, marshall positive or, as the case may be, negative evidence for the themes and hypotheses raised in the first chapter. The chapters by Boddewyn, Willmott, Wilson and Butler, and Hughes were written in response to the formal Call for Papers for the EGOS

Colloquium. From the perspective of the editors, they represent serendipitous discoveries in the sense that there had been no contact with their authors prior to the Colloquium. The chapter by Sargent is an abbreviated version of a policy case study commissioned under the auspices of the Business Project, and the chapters by de Vroom, Traxler, Farago, Grant, van Waarden, and Hollingsworth and Lindberg are, so to speak, spin-offs from work on this same project. The common origin of these chapters is indicated, among other things, by the fact that four of them — Traxler, Farago, Grant and van Waarden — deal with the same economic sector, the dairy industry. These chapters in particular appear to offer rich material for future cross-national comparisons aimed at an improved understanding of the social and institutional conditions for the emergence and functioning of private interest government.

All of the chapters in this volume that were presented as papers at the EGOS Colloquium were considerably revised on the basis of the lively and stimulating discussions in the working group. Some had to be reduced in length because of space limitations, and readers may want to turn directly to the authors for the full versions. Originally, the editors intended to close the volume with another essay reassessing the potential and performance of private interest government in the light of the empirical material contained in the collection. This had to fall by the wayside not just for lack of space. As the papers in this volume clearly demonstrate, the issue under debate is a complex and thorny one, perhaps more so than was originally thought. Summing up the evidence will undoubtedly require a major intellectual effort which one would rather not undertake under the inevitable time constraints imposed by publication deadlines. Clearly, the subject will be around for some time, and the number of participants involved in the debate on 'the prospective contribution of private interest governance to social order' is likely to increase in the future. At the present stage, a volume such as this can be no more than an intermediary report from an exciting collective and interdisciplinary enterprise which may in the end lead up to some important theoretical and practical conclusions.

WS
PCS
Berlin and Florence, December 1984

1

Community, market, state — and associations? The prospective contribution of interest governance to social order

Wolfgang Streeck and Philippe C. Schmitter

Three models of social order — or four?
Ask a contemporary social scientist the question 'How is social order possible?' and she or he will likely answer — if at all — with a model. No one can possibly observe directly or comprehend totally how such an enormous multitude of independent actors with diverse motives can interact in so many different and changing ways, and yet somehow manage to produce (or better, reproduce) something approaching 'order'. Even to begin to grasp how something so incredibly complex works requires a feat of great intellectual pretension and radical analytical simplification. Previously, this could be attempted with organic metaphors or mechanistic analogies; today we feel compelled to offer more explicit and complex 'models of society' or 'social order'. These abstractions reduce the variety of actors to a few ideal types, assign to them a restricted menu of passions or interests, allow them to co-operate and conflict with each other according to certain patterns or rules, and postulate that all this interaction will result in something called an 'equilibrium' — a state in which the actual behaviour of persons and collectivities is both mutually adjusted and predictably variable. Moreover, such models usually pretend not merely to be empirically correct, but also to be normatively proper, i.e. they postulate that if societies were indeed ordered in the stipulated manner, beneficial results would ensue for most, if not all, of their members who would, therefore, accept such an arrangement as natural and legitimate.

Given the magnitude of the intellectual task involved, it is not surprising that there are few such general models available. Three of them seem to have virtually dominated philosophical speculation and social science thought. They tend to be identified by the central institution which embodies (and enforces) their respective and distinctive guiding principles: the *community*, the *market*, and the *state* (or the *bureaucracy*) — although it might be more accurate to label them according to the principles themselves: *spontaneous solidarity*, *dispersed competition* and *hierarchical control*. Clearly, however dominant any one of these three may have been at a given moment and/or for a given set of actors, almost everyone would concede that modern societies/polities/economies can only be analysed in terms of some mix of them. Today, social scientists in their separate disciplines seem to be groping toward concepts for identifying these multifaceted combinations and interactions. While some point out the conflicts and incompatibilities between the three ordering principles, others emphasize their mutual complementarities. Thus, communities may undermine markets by facilitating informal collusion and supporting clientelistic arrangements whereas market competition may decompose community bonds and erode common value orientations. But it is also true that communities encourage mutual confidence and good faith which are necessary for stable economic exchange, while markets provide communities with opportunities for 'extended reproduction'. Similarly, state intervention may distort markets, just as the outcome of free contracts and competition may contradict state policies. At the same time, markets require a legal framework and the authoritative enforcement of contracts, and even the most etatistic states seem to require markets as a supplementary mechanism of allocation. Finally, there are a number of ways in which communities may suffer disintegration as a result of state growth and government intervention, just as communitarian tribalism can frustrate the development of a stable nation-state. Nevertheless, a state without some kind of spontaneous solidarity among its citizens is no more than a bureaucratic or military conspiracy, and modern communities without a state would always be in danger of losing their identity and independence.

This chapter will not explore further the relationships, the linkages and the proper balance between community, market and state. While we agree that it is essentially in different mixes of institutions and in the interaction of different modes of co-ordination that the answer to the question of social order is to be found, we suggest that there exists, in advanced industrial/capitalist societies, a distinctive fourth institutional basis of order which is more than a transient and expedient amalgam of the three others and, hence, capable of making a lasting and autonomous contribution to rendering the behaviour of social actors reciprocally adjustive and predictable. If we labelled this additional source of social order after its embodying institution, we would call it 'the association' — in contrast to 'the community', 'the market' and 'the state'. If we were to identify it by its guiding principle of interaction and allocation, we would call it 'organizational concertation' — in contrast to 'spontaneous solidarity', 'dispersed competition' and 'hierarchical control'.

Why assign to associations such an elevated theoretical status equal to community, market and state? The background of our argument is the emergence in Western societies of systems of bargained interest accommodation and policy concertation in the 1960s and 1970s (Berger, 1981; Crouch and Pizzorno, 1978; Goldthorpe, 1985; Lehmbruch and Schmitter, 1982; Schmitter and Lehmbruch, 1979). On the basis of accumulated research, we are now convinced that the logic according to which these systems operate cannot be reduced to the respective logics of community, market and state, or explained by ad hoc mixes of these.[2] One purpose of this chapter is to explore this 'fourth' logic more systematically and to show in what sense it is different from the others. We believe that it is only through an explicit recognition of the specific contribution of associations and organized concertation to social order that we can arrive at a better understanding of today's 'bargained' economies and societies. We also believe that an improved understanding of the actual and potential role of associations may significantly increase the range of strategic alternatives for the solution of public policy problems. We are aware of the fact that, empirically, associations are of different importance in different countries, sectors and policy areas, but as the same applies no less to the three other ordering principles, we do not think that this, by itself, speaks against our argument.

The idea that associations may provide a distinctive basis for social order is, of course, not entirely new, and we will call upon some prominent witnesses further on. Nevertheless, by the mainstream of modern social and political thought, associations have always been regarded much more as a source of disorder. Usually the history of democratic/industrialized societies is presented as consisting of two main periods: the expansion of *markets* into pre-existing *communities* in the nineteenth century, and the expansion of the interventionist *state* into the new *market economy* in the twentieth century. Associations were in both periods regarded with suspicion: in the first one, they were seen as impediments to the development of a free market; in the second one, they were viewed as obstacles to the growth of the (democratic) state — a perception which was reinforced by the authoritarian corporatist experiences of some countries in the interwar years. In spite of historical evidence to the contrary and occasional theoretical dissent, this tendency to discuss associations mainly in terms of their actual or potential dysfunctions for the three other, more established, bases of order has continued to dominate the scene.

In part, this may be explained by the fact that community, market and state all have their specialized professional advocates within the social sciences, while associations typically had to put up with individual dissidents from a variety of disciplines. Thus, sociologists, following the forceful lead of Robert Michels, have been relentless in demonstrating that modern interest associations tend to become 'alienated' from the values of the communities they purport to represent. Similarly, economists — as far as we know, without exception — have treated associations as cartels, and associative action as a major cause of inefficient, suboptimal resource allocation. Finally, political scientists and public lawyers have, in their great majority, regarded associations as a threat to liberal democracy, parliamentary rule and state sovereignty, pointing to phenomena such as industrial action in defiance of legislation, 'colonization' of state regulatory agencies, or the undermining of parliamentary sovereignty by 'social pacts' negotiated between the government and strong interest groups.

Our point is not that these observations are entirely mistaken. What we are saying, however, is that they are one-sided. The fact that associative action may be dysfunctional for the three (other) institutional bases of social order — a fact which we by no means wish to contest — does by itself not rule out the possibility that it may also contribute to order. As we have seen, community, market and state have dysfunctions for each other as well. What is important is that they at the same time require one another for their respective functioning; and that there are specific problems of order that each of them is better equipped to resolve than the others. The same, we submit, can be said of associations.

A brief excursus on community, market and state

The dominant models of social order are so well known — even if their guiding principles are not often rendered explicit — that we can pass over them quickly. Each of them has its own postulated integrity, autonomy and tendency towards equilibrium and reproductivity. Each has distinctive properties and processes, and each corresponds to distinctive aspects of the human condition. In Table 1 we have laid out schematically twelve elements which might be said to comprise any comprehensive, if radically simplified, understanding of social order, and then suggested the different 'answers' which the three classical models have to offer. Because the market model has been used so extensively to explain the structure, not only of the competitive allocation of material goods and services according to consumer preferences in a capitalist economy, but also of the competitive interaction between political parties in pursuit of voter preferences in democratic elections, we have split this column into two parallel sub-routines for the economic and the political market.

At the core of the different assumptions about actors, conditions, means, resources, decision rules, lines of cleavage, types of goods and

TABLE 1: The properties of 'community', 'market' and 'state' social order

	Community	Market	State
1. Guiding PRINCIPLE of co-ordination and allocation	Spontaneous solidarity	Dispersed competition	Hierarchical control
2. Predominant, modal, collective ACTOR	Families	Firms/parties	Bureaucratic agencies
Other ACTORS	Clans, lineages, communes localities, sodalities	Entrepreneurs/politicians consumers and workers/voters	Subjects (taxpayers, law abiders, conscripts, etc.) civil servants, clients, claimants
3. Enabling CONDITIONS for actor entry and inclusion	Ascriptive member status	Ability to pay/eligibility to vote	Legal authorization, 'jurisdiction'
4. Principal MEDIUM OF EXCHANGE	Esteem	Money/votes	Coercion
5. Principal PRODUCT OF EXCHANGE	Compacts	Contracts/incumbencies	Authorative regulation
6. Predominant RESOURCE(S)	Respect, trust, inherited status	Economic/political entrepreneurship, calculative rationality	Legitimate control over the means of coercion, authoritative distribution of positions, administrative and legal expertise, procedural correctness
7. Principal MOTIVE(S) of superordinate actors	Esteem of followers	Profit/electoral victory	Career advancement, bureaucratic stability
Principal MOTIVE(S) of subordinate actors	Belonging to group, desire to share in common values	Material benefit/exercise of 'voice'	Fear of punishment
Common MOTIVE/CALCULUS	'Satisfying identity'	'Maximizing advantage' 'Minimum winning coalition'	'Minimizing risk', 'Maximizing predictability'
8. Principal DECISION RULE(S)	Common consent, unanimous agreement	Consumer/majority preference	Authoritative formal adjudication, imperative certification
9. Modal TYPE OF GOODS produced and distributed	Solidaristic goods	Private goods	Collective goods
10. Principal LINE OF CLEAVAGE	Natives vs. foreigners	Sellers vs. buyers/parties vs. voters Capital vs. labour/producers vs. consumers/importers vs. exporters/incumbents vs. opposition	Rulers vs. ruled Superiors vs. subordinates Overlaps of jurisdication Conflicts between levels of government, interstate rivalries, etc.
Other CLEAVAGES	Clan rivalries, generation gaps, conflicts over turf, inheritance claims, personal disputes	territorial, ethnic, religious, linguistic, ideological divisions, etc.	
11. Predominant NORMATIVE-LEGAL FOUNDATION	Customary practices	Property rights/constitutional guarantees	Formal administrative procedures
12. Principal PAY-OFF(S)	Mutual affection, collective identity	Material prosperity/citizen accountability	External security, equitable and predictable treatment, efficient mobilization of resources

normative–legal foundations lie the central and controversial questions of what motivates super and subordinate individuals to engage in social action and what makes them respect and accept the collective outcomes which ensue from their efforts at obtaining their specific satisfactions. In the ideal *community*, chiefs, notables, leaders, etc. desire the esteem of their followers, while the latter seek a sense of belonging to and participating in the group as such. Together they satisfy their mutual needs for a shared affective existence and a distinctive collective identity. In the perfect economic/electoral *market*, economic/political entrepreneurs seek to maximize their profits/electoral support in exchange for which their consumers/ voters are expected to be content with the material benefits arising from competition/the impact on public policy of electoral 'voice'. The arrangement is legitimated by greater than otherwise obtainable economic prosperity of consuming publics and political accountability of governing elites. Finally, in the ideal–typical *state* bureaucracy, allocational decisions are made through public policies that are enforced, with the ultimate backing of the state's monopoly on legitimate coercion, by civil servants striving to satisfy their dominant interest in career advancement and bureaucratic stability, on subjects which strive to avoid punishment; both do so by minimizing risks and maximizing predictability through following agreed-upon procedures and regulations. The system 'works' if it is successful in protecting all actors from domination by external actors and in affording equitable and predictable treatment to all.

None of these orders are intrinsically harmonious or conflict-free. All have embedded in them an axial line of cleavage which is a source of continual tension, as well as numerous other cleavages which may arise more episodically. Communities have the general problem of dealing with the relations between native members and 'foreigners' who have somehow gotten into their midst or who wish to do so; economic markets have to deal with the basic conflict of interest between sellers and buyers (of products as well as of factors of production, e.g. capital and labour), just as political markets must cope with the conflicting claims of parties and voters; states are divided by the perpetual dispute over the privileges which rulers arrogate to themselves and obligations which they impose on the ruled. Presumably, however, these lines of cleavage are at least containable, if not resolvable, as long as each order applies and respects its own decision rules. Communities may by common consent incorporate foreigners within their ranks — if properly socialized — or they may expel them if they behave improperly. Markets for goods and services, by responding through investment to the preferences of consumers, may provide for a Pareto-optimal allocation of resources which gives all participants the maximum possible satisfaction, or for sufficient pay-offs to induce workers and consumers to accept the property rights of capitalists and producers. In the electoral marketplace, majoritarian winners may gain the contingent consent of minoritarian losers by assuring them that future contests will be fairly conducted and could result in a reversal of fortune in office-holding and policy-making. States can effectively mitigate the tensions between rulers and ruled by following recognized procedures in establishing entitlements to positions and benefits and by adjudicating fairly and authoritatively all disputes that may arise.

The main threats to the integrity, persistence and legitimacy of these three orders are not likely to come from within but from without. The sharpest and most potentially destructive conflicts are generated when the principles, actors, media of exchange, resources, motives, decision rules, and lines of cleavage from the different 'orders' compete with each other for the allegiance of specific groups, for the control of scarce resources, for the incorporation of new issues, for the definition of rules regulating exchanges between them, and so forth. Politics with, or within, the respective orders is one thing; politics between them quite another matter.

Nor can such dramatic and uncertain conflicts be avoided. Under the conditions described generically as 'modernity', the three orders of community, market and state have come to depend upon each other and to be affected increasingly by each other's unresolved problems and externalities. Communities without states did exist in the past, but there are few left, just as it is hard to imagine even the most isolated or self-encapsulated community which does not draw some of its resources from commercialized economic exchanges. As innumerable analysts have pointed out, capitalist market relations would be self-destructive without the persistence of some degree of trust, deference, esteem and consent rooted in communitarian practices, and they could not even exist if public authority were not present to ensure the policing of contracts — not to mention the myriad of other facilities that the modern state places at the disposition of producers and consumers, capitalists and workers. Even the most ideal−typical bureaucratic state, whatever its linkage with an open, competitive party system and electoral marketplace, must depend upon the performance of its economy (and increasingly that of other economies) to generate the financial resources necessary for protecting its 'legitimate control over the means of coercion' and for remunerating those who occupy its positions of imperative co-ordination and authoritative allocation. No matter how 'formal−rational' a state's administrative apparatus may seem, the efficacy of its everyday decisions depends to a substantial extent on the voluntary compliance and socialized identification of its subjects who associate it with a particular nation, ethnic group, religion or 'community of fate'. Especially in moments of crisis which call for exceptional effort and sacrifice, states will find themselves drawing heavily on their 'community account', as well as upon their economic resources and plebiscitary support. So, to an increasing extent, modern societies find themselves enmeshed in the interstices between the three 'orders'. After lamenting 'the decline of community', attenticn was focused on 'the politicization and bureaucratic regulation of the economy'. More recently, we have become aware of the 'limites of state power' when confronted with market adjustments and communitarian identities. One way in which these 'enmeshed' societies have been coping with this situation is by generating an increasing variety and number of institutions of a new type for intermediating between the conflicting demands of these established orders. As part of this effort to control the externalities of the three classical orders, advanced industrialized societies have rediscovered and begun to revive a fourth, additional basis of order, associations and organizational concertation. This development has not been guided by some recognizable, over-arching principle or justified by an comprehensive ideology. It rather consists of disparate, uneven and pragmatic responses to particular dysfunctions and conflicts. The emerging pattern is, therefore, confused and tentative, and it is not at all clear whether it will in fact consolidate itself, or whether it will turn out to be no more than an ad hoc, temporary and contingent set of mixed responses to ephemeral crises and events. In the following, we will try to describe and analyse the underlying principles of this pattern as best we can discern them.

An associative model of social order

The *idea* of a distinctive associative order is not new to modern social and political thought. Hegel, for example, had an elaborate, if not particularly accessible, conception of how *Korporationen* emerged from civil society as its highest organized expression and laid the basis (the second *sittliche Wurzel*, alongside the family) for 'the universal, substantial state'. He was followed by Fichte, Schlegel, von Ketteler, von Vogelsang, La Tour du Pin, de Mun, von Gierke, Spann and others — all of whom advocated some form of corporative-organic social order as a response to the 'anomic' structure of the emerging market. With *Rerum Novarum* (1891) and *Quadragesimo Anno* (1931), this became an integral part of Roman Catholic doctrine. On a more secular note, Saint-Simon was promoting the idea of *associationnisme*, as early as the 1830s, as an alternative to capitalism. Even more important, perhaps, was Durkheim with his concept of

TABLE 2
The properties of an associative model of social order

1. Guiding PRINCIPLE of coordination and allocation	Inter- and intra-organizational concertation
2. Predominant, modal, COLLECTIVE ACTOR Other ACTORS	Functionally defined interest associations Members (firms, consortia, individuals, social groupings), interlocutors (state agencies, parties, movements)
3. Enabling CONDITIONS for actor entry and inclusion	Capacity for mutual disruption Attainment of monopoly status, willingness and capacity to compromise, symmetry of organizational capacity
4. Principal MEDIUM OF EXCHANGE	Mutual recognition of status and entitlements, compliance of members
5. Principal PRODUCT OF EXCHANGE	Pacts
6. Predominant RESOURCE(S)	Guaranteed access, compulsory contribution and membership, institutionalized forums of representation, centralization, comprehensive scope, jurisdiction and control over member behaviour, delegated tasks, inter-organizational trust
7. Principal MOTIVE(S) of superordinate actors	Expansion of organizational role, organizational development, career advancement
Principal MOTIVE(S) of subordinate actors Common MOTIVE/CALCULUS	Lessened uncertainty, proportional shares 'Satisficing (mini-maxing) interests'
8. Principal DECISION RULE(S)	Parity representation, proportional adjustment, concurrent consent
9. Modal TYPE OF GOODS produced and distributed	Categoric goods
10. Principal LINES OF CLEAVAGE	Members vs. associational leaders vs. (state) interlocutors
Other CLEAVAGES	Included vs. excluded (social movements) Well organized vs. less well organized Established vs. rival associations Over- vs. under-represented Majority vs. minority segments National vs. regional vs. local interests (parties, maverick enterprises, community representatives, local notables)
11. Predominant NORMATIVE-LEGAL FOUNDATION	*Pacta sunt servanda*, freedom of association
12. Principal PAY-OFF(S)	Less class exploitation; more symmetric distribution of benefits; greater predictability and stability of socio-economic outcomes (social peace)

professional corporations as the main institutional basis of 'organic solidarity' in modern societies characterized by a highly developed division of labour. Indirectly, these models inspired contemporary institutions such as *Mitbestimmung*, *Autogestion*, etc., and have prepared an ideological basis, often *via* social democracy, for the growing importance of associations and organizational concertation.

Of course, the *fact* of a distinctive associative order has always been on historical display, so to speak, in the experience of the late medieval cities of Italy, France, Catalonia, the Rhineland and Northern Europe whose social and political system was based on a guild structure. Hence, when John Maynard Keynes reflected on the consequences of 'The End of Laissez-Faire' and searched for a new order 'somewhere between the individual and the modern state', he naturally looked backward to those experiences and proposed 'a return, it may be said, towards medieval conceptions of separate autonomies'. Let us follow Lord Keynes's suggestion and see what such a neo-medieval order might look like if it were to emerge in the contemporary world.

At its core is a distinctive principle of interaction and allocation among a privileged set of actors. The key actors are (Table 2) organizations defined by their common purpose of defending and promoting functionally-defined interests, i.e. class, sectoral and professional associations. The central principle is that of concertation, or negotiation within and among a limited and fixed set of interest organizations that mutually recognize each other's status and entitlements and are capable of reaching and implementing relatively stable compromises (*pacts*) in the pursuit of their interests. A corporative–associative order is, therefore, based primarily on interaction within and between interdependent complex organizations. Secondary interactions involve the relations between these associations and their members (including non-members directly affected by the agreements reached) and their interlocutors—outside actors whose resources or support are necessary for the concerted compromise to take effect (often, state agencies), and/or whose interests are indirectly affected by the externalities generated by such agreements (e.g. political parties and social movements).

It is when we turn to 'enabling conditions' that the distinctiveness of corporative–associative action becomes most manifest, especially in contrast to pluralist theories of pressure politics. For some time, the predominant way of analysing associative collective action relied on an uneasy amalgam of community and market models. According to it, 'interest groups' sprung into existence 'naturally' and acted autonomously on the basis of a unity of shared norms and interest definitions — both communitarian assumptions. They attracted members on a voluntary basis, formed into multiple, overlapping units, entered into shifting 'parallelograms of group forces' according to the issue at hand, used whatever means tended to produce the best immediate results, and won influence roughly proportional to the intensity of their preferences and the magnitude of their resources, all characteristics of market-like relations. The neo-corporatist paradigm which emerged in European political science in the mid-1970s attacked these assumptions head-on. First, the assault was made largely on descriptive grounds, showing that the assumptions of pluralism did not fit recent empirical developments in the politics of advanced industrial/capitalist societies. Only later, after much conceptual speculation and empirical enquiry, did there emerge a growing conviction that the conditions that enable interest associations to enter and be included in certain influence games are so specific, and the rules of these games so distinctive, that they constitute a separate logic of collective action and social order.

In a first approximation, this logic can be characterized as follows. In a community order, actor preferences and choices are *interdependent* based on shared norms and jointly produced satisfaction. In a market order, the actions of competitors are supposed to be *independent* since no one singular action can have a determinant and predictable effect upon the eventual allocation of satisfactions. In a state order, the actors are *dependent* upon hierarchical co-ordination which makes their choices heteronomously determined and asymmetrically predictable according to the structure of legitimate authority and coercive capability. In a corporative–associative order, actors are *contingently* or *strategically interdependent* in the sense that actions of organized collectivities can have a predictable and determinant effect (positive or negative) on the satisfaction of other collectivities' interests, and this induces them to search for relatively stable pacts. To reach this stage, the contracting interest associations have to have attained some degree of symmetry in their respective resources, especially in their capability for representing the interests and controlling the behaviour of their members (and where necessary outside mavericks), and an effective monopoly in their status as intermediaries for a given class, sector or profession. As long as interest associations are fragmented into rival communities, organized into overlapping, competing markets for members and/or resources, completely dependent upon voluntary member support, or manipulated from above by state authority, the enabling conditions for corporative–associative order do not exist.

The medium or 'currency' of the associative model consists

predominantly of mutual recognition of status and entitlements. Of course, concerted groups may bring to bear on a given issue customary solidarities, monetary resources, bloc votes and even threats of coercion should the negotiative process break down, but, fundamentally, they are making demands on each other — informing each other about the magnitude and intensity of their preferences and their likely courses of action if agreement is not reached — and offering in return for the satisfaction of these interests to deliver the compliance of their members. This *scambio politico*, to use an expression which has gained considerable currency in Italy, obviously depends on whether the minimal, enabling conditions have been met, but its efficacy is greatly enhanced if, as the result of iterative efforts at concertation, the participating associations have acquired new resources. Many of those listed under this rubric in Table 2: guaranteed access, compulsory membership and/or contributions institutionalized forums of representation, centralized co-ordination, comprehensive scope, jurisdiction and control over member behaviour and delegated tasks of policy implementation, depend crucially on the response of one key interlocutor, namely the state, which must be willing *and able* to use its key resource: legitimate control over coercion and authoritative distribution of positions, to promote and/or protect such developments. The 'motivational structure' of corporative associability is, perhaps, not as distinctive as many of its other attributes, at least for superordinate actors. Like their *confrères* in state agencies, their motives should be largely determined by the imperatives of the formal organizational context within which they operate and from which they draw their resources. At the centre of these are desires for organizational development, expansion, stability and strategic autonomy (Schmitter and Streeck, 1981). Eventually, this should lead to a professionalization of management within interacting associations and a consequent decline in their dependence on voluntary support and elected leadership.

The motives of subordinate actors (i.e. members) are more difficult to discern since they are obviously being forced to give up what may often be opportunistically attractive possibilities for acting individually or through less formal groups, in exchange for accepting to be bound by compromised, longer-term and more general obligations negotiated for them by their respective class, sectoral or professional associations. This may be less of a problem for categories of interest where individual actors are very weak and dispersed (for example, farmers, workers, *petit bourgeois*), but could pose a serious challenge in those categories where 'going-it-alone' through market power or state influence is a promising alternative (for example, capitalists and some privileged professions). Presumably, what motivates a subordinate to conform to associationally negotiated pacts is lesser uncertainty about aggregate outcomes and higher assurance of receiving aporportionally more 'equitable' share of whatever is disputed. If one adds to these the probability that certain conditions of macro-societal performance (for example, in terms of inflation, unemployment and strike rates) will be superior in societies whose markets have been tamed by associative action, then we have an even greater reason for understanding member conformity. Basically what seems to happen is a shift in the rationality of social choice. In communities, the calculus rests on satisfying identity, in markets, economic or political, on maximizing advantage/building minimum winning coalitions, in states, on minimizing risk and maximizing predictability. What associations in a corporative order strive for is something more prosaic, but quite rational given the structural complexity and informational overload of modern society, namely *satisficing interests*. By deliberate mutual adjustment and repeated interaction, these comprehensive, monopolistically privileged actors avoid the temptation to exploit momentary advantages to the maximum and the pitfall of landing in the worst possible situation. In short, they avoid the prisoner's dilemma through inter-organizational trust backed by what we shall call below 'private interest government'. The price for this is a lengthy deliberation process and a series of second-best compromised solutions which are often difficult to justify on aesthetic or normative grounds.

Communities decide by unanimous consent, markets by consumer or majority preference, states by authoritative adjudication and imperative certification. Corporative associations decide by highly complicated *formulae* which start with parity representation (regardless of members or functional clout), work through a process of sequential proportional adjustments based either on 'splitting-the-difference' or 'package-dealing' arrangements, and then ratify the final pact by concurrent consent. All this takes time and is vulnerable to substantive and normative assaults coming from communitarian, market and state sources. Usually, deliberations are kept informal and secretive in an effort to insulate them as much as possible from outside pressures or from dissidents within the associational ranks. The 'weighting' of influences and the consequent calculation of proportional justice or equity involve often arbitrary standards and mysterious processes — nothing like the neat decision rules of solidaristic unanimity, consumer sovereignty, minimal winning majority or authoritative decree characteristic of the other orders. These elements of citizen unaccountability and proportional inequality — combined with the unavoidably compromised nature of the decisions made — can create a rather serious 'legitimacy deficit' and expose corporative–associative structures to normative challenges by proponents of the competing orders of community, market and state.³

The final structural element we need to discuss in this exploratory description of an ideal–typical associative social order is its lines of cleavage. Here, the principal configuration is tripolar rather than bipolar as in the three other orders. Associational leaders find themselves, *Janus-like*, in conflict with their members on one side and their (state) interlocutors on the other. While the behaviour and the interests of the members are strongly conditioned by competitive market forces, state officials are primarily concerned with upholding and advancing the hierarchical co-ordinative capacities and the bureaucratic jurisdiction of the state. This does not necessarily leave those in the middle with much room for manoeuvre. Either economic market forces may prove too strong to be contained by associational compromise; or electoral competition may bring to power parties representing 'true' citizen interests which will dismantle associational rule; or state officials, wary of excessive devolution of 'their' authority to associations they cannot fully control, will simply outlaw them (not to mention the fact that, in some countries, courts may declare associational pacts illegal under the constitution or anti-trust laws). It may only be a question of which of these gets sufficiently aroused first: opportunistic capitalists, radically mobilized workers, outraged voters, offended civil servants (or strict constructionist judges). In addition, the corporative–associative order also has a number of secondary cleavages to cope with, not the least of which is that between those interests which are organized into it and those, less organized or less functionally specifiable, which are excluded from it.

Public policy and the associative model of social order.
The concept of 'private interest government'

Although it is possible to construct a model of an associative order which possesses a certain internal logic, a rather complete set of attributes and a vague correspondence to possible solutions to some of the functional problems in the interstices between community, market and state in advanced industrial/capitalist societies, this by itself says nothing about its presence and relative importance in social and political reality. Making such an assumption would be to compound a rationalist with a functionalist fallacy. There is, however, a large and growing body of research on the contribution of associational structures to social order, often but by no means exclusively guided by theories of neo-corporatism (Schmitter 1974, 1977).⁴ The lively interest which this concept has stimulated among social scientists may in itself be an indication that the associative mode of social order has gained, or is gaining, in importance. Moreover, it seems that many of the present political controversies in Western industrialized countries can be described, and better understood, in terms of a search for a new balance, not just between community, market and state, but also between these three and a growing realm of associative action.

In the past four decades, the politics of many Western countries seem to have been bound up in a continuous oscillation between state interventionism on the one hand and market liberalism on the other. Today, after the 'long wave' of increasing state interventionism in the late 1960s and early 1970s, the limits and dysfunctions of public bureaucratic regulation have again become a major issue for both the political right and the political left. Catchwords such as 'deregulation', 'de- bureaucratization', '*Entstaatlichung*', '*Staatsentlastung*', etc. have come to figure prominently in political discourse. Most of the current proposals for retrenchment of the role of the state centre on a return to either the *market* or the *community* as sources of social order. While it is the reinstatement of the market which is at the core of the demands of the powerful neo-liberal movement, offloading the welfare state to voluntary community action is by no means incompatible with neo-liberal values. Greater reliance on 'community' is also advocated by a wide range of other groups — from adherents to the Catholic doctrine of 'subsidiarity', to various 'autonomous' and 'alternative' social movements which otherwise have little in common with neo-liberalism and that in particular would not want to ally themselves with its call for 'more market'.

However, for all its powerful influence on the public mind, the widely accepted antimony of *state vs. market/community* appears to be insufficiently complex for both analytical and practical purposes. For one thing, the swing of the pendulum of public policy seems to be different in different countries, with some countries being much less torn between the two extremes than others. As it happens, these countries tend to be those that have relatively strong institutions, often described as 'neo-corporatist', of assocational and interassociational conflict regulation — e.g. Austria, Norway, Sweden, Switzerland, West Germany. Institutions of this kind, in addition to mediating between the state and the market, seem to limit the extent to which the two can invade each other and enlarge their domain at each other's expense. In this way, they seem to inject an element of stability in their respective polities which makes them less subject to changing political fashions. Also, an elaborate intermediary associational structure seems to enlarge a country's repertoire of policy alternatives — its 'requisite variety' — and this may enable such countries to respond to new problems without having to undergo dramatic internal realignments.

From the viewpoint of public policy, neo-corporatism amounts to an attempt to assign to interest associations a distinct role between the state and 'civil society' (market and community) so as to put to public purposes the type of social order that associations can generate and embody. An an alternative to direct state intervention and regulation, the public use of private organized interests takes the form of the establishment, under state licence and assistance, of 'private interest governments' with devolved public responsibilities — of agencies of 'regulated self-regulation' of social groups with special interests which are made subservient to general interests by appropriately designed institutions. The specificity of this strategy lies, above all, in the kind of interests on which it is based, and in the way in which they are treated. This becomes clearer when one compares it to the two alternative strategies of *Staatsentlastung*. The neo-liberal restoration of the *market* aims essentially at the liberation of *individual self-interests* from bureaucratic-regulatory constraints. It is based on the assumption that individuals act most rationally if they are free to pursue their interests as they see fit, and that in the end, this will benefit everybody. Devolving state functions to the *community* amounts to an attempt to marshal *collective other-regarding interests* for social purposes; its underlying premise is that people hold solidaristic values and communitarian identities that, just as their self-interests, can contribute to social order directly and without state co-ordination. Both premises may or may not be correct. What they have in common is that they draw on widely accepted assumptions about the motivation and behaviour of *individuals*. By contrast, the corporative–associative delegation of public policy functions to private interest governments represents an attempt to utilize the *collective self-interest* of social *groups* to create and maintain a generally acceptable social order, and it is based on assumptions about the behaviour of *organizations* as transforming agents of individual interests. This makes the idea of responsible associative governance inevitably more abstract and remote from everyday experience than both the neo-liberal appeal to individual self-interest and the neo-communitarian appeal to group altruism, and here — in the intellectual complexity and, indeed, counterintuitiveness of the idea that organized special interests could be turned into promoters of the public interest — seems to lie one explanation for the lack of public attention which it has so far received.

'Private government' is a concept which has had some currency in the social sciences, and a short definitional excursus may be appropriate. Firstly, the term has been applied to an extremely wide range of phenomena, from sub-judicial legal dispute settlement to the Irish Republican Army (Macaulay, 1983), large business corporations (McConnell, 1966; Buxbaum, 1981) and/or their top management (Bauer and Cohen, 1983), the professions (Gilb, 1966), the universities (Lakoff and Rich, 1973), all kinds of para-state agencies, quangoes, community welfare organizations (Thompson, 1983), etc. In this chapter, we speak of 'private *interest* government' to emphasize that we are exclusively concerned with the self-'government' of *categories of social actors* defined by a *collective self-regarding interest*. Secondly, the concept of 'private government' is often associated with the notion of an illegitimate use of power (Lowi, 1979), for example when Bauer and Cohen (1983) define 'private governments' by their capacity to pre-empt and frustrate public (industrial) policy. For our part, we prefer to reserve the concept for arrangements under which an attempt is made to make associative, self-interested collective action contribute to the achievement of public policy objectives. In generic terms, this is the case where it is in the interest of an organized group to strive for a 'categoric good' which is partially compatible or identical with a 'collective good' for the society as a whole. We maintain that such compatibility or identity may be more frequent than is commonly believed.[5] We also maintain that the extent to which categoric and collective goods overlap depends, within limits, on two factors: on the way in which group interests are organized into associative structures and processes, and on a complex bargaining process between organized group interests and the state — i.e. between the governments of private and public interests.

The following sections of this paper will focus successively on three selected aspects of the phenomenon of private interest government — a genetic, a functional and a structural one. Since the *genesis* of private interest government can in an important sense be conceived of as a process of organizational change, the first part of the discussion will be devoted to the possible contribution of organization theory to an improved understanding of an associative social order. Secondly, in *functional* terms, we will briefly outline in what sense we think private interest government may contribute to the functioning and, hence, compensate for the deficiencies of community action, market competition, and state intervention. Finally, concerning the *structure* of private interest government, we want to point out the essential role played within it by elements of spontaneous solidarity, dispersed competition, and hierarchical control.

The organizational dynamics of private interest governments
Private governance in a corporative–associative order is based on

group self-interest. It is the result of an organizational dynamic by which pluralist interest representation is transformed into neo-corporatist interest intermediation. This dynamic can, we suggest, be analysed in three dimensions: the relationship between *organizations and interests*; the role of *public status* in the shaping of interest organizational structures and functions; and the influence of *political–organizational design*. In each of these dimensions, the phenomenon of private government poses difficult problems for organization theory and may demand a re-orientation of prevailing theoretical paradigms.

(1) Organizations and interests. Mainstream organizational theory has tended to treat interest associations with caution. It has preferred to deal with 'harder', more formalized, types of organizations coming from the more established orders of the market and the state: business firms, public agencies, hospitals, prisons, or military units — whose boundaries are easier to define, whose centres of decision-making are easier to locate, and whose performance is easier to assess against an imputed standard of instrumental rationality. Where interest associations have been studied, they have been conceptualized in the pluralist tradition as 'voluntary organizations' catering to, and exclusively dependent upon, the perceived interests of a given constituency. Tendencies toward organizational autonomy from members' interest perceptions have generally been regarded as a perversion of 'organizational democracy' and have been interpreted, very much in the Michelsian tradition, as oligarchic 'goal displacement' under the influence of a 'dominant coalition' of power-wielding functionaries.

The negligent treatment of interest associations in organization theory seems less than adequate when confronted with the empirical reality of interest group self-regulation. The important present and potential role of intermediary associations for public policy implementation (Mayntz, 1983) makes it costly for a discipline that has a significant contribution to make to implementation theory to pay so much more attention to public bureaucracies than, say, to business associations, especially in a time when, thanks not least to organization research, the deficiencies of state-bureaucratic regulation have become so obvious. The more public policies are, actually or potentially, administered through private-public interfaces and organizational networks, the smaller becomes the share of reality that is accessible to an organizational theory of implementation that contents itself with its traditional research subjects.

Another apparent shortcoming of organization theory is its

reluctance to adopt a political concept of interest. Private interest governments, or neo-corporatist intermediaries, in addition to being mechanisms of policy implementation (Lehmbruch, 1977), are also in a very specific sense *producers* of group interests. Contrary to their dominant image as 'voluntary organizations', they are much more than passive recipients of preferences put forward by their constituents and clients. Empirical observations of neo-corporatist practice, as well as theoretical reasoning, show that organized group interests are not given but emerge as a result of a multi-faceted interaction between social and organizational structure — whereby the substance of the collective interest depends at least as much on the way it is organized, as does the structure of the organization on the interest it is to represent. This interactive relationship is only partly described as one of organizational goal formation; at the same time, it is one of collective identity formation (Pizzorno, 1978) shaped and constrained by established, licensed, oligopolistic (or even monopolistic) organizational structures. Oligarchic staff interests are undoubtedly one of the factors that affect the outcome, but more important seem to be the properties of an association as such — its domain, structure, resources — which determine the institutional context within which group interests and identities are defined and continuously revised. This essentially political view of organizational structure goes beyond traditional concepts of organization centring on the notion of efficiency and effectiveness, just as it transcends objectivistic concepts of interest which postulate their existence outside and apart from their organization. The empirical phenomenon of private governance, just as it requires political science to take more seriously the notion of *organized* interests, seems to require organizational analysis to come to better terms with the *politics* of interests.

(2) *Organizations and public status.* The organizational transformation of 'pluralist' pressure groups into private interest governments is an essentially political process which is based on both bargaining between group interests and the state, and on the (potential or actual) use of state authority. A typical 'path' by which organized interests move into positions of incorporation and authority begins with disputes between interest groups and state agencies on the necessity and the terms of authoritive state intervention into group members' behaviour. In many such cases, the mere presence of a state powerful enough, and willing, to establish direct control adds to the already defined interests of organized collectivities an additional and distinctive interest in preventing that control. This additional interest can be so strong that groups may be prepared to compromise on their

substantive interests if this can save them from regulatory state interference. State agencies, on the other hand, are often prepared to accept 'voluntary' collective self-regulation as an alternative to authoritative state regulation even if this implies certain substantive concessions and a loss of (direct) control on their part. What the state loses in this respect, it can hope to recover through lower implementation costs and higher implementation effectiveness. Note that the substantive and procedural bargaining between the state and organized interests which may give rise to private interest governments would be impossible without the Damocles sword of threatened direct state intervention. Pluralist pressure politics that result in 'agency capture' remove this sword or make it ineffective, and it is here — in the strength and continuing relative autonomy of the state — that private interest government differs most strongly from what Lowi has called 'sponsored pluralism' (1979: 60).

As a result of their assumption of self-disciplinary responsibilities as private interest governments, interest associations can come to develop a special relationship to the state and the 'legal complex' that can be subsumed under the concept of 'political status' (Offe, 1981). This involves much more than just a right to be consulted by the government on legislation. Essentially, it means sharing in the state's authority to make and enforce binding decisions. The delegation of such authority to an association in the course of its transformation into a self-regulating agency will normally be reflected in its structure. But private interest governments may also rely on enforcement mechanisms with which they maintain no formal connection whatsoever — consider, for example, an ostensibly voluntary standardization agency whose norms are used by the courts in rulings on liability. The peculiar facilitative role of the state with respect to private interest government — which typically is highly indirect, subtle and unobtrusive (Streeck, 1979; Streeck et al., 1981) — does not seem to be adequately captured in terms of a relationship between the association and one environment among others. 'Public status' refers to the, direct or indirect, acquisition of a unique resource that no other environment but the state has to offer: the ability to rely on legitimate coercion. Organization theory tends to be 'state-free' in the sense that it does not systematically recognize this crucial distinction (Hughes, in this volume) — crucial, in any case, for understanding the emergence of a corporative–associative order. It appears that, in the same way as organization theory may have to incorporate a political and politicized concept of interest, the reality of modern interest organization confronts it with the need to involve itself more closely with theories of the state.

(3) Organizations and political–organizational design. The emergence of private governments out of pluralist interest representation can in part be reconstructed as the product of direct or indirect, often disintegrated and policy-specific, attempts by state agencies at 'political design' (Anderson, 1977). State political design of organized private interests is aimed at both the structure of associations as processors of group interests, and their public status; its objective is to keep private interest governments responsive to general or public interests. Withdrawal by the state from direct regulation in favour of 'procedurally' (Mayntz, 1983) regulated, self-interested self-regulation, if it is not to result in a loss of public accountability, requires the protection and/or creation of corporative-associative actors and policy-making arrangements which, by their inherent institutional dynamics, arrive at interest definitions which are, at least in part, compatible with the objectives of public policy — i.e. that produce, in the pursuit of 'categoric goods', 'public goods' for the society as a whole (cf. Teubner, 1978). Otherwise, what may have been intended as a devolution of public responsibility to private group interests will end up as a pluralist 'colonization' of the state by the very interests that were to be subjected to public discipline.

Organization theory and research have a crucial contribution to make to the political design of responsible interest intermediaries. For example, a central problem of public control over self-regulating groups is to make organized groups internalize as much as possible the costs of their self-interested behaviour for other interests. This can be achieved either by the facilitation of 'encompasssing organization' (Olson, 1965) which includes and, therefore, balances internally a wide variety of interests (intra-organizational concertation) or by setting up arrangements for bargaining between a spectrum of narrower organizations mandated with reaching mutual agreement (inter-organizational concertation). Political design, then, seems to have some degree of choice between intra- and inter-organizational relations as politically privileged structures for publicly responsible interest accommodation. What is, in a given case, the adequate mixture between the two? To what extent are they functionally equivalent? How much interest diversity can be brought together under the roof of one comprehensive organization? How do the results of intra-organizational interest negotiation differ from those of inter-organizational bargaining, given the same underlying group interests? And what are the limits, and the possible unintended side-effects, of the authoritative structuring of, and the award of public status to, organized interest groups in a democratic society? The political theory of neo-corporatism has only begun to address these questions; it will have to absorb much more thoroughly the lessons of organization theory if it is to advance in this difficult territory.

The functional advantages of private interest government

'Regulated self-regulation' by organized interests seems to be capable of solving a number of problems that have been found to be associated with either state intervention, market competition, or voluntary community action. As far as the *state* is concerned, two specific deficiencies stand out as of particular importance. One is the *limits of legal regulation*, especially in terms of the *implementation* of regulatory programmes (Luhmann, 1981; Teubner, 1983; Voigt, 1983; Willke, 1983). Private interest government provides for a peculiar amalgamation of policy formation on the one hand and policy implementation on the other, within one and the same organizational structure (Lehmbruch, 1977). The same associations that negotiate the terms of regulation of their members' behaviour, are charged as private governments with responsibility to enforce them. As a result, not only do considerations of enforceability enter directly into the process of policy formation (on the importance of this, see Mayntz, 1983), but the agents of implementation — the professional staff and the officials of the association — are closer to the target group (their members) than state bureaucracies, and they have more intimate knowledge of its situation and concerns. It is likely that this enables them to apply rules less formalistically and to take the specific conditions of individual cases better into account — which, in turn, tends to increase the acceptance of regulation by those affected by it (Streeck, 1983a).

Another problem with state hierarchic co-ordination is that it has always been associated with specific difficulties of *legitimation* (Offe, 1975). These are basically of two kinds: one involves winning the support and the co-operation of groups that are asked to sacrifice some of their interests in favour of general interests; the other involves presenting a constistent image of the societal role and the jurisdiction of legitimate state intervention as such — in other words, a normative definition of the boundaries of the modern state. Private interest government, by providing for a close institutionalized interface between public authorities and specific groups in civil society, can make a significant contribution to the solution of both kinds of problems. By turning behavioural regulation into a matter of the organized self-interest of affected groups, it leaves the legitimation of regulatory interference to group representatives who, instead of having to call upon general, society-wide values and obligations, can have recourse to more tangible group-specific norms and interest perceptions. The most well-known, but by no means the only, example is that of the leaders of a trade union and a business association who defend an industrial agreement as viable and equitable to their respective constituents, with each side using very different arguments and appealing to very different common values. This differentiation of legitimation by conflicting social interests relieves the public government of the need to develop a generally acceptable political formula to defend allocational decisions. It amounts to the utilization, for the purpose of creating public order, of divergent interest perceptions whose ideological integration is difficult or impossible.

Secondly, the notion of collective responsibility of interest organizations for controlling their members in the public interest can serve as a general principle demarcating the limits of direct state responsibility. Here, one comes close to traditional ideas of the state being only subsidiary to society — in the sense that it should content itself with assisting smaller collectivities to help themselves, and intervene directly only if such self-help has turned out to be impossible. Of course, Catholic social doctrine, with its underlying concept of 'natural law' and its organic, collectivistic image of society, cannot really provide a normative justification for today's secular corporative–associative structures and practices. The most effective legitimation for a withdrawal of the modern state from substantive regulation to the 'procedural' regulation of collective actors (Mayntz, 1983) is likely to come from accumulated negative experiences with *étatiste* modes of policy-making — i.e. is pragmatically and empirically rather than normatively based. One implication of this is that, however important the use of private associability for public policy purposes may be or become, it will consist of a series of pragmatic adjustments within the existing ('liberal', 'democratic', 'capitalist') system of government, not in the latter's wholesale replacement with an 'associative' or 'corporatist' system (Olsen, 1981).

Concerning *markets*, their obvious and often analysed problem is that the unregulated interaction of self-interested parties may fail to produce certain collective or categoric goods which are a necessary precondition for an effective functioning of the market ('market failure'). In such cases, the rational behaviour of market participants needs to be subjected to some form of authoritative control — exercised either by the state or by some other agent — to prevent it from becoming self-destructive. Furthermore, free competition may result in social cleavages and inequalities which in turn give rise to 'pluralist' collective action aimed at 'distorting' the market. 'Factionalism' of this kind is not easy to suppress in a democratic society; a state which would try to do so would have to be so autonomous that it would in effect cease to be democratic.[6] In this sense, economic liberalism and political democracy are indeed ultimately incompatible, as has been argued by observers from both the right (von Hayek, 1976−78) and the left (Goldthorpe, 1985). The neo-corporatist transformation of pluralist interest groups into publicly responsible self-regulating bodies can be seen, from this perspective, as an attempt not only to provide for the production of categoric/collective goods by other, and more effective, means than state regulation; it is also an attempt to impose discipline on the inevitable factions which arise in a democratic polity combined with a market economy, and, thereby, to make organized interest politics more compatible with the requirements of the market.

Finally, the Achilles heel of *community* action is that it lacks authoritative means to mobilize resources above and beyond what can be obtained on a voluntary basis. This is a problem which is particularly relevant the less normatively integrated communities are, and there is reason to believe that with increasing mobility of individuals and cultural identities, the sense of altruistic obligation — of 'other-regardingness' — has tended to become weaker in most social groups. In fact, this is precisely the rationale behind the modern transfer of traditional community welfare functions to a growing 'welfare state'. Moreover, communities can be parochial in that their values and accepted mutual obligations may be at odds with the values and requirements of society at large. The backing by public authority of strong intermediary organizations representing specific social groups may offer a way of increasing the latter's self-regulating capacity beyond the limits of voluntarism, and of guiding their collective behaviour in accordance with general rather than exclusively group-specific values and interests.

Interest associations which have been transformed into private interest governments compensate for a number of specific state, market and community failures. By relieving the three other orders of problems they are less well equipped to solve, they not only do not preempt them but in fact contribute to their respective functioning. A state that withdraws, in selected areas, from direct to procedural control does not become a weak state; in terms of the effectiveness of its policies, it may in fact gain in strength. Similarly, in order to be efficient mechanisms of allocation markets need to be protected from distortion by pluralist interest politics, and they require regulatory constraints on competitive behaviour as a precondition of stable, long-term exchange and competition (for example, in areas such as technical standardization or vocational training). Finally, communities in a society with a strong state and a free market can better preserve their cultural identities and bring them to bear on the political process if they are effectively organized so as to command more and other resources than those that modern communities can generate on their own.

Private interest government as a 'mixed mode' of policy-making
It is important to emphasize that the state is not absent in the associational mode of social order, and nor is the market or the community. Corporative–assocative order emerges in thoroughly 'mixed' polities. Typically, institutions of private interest governance are geared to selected sectors, industries and policy areas — with other collectivities and issues being directly governed by the state, left to the forces of the market, or taken care of by community action. Moreover, community, market and state constitute important limiting and facilitating conditions for and inside any given associative arrangement, and without them such arrangements could not exist and function. While we believe that the same can be said, respectively, for each of the four modes of order, we will in the following focus exclusively on private interest governments and their relationship to the three others.

State
Interest associations can usually govern the interests of their members only with some kind of state facilitation and authorization. At the very least, private interest government requires an *Ordungspolitik* of deliberate abstention from interference with the exercise of authority by powerful associations over their members. Where the state strictly upholds the right of individuals not to be organized and not to be subject to any coercion other than that exercised by the state itself, a corporative – associative order cannot exist. As a rule, however, mere abstention is not enough. The power of associations to govern does not normally arise spontaneously from the process of civil associability. To turn into private interest governments, associations need to be supplied with more and stronger authority than they can possibly mobilize by themselves on a voluntary basis. In fact, the limits to autonomous mobilization of authority, just as of other resources such as money, organizational stability and effective recognition, are an important reason why associations are often prepared to trade some of their members' interests against *public status* when it is offered to them by the state (Streeck, 1982). State facilitation of organizational development and the institutionalization of interest associations can take a wide variety of forms, and usually they are much less conspicuous than in a country such as Austria where there is compulsory organization of industry, commerce, agriculture and labour in their respective chambers.
    An active role of the state is necessary in yet another respect. One important mechanism by which private interest governments are kept responsive to wider societal needs is the threat by the state to intervene directly if the group fails to adjust the behaviour of its members to the

public interest. In this sense, the public use of private organized interests requires a strong rather than a weak state. It is true that an associative social order implies a devolution of state functions to interest intermediaries. But this has to be accompanied by a simultaneous acquisition by the state of a capacity to design, monitor, and keep in check the new self-regulating systems ('procedural control', Mayntz, 1983). Moreover, reliance on associative self-regulation in specific cases and at a given time must not undermine the state's general capacity to resort to direct regulation if it so decides; otherwise, an important source of strength for the state in bargaining with organized interests over their acceptance of obligations to the society as a whole disappears. It is only to the extent that the state — by a combination of procedural, instead of substantive, regulation with a credible threat of direct intervention — can hold private governments at least partially accountable to the public, that the associative–corporative mode of social order can become a legitimate alternative to communitarianism, *étatisme* and market liberalism.

Market
Private governments do not eliminate competition per se. In all Western countries, legal rules about 'restraint of trade' impose limits on associations interfering with the market. In principle at least, the subjects of private governments remain free to engage in contractual relations with each other and with members of other groups. Group self-regulation is concerned with the non-contractual preconditions, not with the substitution of private contracts. It is true that self-regulation, just as state regulation, often extends to the substantive content of private-law contracts; but it is also true, even in the labour market, that there always remains a significant area of discretion for individual contracting parties ('wage drift') that is protected from associative interference.

The market order continues to be present also in a political sense. The emergence of private interest government is closely related to the acquisition by formerly 'voluntary' interest associations of organizational privileges which protect them from competition for members and resources. The element of interest–political 'monopoly' which is inherent in all such arrangements must, however, be seen in perspective. Even associations with compulsory membership, such as continental Chambers of Commerce, depend to a significant extent on voluntary contributions and voluntary compliance by their members. Refusal to participate in associational bodies and to support associational policies remains a strong sanction in the hands of the membership. The authority of private interest governments to compel, even where it is strong, is never strong enough to exempt associations completely from the need to mobilize, on a voluntary basis and in competition with other institutions and collective actors, additional political resources and loyalities. For such mobilization to be possible, associational policies, for all their undoubted autonomy, must be attractive enough to the members to be competitive in the political market — a market that, while it may be highly oligopolistic, nevertheless remains a market.

Community
Private interest governments, however much facilitated and institutionalized by state authority, must be rooted in the values and interest perceptions of existing social collectivities. The (organized) collectivities that are to be drawn into public status cannot be arbitrarily created by state decree; they must have some kind of prior, independent existence and identity. This does not mean that they have to be intact communities. As their organizations acquire further 'external' means of control through their assumption of public status, their collective capacity to act and exercise internal discipline depends not only on normative integration. Similarly, the interest perceptions of collectivities that are potential subjects of group governance need not by themselves be clear and unambiguous enough to guide group collective action; in fact, they may become manifest only through authoritative (re)definition by professional, 'established' representatives with monopolistic status. Nevertheless, the leaders of private interest governments, in asking for the compliance of their constituents to concerted pacts, must be able to draw on some kind of shared norms and collective identity which they cannot create, and the members must recognize in the policies of their leaders some reflection of what they themselves regard as their interests. Moreover, the value systems supporting corporative–associative institutions must include some residual commitment to the society at large which goes beyond the boundaries of just one interest aggregate. Such commitments — for example, to professional norms of good performance or to a group's prestige and respect with other groups — can be, and are likely to be, reinforced by organizational efforts to build a collective identity; but where they are not even residually present, and where community values and identities are exclusively self-regarding and self-sufficient, corporative–associative arrangements become extremely tenuous and unstable.

Conclusion
Private interest government is not about to replace community, market and state. Even where a large share of public policy is made by and implemented through intermediary associations, these are always

to some important extent dependent on community values and cohesion, kept in check by economic and political market forces, and subject to hierarchical control, political design and the pressure of possible direct state intervention. Moreover, not all social groups and political issues lend themselves equally well to associational self-regulation, and there undoubtedly are social order problems in modern societies for which the three competing institutions offer more appropriate solutions. The idea of a comprehensive corporative–associative social or political 'system' is therefore fundamentally misleading. At the same time, there is growing evidence that there is a certain range of policy areas for which institutions of group self-regulation may produce more socially adjusted and normatively acceptable results than either communal self-help, free trade, or *étatisme*. Empirical research and theoretical reflection on the preconditions of successful utilization, in a 'mixed polity', of corporative associability for public policy purposes has only begun. Increased efforts in this direction may make it possible to employ more consciously an additional mode of ordering social relationships that compensates for important dysfunctions of community, market and state, and may thus significantly enrich the policy repertory of modern societies.

Notes

We thank Bill Coleman, Henry Jacek, Patrick Kenis and other participants in the 1983 EGOS Colloquium for their comments and criticism.

1. Actually, it would be more accurate to call it 'the corporative association' since it differs significantly from 'the voluntary association' which preceded it in social and political theory. If the concept 'corporation; had not already been appropriated for use to describe a particular type of market institution, we would have preferred to use that term. We were tempted to invent a new noun, 'the corporative', to replace 'the association', but declined to do so on the grounds that there were already too many neologisms in this kind of field and that it would, in any case, probably be confused with 'the corporation' or 'the co-operative'.

2. A similar argument has been put forward by Colin Crouch (1981), in a paper from which the present one has greatly profited.

3. For a more detailed discussion of the legitimation problems of a corporative–associative order, see Schmitter (1983).

4. Part of the relevant literature has been reviewed by Olsen (1981), under the label of 'integrated organizational participation in government'. Related concepts — of which each stands for another unending list of publications — are 'para-state government', 'public-private interface', 'quangoes', etc. It is impossible to cite all or most of the studies that have in one way or another influenced the ideas presented in this article. A list of recent *empirical* studies on interest associations as contributors to public policy and social order includes: Ackermann (1981) and other research reports from the *Forschungsprojekt Parastaatliche Verwaltung* at the *Eidgenossische Technische Hochschule*, especially nos. 5, 7, 9, 12 and 13; Boddewyn (1981a); Coleman and Jacek (1983); Grant (1983a); Jacobsson (1983); Ronge (1980); Streeck (1983b).

5. That it is *possible* is admitted even by such a formidable critic of 'distributional coalitions' as Mancur Olson: 'Occasionally there are ... situations in which the constituents of special-interest organizations seek to increase social efficiency because they would get a lion's share of the gain in output; this occurs when the special-interest organization provides a collective good to its members that increases their production efficiency and also when it gets the government to provide some public good that generates more income than costs, yet mainly benefits those in the special-interest group' (Olson 1982: 46).

6. This seems to be the central 'policy' problem in Mancur Olson's recent book, *The Rise and Decline of Nations*. While Olson demonstrates convincingly the allocational superiority of free competition, his sophisticated knowledge of interest politics prevents him from siding with economists like Milton Friedman in their call for a *laissez-faire* liberal state. Olson is well aware of the fact that a free market in order to remain free, requires continuous, vigorous state intervention. He even goes as far as to say that, 'the absence of government intervention (even if it were invariably desirable) may not be possible anyway, because of the lobbying of special-interest groups, unless we fly to the still greater evil of continuous instability' (1982: 178). But Olson stops still short of explaining what kind of interventionist policy he recommends to governments in relation to group interests, and how a state would have to look like in order to provide politically for 'freer trade and fewer impediments to the free movement of factors of production and of firms' (p. 141). Olson does not, at least not explicitly, argue in favour of state support and facilitation of 'comprehensive organization' which for him is no more than a second-best solution. Nor does he advocate the abolishment through government repression of the democratic freedom of association. But he does quote Thomas Jefferson's remark that 'the tree of liberty must be refreshed from time to time with the blood of patriots and tyrants' (p. 141) — the latter clearly being, in the context of Olson's argument, the 'private tyrants' that govern a society's 'distributional coalitions'.

2
Advertising self-regulation: organization structures in Belgium, Canada, France and the United Kingdom

J.J. Boddewyn

There is general agreement that advertising ought to be truthful, non-deceptive (straighforward), fair, wholesome, informative and the like even though the precise meaning of these terms as well as the composition of such a list of objectives remains controversial and evolves over time.

In any case, obtaining 'good' advertising behaviour requires that the following tasks be performed: 1. developing standards; 2. making them widely known and accepted; 3. advising advertisers about grey areas; 4. monitoring compliance with the norms; 5. handling complaints from consumers and competitors; and 6. sanctioning 'bad' behaviour in violation of the standards, including the publicizing of wrongdoings and wrongdoers (Boddewyn, 1985a).

Types of advertising controls
Such tasks can be performed through either *laissez-faire*, industry self-regulation or government regulation — or a mixture of the three. In fact, there is growing recognition that these approaches are complementary since none of them can, by itself, achieve full and effective control of advertising behaviour. Hence, a number of developed-nations' governments are increasingly encouraging and supporting self-discipline and self-regulation as a matter of public policy.

Pure self-regulation
This system refers to 'the control of business conduct and performance by business itself rather than by government or by market forces' (Pickering and Cousins, 1980: 17). In its pure form, the industry on its own assumes *full* responsibility for the six tasks outlined above. Control is exercised by one's peers so that 'outsiders' such as consumer representatives or government officials are kept out of the development, use and enforcement of an industry's code of practice or guidelines. This approach does not preclude informal consultations with outsiders but it excludes a *formal decision-making role* for them (Boddewyn, 1983b). In the case of advertising, coverage applies even to non-association members to the extent that media members agree to refuse advertisements found in violation of self-

regulatory codes — irrespective of whether such advertisements originate from members or non-members of the association.[1]

Alternatives to pure self-regulation
Under *laissez-faire*, the control of advertising behaviours is left both to individual firms and customers — not to associations or the government. Business' temptation to fool the clientele or abuse competitors is tempered by *self-discipline* based on current notions of fair business behaviour and on *self-interest* since advertisers fear both consumer retaliation and the threat of regulation — the same motives which are supposed to keep *industry* self-regulation on the straight path, but on a personal or company basis this time.[2]

Under *regulation*,[3] all or part of advertising behaviour is mandated and/or circumscribed by various government rules on the grounds that the public interest is best served through statutory controls because business cannot be trusted to self-discipline or self-regulate itself, and consumers and competitors lack the will or the means to countervail business power. Besides, the law can achieve universal reach and compulsion, compared to *laissez-faire* and to self-regulation where only 'members' and those who can be reached through these members (for example, the media in the case of advertising) do apply standards of good advertising behaviour.

This classification parallels the 'institutional bases of social order' discussed by Streeck and Schmitter in this volume. Regulation rests on 'hierarchical control' by the 'state'; *laissez-faire* is 'dispersed competition' through the 'market'; self-discipline reflects the 'spontaneous solidarity' of the 'community' to the extent that it draws on general notions of what constitutes 'good behaviour'; while pure self-regulation rests on the 'organizational concertation' of 'private interest government' although few advertising self-regulatory bodies draw the support of the state and achieve the control of their members to the extent assumed by their model.

Hybrid and emerging forms
This triple classification of achieving control of advertising behaviour through either *laissez-faire*, self-regulation or regulation should not suggest an 'either-or' situation.

First, the three systems coexist in various doses throughout most of the world where there are at least thirty-five fairly developed self-regulatory systems (Neelankavil and Stridsberg, 1979; Boddewyn, 1981a). Elsewhere, regulation or *laissez-faire* largely predominates in various states of development.

Second, governments (for example, in France and the United Kingdom) frequently encourage and support the existence of self-regulatory systems that *complement* the law because: (i) they relieve the administration and the courts of some burdensome, costly and/or complex tasks; (ii) they even apply statutory rules (for example, in Belgium and France where it is said that 'the first principle of ethical behaviour is respect of the law');[4] and (iii) they serve at times a 'pilot' role in testing and spreading new norms of behaviour which can be incorporated into law at a later stage.[5]

Third, 'pure' advertising self-regulation conducted only by industry members is giving way in many countries to the inclusion of 'outsiders' — whether consumer representatives (as in Canada and the Netherlands), public members (as in Brazil and the United States) or independents (as in Italy and the United Kingdom). While most of these outsiders are in a minority position, the British Advertising Standards Authority includes a two-thirds majority of them; and in Italy, the totality of the Guiri is made up of independents. In any case, even pure self-regulatory bodies (for example, in France) sometimes involve outsiders (including government representatives) as advisers or experts.[6] Consequently, public-opinion and public-policy representatives have acquired 'voice' and even 'loyalty' within some self-regulatory systems (Hirschman, 1970).

Fourth, further down the road are codes of practice negotiated or 'concerted' between self-regulatory and consumer associations and/or the government. Thus, the European Advertising Tripartite (of advertiser, agency and media associations) and COFACE (EEC Committee of Family Associations) are jointly developing guidelines for toy advertising as well as an enforcement system. In the United Kingdom, the Office of Fair Trading encourages and assists the development of voluntary codes of practice by trade associations, and had approved some twenty of them by 1980 (Pickering and Cousins, 1980: 3). In that country:

> Day-to-day implementation is the responsibility of the trade association but monitoring of the code takes place from time to time by the official negotiating body. Because such codes are negotiated with the industry, they are clear, unambiguous and practicable to implement. The official body can be very useful in publicizing new codes and ensuring their wide dissemination, and may subsidize or pay for appropriate educational literature (EAT, 1983: 14).

Fifth, such negotiated agreements can be sanctioned by government and become 'collective conventions' applying to an entire industry, including non-members of the association. This corporatist stage has not been reached in advertising, as far as is known, although there are elements of it in Brazil and the Philippines. The advertising industry, however, is generally opposed to it because a corporatist approach tends to 'freeze' codes and guidelines which cannot be changed without government approval, thereby reducing their crucial flexibility.

Sixth, codes such as the World Health Organizations' Code of Marketing of Breastmilk Substitutes (which bears on advertising) are *imposed* on business from the outside. They often lack clear instructions and procedures for the monitoring of advertising practices and the adjudication of complaints (EAT, 1983: 14–15). Commenting on such external codes, the European Advertising Tripartite remarked that:

> Industry should not be expected to enter into agreements against its own interests or better judgment. In such cases, national legislation fought through the democratic process may be the most effective means of establishing controversial controls (EAT, 1983: 15).

Seventh, the Swedish case (Boddewyn, 1985b) illustrates another development — namely, the inclusion of the self-regulatory system into the Consumer-Ombudsman apparatus to the extent that: (i) the norms applied have been largely borrowed from the International Chamber of Commerce's and the now defunct Swedish Council on Business Practice's Code, and (ii) business representatives sit as decision-makers on the National Board for Consumer Policies and the Market Court, together with other outsiders such as consumer representatives.

Tables 1, 2 and 3 briefly define these different types of advertising controls and their characteristics as well as outline the respective advantages and disadvantages of self-regulation and regulation.

In Table 1, one must observe the special role of the media in advertising self-regulation. All advertisements — except those reaching the public directly as in the case of direct-mail/direct-response advertising which usually has its own self-regulatory associations — have to use the media. This means that someone else plays a crucial role in screening and/or stopping an advertiser's messages on the basis of his own acceptance rules and/or his adherence to the advertisers' and advertising agencies' self-regulatory system — a feature which appears to be absent in other industries. Therefore, the 'Type B' systems in advertising self-regulation can assume both a 'horizontal' (limited to the advertisers and their agencies) and a 'vertical' (also encompassing the media) form.

Private government or agent of public policy
There is growing interest in the actual and potential functions of private intermediary organizations in and for public policy (Schmitter and Streeck, 1981; see also their introductory chapter in this volume). The underlying idea is that public-policy functions may be performed and the public interest safeguarded not just by the state but also by

TABLE 1
Types of advertising controls

Self-discipline	Norms are developed, used and enforced by the *firm* itself.
Type A	The norms apply only to members of the organization
Type B	The norms apply to everybody (for example, acceptance codes of broadcasting authorities, newspapers and magazines that are applied to advertisers using their services).
Pure self-regulation	Norms are developed, used and enforced by the *industry* itself ('one's peers').
Type A	The norms apply only to members of the association.
Type B	The norms apply to everybody, even to non-members.
Co-opted self-regulation	The industry, on its own volition, involves *non-industry* people (for example, consumer and government representatives, independent members of the public, experts) in the development, application and enforcement of norms. These 'outsiders' are 'internalized'.
Type A	The norms apply only to members of the association.
Type B	The norms apply to everybody, even to non-members.
Negotiated self-regulation	The industry voluntarily negotiates the development, use and enforcement of norms with some outside body (for example, a government department or a consumer association). In this case, 'outsiders' remain 'outside'.
Type A	The norms apply only to members of the association.
Type B	The norms apply to everybody, even to non-members.
Mandated self-regulation	An industry is ordered or designated by the government to develop, use and enforce norms — whether alone or in concertation with other bodies. This system is akin to 'corporatism'.
Type B	The norms apply to everybody since everybody has to be a member.
Pure regulation	The government monopolizes the development, application and enforcement of norms.
Type B	The norms apply to everybody since everybody comes under the law.

social groups such as business associations, trade unions, community-action groups and the like — provided they are properly institutionalized and supervised. Self-regulation by an industry such as advertising fits into this scheme.

Industry self-regulation certainly constitutes a form of private government to the extent that *peers rather than outsiders* formally control or at least dominate the establishment and enforcement of

TABLE 2
Aspects of advertising controls

	Pure laissez-faire	Pure self-regulation	Co-opted self-regulation	Negotiated self-regulation	Mandated self-regulation	Pure regulation
Consumer	Exit	Voice[a]	Voice and loyalty	Voice and loyalty	Voice	Voice
Business behaviour	Self-discipline (personal and corporate)	Voluntary adherence	Voluntary adherence	Voluntary adherence	Semi-voluntary adherence	Law-obedience
Types of formal rules	None for individuals but there may be company codes	Coluntary codes, guidelines, recommendations, etc.	Voluntary codes, guidelines, recommendations, etc.	Negotiated codes, guidelines, recommendations, etc.	Collective conventions (pacts)	Legislation, regulation, decrees, etc.
Reach of controls	All firms	Members of the association[b]	Members of the association[b]	Members of the association[b]	All members of the industry	All members of the industry

[a] 'Voice' takes the form of complaints by consumers, lobbying by consumerist organizations, etc.
[b] Non-members can also be reached in the case of advertising, if the media abide by the association's code and rulings, and refuse advertisements contravening the code as well as those criticized or condemned by the association.

TABLE 3
Respective strengths and weaknesses of advertising regulation and self-regulation

Advertising-control tasks		Regulation		Self-regulation
Advertising standards	+	Greater sensitivity and faster response to emerging public concerns	−	Greater lag in responding to emerging concerns
	−	Difficulty in elaborating standards in areas of taste, opinion and public decency	+	Greater ability to develop and amend standards in areas of taste, opinion and public decency
	−	Difficulty in amending standards		
Making standards widely known and accepted	+	Everybody is supposed to know the law	−	Difficulty in making the public aware of the industry's standards and consumer-redress mechanisms
	−	Compulsory nature of the law generates more hostility and evasion	+	Greater ability to make industry members respect both the letter and the spirit of voluntarily adhered to codes and guidelines
Advising advertisers about grey areas before they advertise	−	This service is usually not provided by government	+	This service is increasingly being promoted and provided by industry — sometimes for a fee
Monitoring compliance	+	Routinely done but often with limited and even relatively declining resources	+	Increasingly done by the industry although restricted by available financial resources
Handling complaints	+	Impartial treatment	−	Treatment may be perceived as partial
	+	Extensive capability to handle many complaints	−	Limited capability to handle many complaints
	−	Slower and more expensive	+	Faster and cheaper
	−	Cannot put the burden of proof on advertisers in criminal cases	+	Usually puts the burden of proof on the incriminated advertiser
Sanctioning bad behaviour, including the publicity of wrongdoings and wrongdoers	+	Can force compliance	−	Problem of the non-complier but the media will usually refuse to print or broadcast incriminated ads or commercials
	−	Generates hostility, foot-dragging, appeals, etc.	+	More likely to obtain adherence to decisions based on voluntarily accepted standards
	−	Limited publicity of judgments unless picked up by the press	+	Greater publicity of wrongdoings and — to a lesser extent — of wrongdoers

self-imposed and voluntarily accepted behaviour rules. Besides, it is being increasingly recognized as a tool of public policy.

For one thing, the limits of regulation (and of *laissez-faire*) are evident even if not static nor remediable to some extent (Thompson and Jones, 1982). Hence, there is always a need for *complementary forms of behaviour control*. Actually, courts in a number of countries use the International Code of Advertising Practice of the International Chamber of Commerce as well as national voluntary codes as expressions of fair commercial practice:

> The distinction and preference between rules of self-regulation and statutory regulation are too simplistic. There is a large category of rules of self-regulation which are applied by the courts as rules of law, and there are statutory rules which the self-regulation bodies use as professional recommendations. It is also a mistake to think that professional rules are less restrictive than laws: they affect the freedom of business quite as much, and sometimes more (ICC, 1978: 35).

Second, discussions of the control of economic systems have generally ignored or underplayed what might be called the 'meso' level between the 'micro' (the firm or consumer) and 'macro' (the government) levels. A good part of this ignorance can be ascribed to over-reactions against the corporations of the fascist state — not to mention the US National Recovery Administration of the 1930s and its proposed industry-wide cartels (Schmitter, 1974; Streeck and Schmitter in this volume).

The industry level has first-hand expertise about problems and possible solutions within its own domain. Such expertise is not complete nor impartial — but whose is? The industry's conception of the public interest is bound to be partial and limited — but whose is not, even through the government is more likely to provide a better forum for the expression, however imperfect, of the public interest. In advertising, self-regulatory codes and guidelines are constantly being improved and expanded on the basis of experience and public pressure while governments tend to under- or over-react with various lags to new issues. (The advertising industry also tends to react rather than proact in the face of new issues — see below.)

Third, public policy in most developed countries has already encouraged the development and use of associations for various purposes, including the elaboration and application of technical and ethical standards, although not unaware of the real and constant danger of anti-competitive behaviour on their part. The European Communities (1981), the European Parliament (1980), the Council of Europe (1972) and, to a lesser extent, the United Nations (1981–5) have done the same although they tend to prefer 'negotiated' codes.

The true challenges in this area lie in the development and supervision of self-regulation. Some nations already have effective systems but the latter are largely missing in less-developed countries (LDCs) at a time when the United Nations is urging the expansion of bureaucratic systems of consumer protection, which would include major consumerist inputs but relatively little industry participation (UN, 1981–5). Self-regulatory bodies from developed nations will need to assist their parallel development in LDCs, lest this crucial mechanism of behaviour control remains untapped.

Governments must not only encourage the development of self-regulatory bodies but also supervise their functioning lest they be either too weak or too strong, ineffective as far as consumer protection is concerned or anti-competitive. In particular, a system similar to the UK Office of Fair Trading would seem desirable. The latter is charged with the promotion and supervision of voluntary industry codes but has the reserve power to recommend legislation where the code approach has failed. (For similar comments about the need for strong state involvement, see Streeck and Schmitter, in this volume.)

Associational structures and public-policy functions
Studies of advertising self-regulatory system in Belgium, Canada, France, Sweden and the United Kingdom (see various entries under this author's name under References) reveal that three distinct groups are involved: (i) industry representatives (typically on a tripartite basis from advertisers, advertising agencies and the media); (ii) a permanent staff or secretariat, and (iii) various types of 'outsiders' (consumer representatives, government officials, independent members of the public, experts, etc.). Who dominates in what respects?

Insiders and outsiders
Typically, industry representatives insist on playing the key role in *code and guideline development*. Their major rationale is that self-regulation will be accepted by industry only to the extent that such norms are internally produced. Yet, the Belgian (JEP) and French (BVP) systems also implement external government regulations on the ground that respect of the law is the first principle of ethical behaviour. Still, these external norms are voluntarily accepted as part of self-regulation.

Having the industry develop its own norms works most obviously when limited to what may be called the traditional areas of advertising control — namely, false, misleading/deceptive and unfair advertising. However, the major thrust of the current criticisms addressed at advertising deals with such 'softer' issues as good taste, decency, privacy, sex-stereotyping and the representation of minorities in advertisements (Boddewyn, 1982; 1985c).

The advertising industry tends to react grudgingly and slowly to these emerging or growing concerns although it claims that it is better equipped than government to deal with such subjective matters which are difficult to handle through regulation. In other words, the industry 'can' handle such matters more flexibly than government but does not 'will' it until threatened by outside pressures and threats.

The Canadian experience is particularly revealing here as its self-regulatory bodies have had to set up separate unites to handle advertising to children, feminine-hygiene products and sex-stereotypes in advertising. These units include consumer representatives in a minority position, and their role in code development is still somewhat indirect. Still, the trend is unmistakable: *softer issues cannot be handled without outside participation* (Boddewyn, 1984b).

The French approach is to include outsiders only as *advisers* — mainly representatives of the relevant ministries and of the government-sponsored Institut National de la Consommation (Boddewyn, 1984a). However, it is only a matter of time before the softer issues such as 'the image of women in advertising' will force recourse to the more formal use of other types of outsiders — most likely independent experts such as psychologists, sociologists and moral philosophers.

The British Advertising Standards Authority claims that the two-third majority of 'independents' on the ASA Council can develop some sort of a jurisprudence about softer issues without having to develop formal norms about these matters with the help of specially appointed outsiders (Boddewyn, 1983a). In other words, *the independent members are the specialists about soft issues.*

The Belgian advertising self-regulatory agency has been unable to induce consumer representatives to participate in its activities (Boddewyn, 1983c) on account of strong ideological cleavages in the fragmented consumer movement, weak government support of self-regulation, and lukewarm efforts on the part of the association.

Internal staff
The permanent staff of self-regulatory bodies handles many routine functions such as prior advising of advertisers, monitoring of ads and commercials, sorting out the complaints received from consumers and competitors (many of them are irrelevant or duplicative), and preparing the cases that will require deliberation by a broader body in Belgium, Canada and the United Kingdom (in France, all decisions are made by the staff which includes, however, an independent chairman), and following up with the advertisers and the media the implementation of its recommendations to modify ads or suspend their publication as well as other sanctions.[7]

The composition of such a staff is crucial in this respect, as the British experience reveals:

In the sorting-out, analysis, and recommendation processes, the composition of the Secretariat plays a very important role. Were this staff to be made up of 'activist' or 'militant' people, it is likely that more cases would come up for decisions, and that the staff recommendations would be more stringent. Here again, one needs 'people sympathetic to advertising' since their job is to enforce a code which presupposes that advertisements can be legal, honest and truthful. As one respondent put it: 'What are wanted are people with perception and judgment who will not let their personal antipathies interfere with their work, or see the enforcement of the Code as an opportunity for an ego trip' (Boddewyn, 1983a: 86).

State involvement
The role of government is essential in prodding the development of self-regulation and in monitoring its performance. In Canada, France and the United Kingdom, the authorities encourage it and keep a watchful eye. The Canadian Consumer and Corporate Affairs Ministry has played a major role in pushing industry to establish new norms and procedures in such areas as advertising to children, comparison advertising, sex-stereotypes, feminine-hygiene products and the representation of minority culture in advertising.

French government representatives sit as advisers on the self-regulatory body's Technical Committees that develop new norms for particular industries; and the association remains in close contact with the relevant ministries to keep track of new regulatory proposals and influence their content — often offering self-regulation as a superior alternative (e.g., in the recent case of liquor advertising). As was mentioned before, the British Office of Fair Trading plays crucial promoter and watchdog roles.

In all these countries, the implicit threat is that regulation will be proposed and enacted if the industry does not police itself effectively. Hence, the government does not have to be 'inside' the self-regulatory structure in order to influence it — but it helps.

The Swedish system (Boddewyn, 1985b) is unusual in that the advent of the Consumer-Ombudsman system after 1970 let to the disbanding of the very effective self-regulatory Council on Business Practice, and the borrowing of most of its norms and the co-optation of some of its members in key decision-making bodies (essentially, the Market Court). Here, it is the structure of the bureaucracy that has been changed in order to accommodate the main elements of self-regulation rather than the latter trying to pre-empt or complement regulation.

Advertising media's special role
The media play a crucial role in advertising self-regulation. On the one hand, they are usually represented on self-regulatory bodies; on the

other, they play separate and additional 'screening' roles through their own acceptance rules for advertisements and commercials, and their voluntary compliance with the recommendations from self-regulatory bodies to suspend the publication of errant advertisements and commercials. (This is not true in the United States where the anti-trust laws largely preclude such co-operation perceived as anti-competitive, at least potentially.)

These roles of the media allow advertising self-regulation to be particularly successful in terms of compliance because the suspension of an advertisement or commercial is a more effective sanction than frequently non-enforceable fines imposed on members, membership exclusion and even negative publicity, which often do not deter marginal advertisers who do not care. (Post Office departments play a similar role in suspending the distribution of unacceptable direct mailings but this still leaves unaffected those advertisers that use handbills, window signs, etc. that do not satisfy regulatory or voluntary norms.)

Conclusion

These country studies as well as more general analyses point to: (i) the healthy growth of self-regulation in a number of developed countries; (ii) its growing acceptance as a useful complement to regulation; and (iii) the increasing interaction between industry, government and other stakeholders (e.g., consumers).

Consequently, discussions of regulatory reform need not be cast solely in terms of less or more governmental involvement, nor must 'non-market' control be limited to direct regulation by government (Gupta and Lad, 1983: 416). Instead, advertising self-regulation as a form of 'organizational concertation' often interacts effectively with 'the Community, the Market and the State'.

Governments (the 'state') are increasingly paying attention to it in the context of the current deregulation movement but mainly because the law cannot realistically hope or pretend to be effective in controlling all forms of advertising behaviour — a fast changing and complex field in any case. Yet, the law remains crucial as a threat and prod for self-regulation to perform better. The growing issues of taste, decency, sexism, privacy, 'vulnerable groups' (children, uneducated consumers in less developed countries, etc.), 'objectionable products' (liquor, tobacco, etc.) and the like reflect the influence of 'community' values on the agenda of advertising associations. Competitive pressures resulting in aggressive advertising occasionally testing the limits of voluntary norms reveal that the 'market' is alive and well.

Not all industries are amenable to effective self-regulation. As one

Quebec-Province consumer-protection officer put it: 'There has to be cohesion in the sector, it must be well organized, and there cannot be too many recalcitrants [non-compliers]. Besides, businessmen have to accept the primacy of the law (Boddewyn, 1984b).' The advertising industry has fared rather well in this context — largely because media co-operation helps to put teeth in the voluntary compliance system.

Besides, as was mentioned above, new important issues are beginning to define the agenda for advertising control, and they transcend the traditional concerns about false, misleading and unfair advertising. It is likely that their resolution will require new structures for self- regulation, including greater outside participation in it. As such, 'pure' self-regulation is an endangered species and is likely to keep evolving in order to cope with such issues.

The true challenges in this area lie in the governmental support and supervision of self-regulation. Some nations already have effective systems but the latter are largely missing in less-developed countries at a time when the United Nations is urging the expansion of bureaucratic systems of consumer protection, which would include major consumerist inputs but relatively little industry participation (UN, 1981—5). In many developed countries, the authorities encourage self-regulation, keep a watchful eye on it and have, of course, the reserve power to recommend legislation where the code approach has failed.

In these countries, the implicit threat is that regulation will be proposed and enacted if the industry does not police itself effectively. Hence, the government does not have to be 'inside' the self-regulatory structure in order to influence it; and it can enlist the real capabilities of advertising self-regulation to complement its own resources. As such, self-regulation truly becomes an agent of public policy besides remaining a private government; and it complements the community, market and state in achieving control of advertising behaviour.

Notes

This research was made possible by a grant from the City University of New York's PSC-CUNY Research Award Program. This chapter is based on three papers presented at the Fifth Annual Macromarketing Seminar (18—21 August 1983, University of Rhode Island), at the Sixth EGOS Colloquium on 'Beyond Bureaucracy' (3—5 November 1983, Florence, Italy), and at the European Marketing Academy (25—7 April 1984, Nijenrode, Netherlands).

    1. For a discussion of the pros and cons of industry self-regulation, see: Boddewyn (1985a), ECLG (1983), LaBarbera (1980), Pickering and Cousins (1980) and Thomson (1983). The introductory chapter by Streeck and Schmitter in this volume is, of course, most relevant in understanding the relationship between industry 'self-regulation' and 'private interest government' although the correspondence between the two concepts is not complete — as will be illustrated in this chapter.

    2. 'Self-regulation is a concept distinct from self-discipline. The latter describes the

individual's control, or attempts to control, his own actions; the former entails control by the individual's peers, subjection to whose judgment is central to the description of such systems as regulatory. Self-discipline's only sanction is the individual conscience. The most characteristic sanction of self-regulation is exclusion from participation in the activity regulated' (Thomson, 1983: 4).

3. 'Economic regulation may be defined as the imposition of rules by a government, backed by the use of penalties, that are intended specifically to modify the economic behavior of individuals and firms in the private sector. This definition distinguishes economic regulation as an instrument of public policy from others such as exhortation, direct expenditure, taxation, tax expenditures, and public ownership' (Thomson and Jones, 1982: 17).

4. The International Chamber of Commerce's International Code of Advertising Practice starts by saying that 'all advertising should be legal'.

5. The law can also be used by competitors and consumers (and sometimes their associations) who can sue advertisers or petition for cease-and-desist injunctions — at least in some countries. This paper focuses on consumer-protection issues rather than on the use of self-regulation to handle conflicts among competitors.

6. The references to various national advertising self-regulatory systems in this chapter are usually based on this author's country studies identified in the Bibliography (see, for example, Boddewyn, 1984c, on Brazil). Additional reports are being prepared on Germany, Italy, Japan, the Philippines and the United States.

7. Typical sanctions applied by self-regulatory bodies include denial of access to member media (mainly), publicizing the names of recalcitrant advertisers (occasionally), denunciation to the authorities (rarely), expulsion from the association (rarely), and suing to protect the intersts of the profession (rarely). Most of these sanctions can also be applied to non-members of the self-regulatory system.

3

Setting accounting standards in the UK: the emergence of private accounting bodies and their role in the regulation of public accounting practice*

Hugh C. Willmott

Introduction

The expertise of accountants plays a dominant and pervasive role in the regulation of modern industrial societies (Brown, 1905; Yamey, 1978). Their skills are deployed not only to quantify and audit the performance of all types of organizations but also to budget, cost and generally regulate the flow of stocks, cash and behaviour within them (Stacey, 1954; Hopwood, 1974). Accounting information is thus used to determine where funds are to be raised and allocated and also to control how these funds are managed.

In the context of developing capitalist economies, Johnson (1980: 356) has noted how modern accounting 'is the creature of corporate business'. It has served the modern corporation in three ways. First, it has been developed to improve internal company control, this being the realm of 'management accounting'. Second, following the development of the joint-stock company, accounting has been developed to regulate transfers of value, this being the province of 'financial accounting'. Finally, and more recently, it has been employed to construct projections of economic trends that serve as an aid to investment decision-making by large corporations and government departments. In short, Johnson has shown accounting to be a prominent and pervasive, yet routinely hidden, agency involved in the regulation of the reproduction of economic relations — not only in respect of the appropriation and realization of surplus value but also in connection with economic regulation by the state (cf. Burchell et al., 1980).

Given the centrality of accounting in the regulation of advanced industrial societies, a question arises as to how accounting practices

---

*I would like to acknowledge the helpful comments and suggestions received from the following in response to an earlier draft of this article: David Cooper, Colin Gilmore, Rob Gray, Tony Puxty, Wolfgang Streeck and David Tonkin. Responsibility for remaining muddles and errors is, of course, mine.

are, and should be, organized. In the British context, some basic requirements are legally mandated. But, traditionally, the standardization of practice has been generally left to the professional associations of accountants. It is these bodies that presently issue accounting standards, in addition to training, certifying and controlling the bearers of accounting practice. So, whereas elsewhere (e.g. France) policy on accounting standards is directly determined or substantially influenced by the state, in the UK standards of practice are ostensibly authorised and regulated by private organizations in the form of professional associations.

The object of this chapter is to consider some features of the role and organization of the major professional associations of accountants in relation to the setting of accounting standards. To this end, the chapter first explores the historical conditions that have supported the growth and strength of these professional bodies. It is shown how until recently the accountancy profession has succeeded in establishing and defending an extensive preserve of self-regulation and 'professional' discretion, despite the existence of the considerable tensions associated with its segmented organization. This historical introduction leads on to a consideration of recent efforts to close the ranks of the six major professional bodies in the face of mounting public criticism of the abuse of self-regulation in general, and the perceived inadequacy of accounting standards in particular. The organizational mechanism for setting accounting standards is then examined in some detail, with particular reference to the constitution and work of the Accounting Standards Committee. This is followed by a critical discussion of technical and political perspectives on the regulation of accounting practice. In conclusion, the issue of how the role and accountability of accountants in forming and enforcing public policy is addressed.

The historical and organizational background of self-regulation

With a minimum of statutory intervention and prescription, accounting standards in the UK are currently established and regulated by professional associations of accountants. To understand how this has come about it is necessary to examine the historical conditions that have favoured and continue to support the privilege and responsibility of self-regulation. Among the factors relevant to such an examination are the distinctive character of the UK legal system, the historical stimulus for self-regulation and the peculiarities of the British constitution, as reflected in the segmented organization of the profession.

The legal system and the stimulus for self-regulation

The significance of the British legal system is that is is based upon common law. Instead of consisting of a comprehensive and prescriptive set of statutes, it comprises only a basic framework that is filled in and revised on an ad hoc basis by judgements in the courts. As the Accounting Standards Committee (ASC) points out in *Setting Accounting Standards*, this situation contrasts directly to legal systems based upon Roman Law where 'mandatory accounting standards would be solely a matter for statute law (supplemented by) a widespread network of commercial courts which can readily produce interpretations or fill small gaps' (ASC, 1981: 13). For, in the UK, the Company Acts indicate only in very general terms how accounts should be prepared and presented, their emphasis being upon the (ill-defined) need for a 'true and fair view'. As the ASC comments, *'this leaves a great deal of detail to be filled by ... the work of regulatory bodies outside the statute law, such as the ASC* (ibid,: 13, emphasis added).

Historically, accounting in the UK has been continuously troubled by difficulties associated with the setting and enforcement of standards of practice (Pollard, 1965; Lee, 1975; Jones, 1981). The origins of the contemporary problem can be traced to the mid-nineteenth century when an increase in demand for accounting labour, accelerated by business failures and especially by the advent of the Companies Act of 1862, invited the entry of a host of incompetent and unscrupulous persons into this lucrative labour market. The outcome was a series of scandals in the 1850s–1870s which brought accountancy into considerable disrepute. In response to this crisis of credibility, 'respectable' accountants developed professional associations to differentiate their competence and market value from those whose activities posed a threat to their reputation for probity. To this end, in 1870, the Institute of Accountants in London was formed, an association which was eventually to become the largest and most influential of the professional bodies — the Institute of Chartered Accountants in England and Wales (ICAEW). Reflecting a concern to differentiate its membership from the unreputable and incompetent, the stated objectives of the founding Institute were 'to elevate the attainments and professional status of accountants in London, to promote their efficiency and usefulness, and to give expression upon all questions incident to their profession' (Hopkins, 1980: 3). This brings us to a consideration of the establishment of the professional accountancy bodies which, in the UK context, play a central role in regulating accounting standards and practice.

The establishment and segmentation of professional associations

Professional accountancy bodies are established in one of two ways. The first, less prestigious method is by incorporation through the Companies Acts. This involves making an application to the Board of Trade. If, as in the case of professional associations, no profit is to be made, a licence to omit the word 'Limited' can be obtained. As Millerson (1964: 94) observes, this method is 'cheapest and easiest' and 'ensures a minimum of interference from outside, plus a maximum level of legal protection'. The more prestigious method of obtaining official recognition is by petitioning the Queen in Council, through the Privy Council, for a royal charter.[1] Charters have become symbols or badges of honour that allegedly signify exceptional virtues and trustworthiness in the provision of specialist expertise.

At the time of its formation (1870), the English Institute's initial attempt to obtain a royal charter was unsuccessful. However, rather than seek incorporation through the Companies Act, its founders preferred to bide their time. Their moment came ten years later when, after a protracted squabble with the rival Society of Incorporated Accountants (SIA) over the state registration of accountants, it was unexpectedly suggested that an application for a royal charter would be more favourably received. The by-laws of the charter eventually sanctioned by the Privy Council in 1882 placed great emphasis upon raising and maintaining technical and ethical standards. With the exception of founder members and practising accountants with at least ten years experience, entrance into the elite club of chartered accountants was by examination only. Combined with the expense of being articled to an existing member for no less than five years, with each member being allowed to article two clerks at most, membership was highly restricted.

In the absence of any state registration of accountants (see note 3), numerous bodies representing accountants sprang up in the period between 1880 and the Second World War (Willmott, 1983). Although a series of mergers substantially reduced their number, there still existed seven major bodies in 1957 when circumstances conspired to create the conditions conducive to a self-interested merger between the two largest bodies — the English Institute and the Society. Following its absorption of the Society, the English Institute has towered above the other bodies in terms of membership and resources as well as prestige.[2] Since the merger, the English Institute has been much better placed to fulfil its traditional claim to speak for the profession as a whole. However, for a variety of reasons — including the robust independence and speedy growth of the other five major bodies and the increasing heterogeneity of its own membership — difficulties have been encountered in the attempts of the English Institute to act as the voice of its sister bodies.[3] This difficulty was vividly illustrated in 1968 when the Council of the Institute initiated a proposal to integrate the six major bodies. As on previous occasions, when unification had been recommended, those in favour of such a move contended that it would put the profession 'in a position to speak with a unified voice on matters of professional, national and international importance' (*The Accountant*, 17 July 1968). But this proposal was criticized by those who wished to maintain a distinction between accountants working in public practice and those employed in industry.[4] As a correspondent to *Accountancy* put the case against integration:

> It is a pity that the Council of the Institute let its eyes wander from the original objects in the Charter. The words 'Chartered Accountant' now only denote a qualification and not a profession ... I know of stockbrokers who can boast of being Chartered Accountants — what is their profession? They might become turf accountants and still describe themselves as Chartered (*Accountancy*, March 1968).

The counter-argument was that concerns with status were short-sighted and that every member of the profession had a duty to act responsibly in fulfilling his (or her) public role. Failure to do so, it was suggested, would needlessly increase the risk of government intervention to regulate the profession. This argument was put forcefully by another correspondent to *Accountancy*:

> The accountancy profession is lucky, as it has so far escaped the control of Parliament and is responsible to itself for how it orders its affairs.... I believe that the Government would have a duty [to 'step in to sort the profession out'] if ever the profession was failing badly to fulfil its public role.

In the event, the integration proposal failed. This was damaging not only to the public image of the profession but also to relations between the six major bodies. On the face of it, the profession appeared divided against itself and unable to speak with one voice.

Setting accounting standards
Before 1970, a variety of accounting conventions and practices were recognized, and it was left to the 'expert' judgement of the accountant to determine which convention to apply. Speaking to a summer school of the Institute of Chartered Accountants of Scotland in 1970, Morrison summarized the position as it existed then:

There are at present a great many permissible accounting conventions which the accountant can choose from; *nothing in the logic of the discipline itself prescribes which one he shall choose.* And the area of the permissible is itself continually changing. The object is simply to present a picture of the facts; the means are a set of conventions using both figures and (may we not forget) words. The restraints on what is said are therefore empirical and subjective, not logical or demonstrative (Quoted by Slimmings, 1979: 14; emphasis added).

Pressures to regulate the profession were further increased by a series of spectacular and highly embarrassing instances of accounting 'failure',incompetence and misconduct which occurred during the late 1960s and 1970s (Stamp and Marley, 1970; Lowe and Tinker, 1977). Amongst the more notorious were Rolls Razor (John Bloom), the AEI–GEC take-over battle, the Pergamon/Leasco affair (Robert Maxwell), the British Bangladesh Trust scandal (John Stonehouse) and the collapse of Court Line. Apart from the undesirable media exposure given to such instances of accounting, these cases provided an impetus for a strengthening and a more ready application of the Department of Trade's powers to conduct an independent inspection of company accounts.[5] During this period, reports of the Department not only exposed malpractice in specific companies but, more seriously for the public standing of the profession, made a series of critical observations upon the adequacy of accounting standards.

During the 1960s concern about accounting and auditing standards had been expressed within professional circles and in the pages of the academic journals. But matters came to a head in September of 1969 when Edward Stamp, a qualified accountant and influential academic, published an article in *The Times* (11 September 1969) in which he commented on the Pergamon affair, suggesting that the profession was rapidly approaching a crisis of credibility and argued the case for the development of a new approach to the development of accounting standards. This provoked a response (22 September 1969) from the then President of the English Institute (ICAEW) to which Stamp replied (26 September 1969)[6] Thus, an issue of public policy and accountability that had lain dormant and largely concealed from the public eye for many years had at last been brought into the open.

With the response drawn by Stamp from the President of the English Institute, it became evident that the Institute intended to initiate reforms in the construction and regulation of accounting standards. Its initiative was formally announced with the publication, in late 1969, of its *Statement of Intent on Accounting Standards in the 1970s*. In summary, its objectives were:

1. To narrow the areas of difference and variety in accounting practice.
2. To disclose the accounting bases adopted when items in accounts depend substantially on judgements of values.
3. To disclose all departures from definitive standards.
4. To provide an opportunity for 'appropriate bodies' to express their view on draft proposals for new standards.
5. To suggest improvements in accounting standards established by legislation (e.g. Companies Acts).

Almost immediately, in January 1970, the Council of the Institute created an Accounting Standards Steering Committee (ASSC) to fulfil the objectives outlined in the statement of intent. The Committee was composed of fifteen people, but only *one* place was to be reserved for nominees of the Scottish and Irish Institutes. Moreover, ultimate approval of proposed standards was to be given by the Council of the English Institute *alone*. As the then President of the Scottish Institute later reflected, this put the ICAS in an impossible position (Slimmings, 1979). Either the Scottish Institute could participate in the ASSC but have no influence, or it could refuse to participate and tacitly accept the standards drawn up by the English Institute. Or, finally, it could disagree, and thereby provide more ammunition for the critics of the profession.

But, at the same time, it was acknowledged that the profession had to respond positively to the criticisms being levelled against it. Within the Scottish Institute, these criticisms were perceived to follow from its lack of success in educating the public about the role of judgement in the preparation of accounts. Recognizing that these shortcomings required attention and correction, the Scottish Institute sought to negotiate a change in the constitution of the ASSC which would increase its representation, make the approval of standards subject to the agreement of the councils of the Scottish and Irish associations and, finally, make it a joint committee. Of these three proposals agreement was reached on the first two only. Nonetheless, in 1971 the ICAS as well as the ACA and the ICMA joined the ASSC. Five years later, CIPFA were also represented when the ASSC was reconstituted as a joint committee of the CCAB, an umbrella organization of the major accounting bodies which was formed in 1973.

The organization and development of the accounting standards committee

The constitution and procedures of the ASC

In February 1976, the ASC was composed of twenty-three members appointed by the six major accountancy bodies. Distribution of the nominations were as follows:

ICAEW	12
ICAS	3
ICAI	2
ACA	2
ICMA	2
CIPFA	2
	23

The contribution of the ASC, drawn up by its members under the auspices of the CCAB, requires that those appointed to it are '*to be guided by the need to act in the general interest of the community and the accountancy profession as a whole*' (ICAEW, 1979: 15, emphasis added). To enable it to fulfil this objective, the ASC has created a group to advise it on its work. This Consultative Group is drawn from finance, commerce, industry and government.

To perform the tasks outlined in the *Statement of Intent on Accounting Standards* (see above), the ASC has evolved a process consisting of the following stages:[7]

1. *Research*. Studies of the problem area are commissioned by the research committee of one of the six CCAB bodies.

2. *Preliminary drafting*. A sub-committee of the ASC prepares a draft of the proposed standards.

3. *Early consultation*. The preliminary drafts are circulated for discussion with the technical committees of the CCAB bodies. Discussions may also take place with bodies 'likely to be significantly affected' by the proposals.

4. *Publication of exposure draft* (ED). These are mailed to major organizations and companies and are published in the leading accountancy journals. Comments are invited during a six-month exposure period.

5. *Comments*. ASC members evaluate comments.

6. *Later consultation*. Meetings are held with bodies whose comments are not accommodated in the redrafting of an ED.

7. *Draft for CCAB councils*. Final draft is sent to councils of CCAB bodies for their approval.

8. *Publications.* A statement of Standard Accounting Practice (SSAP) is issued accompanied by a technical release that explains the background, the amendments to the ED and reasons for substantial comments not being reflected in amendments.

Once an SSAP has been approved by CCAB members' Councils, their members are obliged to adhere to its requirements.[8] Standards are *formally* enforced by the disciplinary procedures developed within each of the major bodies. Beyond this, the only penalty for enterprises that breach the standards is its revelation in the audit report.

The review of the standards setting process

Following criticism of the organization and activity of the ASC which had been mounting in the mid-1970s, the ASC established a Review Group in January 1978 to review the process of standard setting. The report of this Group was published in September 1978 as a discussion document on which all interested parties were invited to comment. In this report, the Review Group summarize three of the major criticisms that had been made of the ASC.

> Some accuse the ASC of failing to react properly to public and professional opinion; others, of lacking the courage of its own convictions by giving in too easily to pressure from these quarters — for instance, some say that the about-turn on deferred tax was a weak change of mind; others that it was a proper recognition of the arguments.
>
> Some believe that standards should seek uniformity; others, that they should be more flexible and specify alternatives.
>
> The ASC has been said to lack consistency because it has failed to develop an agreed conceptual framework from which to build a logical series of SSAPs (ICAEW, 1979: 26–27).

In response to these criticisms, the main general recommendations contained in the ASC's *Setting Accounting Standards: A Consultative Document* were, first, that it should continue to strive 'to make financial statements reasonably comparable one with another'; second, that SSAPs should continue to be used as 'definitive principles' and not as a benchmark for measuring deviations; third, that departures from SSAPs should be allowed only in cases where to follow them would distort 'a true and fair view'. In addition, the report recommended that the Stock Exchange or the Council for the Securities Industry should take a more active role in the enforcement of standards. It also suggested that there should be an extension of consultative procedures in the standard setting process but that the existing organizational structure of the ASC be retained.

The consultative document of the ASC attracted 132 written

submissions, running to nearly 700 pages (ASC, 1979), in addition to reactions received at numerous informal meetings and three formal public hearings. Later, specific reference is to be made to the contents of these submissions. For the moment, attention will be focused upon the report and recommendations made by the ASC following receipt of comments upon its consultative document. These are presented in *Setting Accounting Standards*, published in 1981.

In the preface to *Setting Accounting Standards*, the ASC offers its own account of the Committee's existence and explanation of why a Review of the standard setting process was thought necessary:

> In late 1969 and early 1970, the principal accountancy bodies *took upon themselves* the public duty of setting mandatory accounting standards (ASC, 1981; 7).

This move is said to have 'received tacit public acceptance'. However, over the years.

> It became evident that public consultation and debate was required about how, and by whom, standards should be set. And on the basis of that consultation and debate, standards setting could then proceed with overt public acceptance (ibid).

The consultation and debate with 'the public' referred to here is the response invited to the ASC's consultative document. It is worth recording that in the case of the written comments, at least, these were mainly received from accountants:

Companies	22
Practising firms of accountants	23
Representative bodies of accountants	31
Other representative bodies	22
Individuals (mainly accounting academics)	34
	132

In *Setting Accounting Standards*, the major concessions made to the critics of the ASC were, firstly, that it should reserve four or five seats (in addition to the existing membership of 23) for 'suitable people' who were not members of the accountancy bodies; and, secondly, that the enforcement of standards be strengthened by establishing a joint panel, with the CSI and Stock Exchange, to review non-compliance with accounting standards by listed companies. The reasons given for preserving the present role and constitution of the ASC, subject to minor changes, were:

1. Since setting standards involves a high degree of professional skill, it is impracticable to separate the standards body from the accountancy bodies.

2. Without statutory or quasi-statutory authority, the body responsible for setting standards requires the power and authority of the CCAB to be independent and effective.

3. Members of the CCAB who deviate from the standards can be disciplined by their bodies only when these standards are issued by their respective Councils.

Having outlined the organization and operation of the ASC, the process of setting accounting standards will now be examined from three different perspectives.

Perspectives on the regulation of accounting practice
Commentary upon the process of setting accounting standards has been informed by two contrasting orientations. One school of thought has argued that accounting consists, or should consist, of those measurement techniques that most accurately *mirror* economic reality. This may be termed the *technical* perspective on accounting practice and regulation. In contrast, the *political* perspective attends to accounting as a selective *reconstruction* of reality. From the latter standpoint, practices and standards are seen to be developed and revised in the light of their material and ideological significance for the preparers and users of accounts. Whereas, ideal-typically, the technical perspective apprehends accounting as a value-free reflection of reality 'out there', the political approach highlights the role of value judgements and social and economic pressures in the shaping of accounting standards.

The technical perspective
The technical perspective on accounting has been most strongly expressed and defended by Solomons (1978). Central to his position is the contention that accounting involves the measurement of facts; and that it must be sharply distinguished from the realm of politics in which values are realised. Otherwise, he argues, 'if it ever became accepted that accounting might be used to achieve other than purely measurement ends, faith in it would be destroyed' (p. 69).

From a technical perspective, it is acknowledged that accounting information necessarily affects human behaviour. But, it is argued, this in itself does not make it political. This is because accounting is neutral in respect of ends: it merely provides factual information which others use to guide their action. From this standpoint, the accountant is seen to have a responsibility to disregard the social and economic consequences of accounting standards and to concentrate one-pointedly upon mapping the financial landscape.

This position, it is recognized, may make accountants appear indifferent to the achievement of 'national objectives'. But the only alternative, Solomons warns, is to bow to political pressures, and thereby endanger the integrity of accountants' measurement techniques. And since the accountant's capacity to serve society is perceived to depend upon the technical ability to provide neutral information, the choice is clear:

> It is our job — as accountants — to make the best maps we can. It is for others, or for accountants acting in some other capacity, to use those maps to steer the economy in the right direction. If the distinction between these two tasks is lost sight of, we shall greatly diminish our capacity to serve society, and in the long run everybody loses (ibid.: 72).

Within the technical perspective on accounting practice there are differing views on how the goal of accurately representing economic reality is to be achieved. One view stresses the role of each accountant's independent, *professional judgement* in selecting from available techniques the one that yields the most 'true and fair' account of reality in specific circumstances. This approach is challenged by those who argue that consistency and comparability in accounting can be achieved only through a *bureaucratic standardization* of the techniques that produce the most reliable and accurate picture of economic reality.

The professional view. Those who stress the role of professional judgement are critical of the introduction of mandatory standards on a number of grounds. First, rules are seen to harbour inflexibility and to invite a trained incapacity to exercise discretion. Second, they are perceived to encourage individual accountants to abdicate their responsibility for understanding matters of principle. Third, a profession restricted by standards is seen to be more easily manipulated by governments than one in which individuals are free to exercise independent judgement. Fourth, and crucially.

> Standard-makers may have to bow to political pressures. Already one hears the argument that standards ought to further desirable political and social ends. Most of us would answer that figures can best further desirable ends by being unbiased and accurate (Baxter, 1981: 7).

In general, the 'professionalist' variant of the technical perspective on accounting practice is critical of the assumption that there is a standardizable way of communicating economic truth. While regarding accounting technique as potentially objective, there is an insistence that objectivity is *actually achieved* only when professional judgement is applied in selecting the accounting method most appropriate (i.e. true and fair) for the specific job in hand. From this standpoint, calls to standardize practice are regarded as unrealistic and undesirable. They are seen to be unrealistic in so far as they disregard the inherently problematic status of the concepts upon which accounting is based. And they are viewed as undesirable inasmuch as they are perceived to undermine professional expertise and to invite political distortion and control.

The bureaucratic view. Within the technical perspective, the opposing view is that the absence of standardization results in accountants employing techniques that are imperfect and inconsistent in their representation of economic reality. Two different 'bureaucratic' approaches to standard setting have emerged. A *systematic* effort to devise a comprehensive and permanent framework for determining and unifying standards continues to be made by the Financial Accounting Standards Board (FASB) in the United States. Its aim has been to fashion formal propositions relating to eight different dimensions of standard setting such as 'objectives', 'elements of financial statements' and 'accounting measurement'. In contrast, in the UK, the dominant view has been that the chances of constructing a conceptual framework for guiding the setting of standards are slim. A more ad hoc bureaucratic approach has prevailed.

In its consultative document of 1978, the ASC allowed that an agreed conceptual framework would be advantageous, but considered its formulation unlikely for a number of reasons. First, because accounting is 'in a transitional stage' between two types of accounting: historical cost accounting and accounting based on current values (ASC, 1979: 45). That is to say, accountants haven't (yet) agreed upon how to measure value. Second, agreement on the construction of a conceptual framework, it is argued, is impeded by a conflict between the prudence concept of accounting and the accruels concept of accounting. In other words, accountants haven't (yet) agreed what constitutes a 'realistic' view of economic reality. Finally, it is said that agreement over a conceptual framework is impeded because 'the users of financial statements have different objectives' (ibid.: 45). For these reasons, the consultative document concludes that

> If an 'agreed conceptual framework' is equated with a single undisputed 'model', then this is a luxury which evades us at the moment. . . . Research into this problem could be encouraged or commissioned by the ASC. For the time being however it is necessary to proceed from a historical cost starting point on a pragmatic and experimental basis (ibid.: 46).

The ASC's attitude to the development of a conceptual framework attracted considerable criticism from those who responded to the ASC's consultative document, especially from the large firms of accountants. For example, Price Waterhouse suggested that many of the problems experienced both before and after publication of some SSAPs were attributable to the lack of a conceptual framework (ASC, 1979). Similarly, Thornton Baker noted that the section on the conceptual framework in the consultative document 'is somewhat incongruous, as the determination of an agreed conceptual framework should logically be the first step towards the development of a comprehensive and consistent set of accounting standards' (ibid.: 173). Touche Ross spoke for the majority of the big firms when they asserted that

> Until the foundations have laid more soundly based financial statements designed to meet clearly defined objectives, it will not be possible to do more than reduce the number of conceptual inconsistencies between different SSAPs. For the credibility of the accounting profession it is therefore imperative that the development of one or more 'agreed conceptual frameworks', should proceed as rapidly as possible (ibid.: 183).

In reaction to the submissions on its consultative document, the ASC commissioned Professor Macve to survey the literature and opinion in the UK and elsewhere with a view to examining the possibility of constructing such a framework and identifying further areas of research. Macve's (1981) conclusions broadly confirmed the earlier view of the ASC: that a framework for giving *direct* guidance on the setting of *actual* standards was unlikely to be achieved. In doing so, they have effectively legitimated the ASC's ad hoc approach to the setting and revision of accounting standards.

Discussion. It has been suggested that within the technical perspective a division of opinion exists between the proponents of 'professionalist' and 'bureaucratic' means of providing an objective representation of economic reality. 'Professionalists' have regarded the development of mandatory standards as a threat to the use of discretion and professional judgement in the selection of situationally appropriate accounting methods (see Jamous and Peloille, 1970; Oppenheimer, 1973). In doing so, they have highlighted the problem of constructing standards that will yield a 'true and fair' view in widely differing circumstances (cf. Bromwich, 1980; 1981). Moreover, in pressing this opinion, they have willingly exposed the inherently problematic foundations of accounting. Indeed, they have even suggested that central tasks of accounting, such as the estimation of wealth, are 'probably closer to judging a beauty competition than to physical measurement' (Baxter, 1981: 8).

Such views are potentially embarrassing for those who seek to standardize accounting practice. Any exposure of the problematical grounds of accounting stimulates enquiry into the question of how standardization is possible and why it is favoured. This is because, from a 'professionalist' standpoint, standardization is *incompatible* with the obligation to provide a 'true and fair' view. At best, it can provide only an artificial or contrived form of consistency and comparability. Moreover, from a 'professionalist' standpoint, standardization involves an attempt to cover up the inherent difficulties in presenting a 'true and fair view'. And, in doing so, it is perceived to conceal as well as devalue the inescapable role of judgement in the preparation of accounts (Perks and Butler, 1979). In preference to standardization, the course favoured by 'professionalists' is a more open and well-publicized recognition of the role of judgement in accounting — a role which is inescapably accompanied by occasional disagreements, discrepancies and inconsistencies.

Mainly by default, the 'professionalist' view prevailed until 1970, although it must be said that little effort was made to disabuse the public of its conception of accounting as an unproblematically objective discipline. In 1970, instead of attempting to educate the public, the profession responded by seeking to restore the image of objectivity by creating standards that would eliminate embarrassing inconsistencies. However, because this response was not based upon, or disciplined by, any guiding conceptual framework, inconsistencies have emerged between standards. Moreover, because there is no longer a proliferation of practices from which to pick and choose, the determination of *the* standard has become more critical for preparers and users alike. By establishing a body to produce mandatory standards, the profession has retained formal control over its practice. But, to do this, it has had to respond to pressure from users of accounting information to severely reduce its areas of discretion. Furthermore, since its formation, the ASC has repeatedly yielded to powerful interest groups who have lobbied for a change in the content or slant of particular standards (Zeff, 1979; Tonkin, 1981; Hope and Gray, 1982; see also Watts and Zimmerman, 1978). Indeed, as noted earlier, the ASC has continuously, if reluctantly, revised its procedure and widened its membership to accommodate such critical pressure (ASC, 1978; 1981; 1983).

The political perspective
The previous observations lead us to an appreciation of the concerns of a political perspective on accounting. Fundamental to this perspective is its understanding that information about the world is never produced within a social or political vacuum. Rather, its production is seen to be guided by the institutionally located interests and priorities of those who prepare and/or use it. Unavoidably, *specific* types of information are collected in *particular* kinds of ways and presented in *acceptable* forms

as a result of on-going negotiations between the preparers and users of such information (Tonkin, 1981).

More fundamentally, it is stressed that concepts basic to accounting — such as wealth and income — are founded upon válue-judgements about what counts as wealth and how it is to be accounted for. From a 'political' standpoint, the lesson to be drawn from this observation is not that standardization is necessarily undesirable, nor that objectivity is conditional upon the exercise of professional judgement. Rather, the lesson is that accounting rules cannot mirror economic reality. Why not? Because 'if income and wealth (for example) are not absolutes but value-judgements, the financial community has no manifest reason to accept accountants' rules for computing them' (Gerboth, 1973: 479).

Central to Gerboth's observation on the politics of accounting rules is the insight that accountants are obliged to legitimate their practices in the eyes of significant others — namely, their patrons, the government and 'the financial community' (cf. Horngren, 1973). When examined in this light, the fundamental and critical issues of standard setting are disclosed as political. Rules are seen to be developed within *institutions* whose existence and rationality is shaped by groups possessing resources that enable them to shape or influence the machinery as well as the products of the standard setting process (Burchell, Cooper and Sherer, 1983).

Politics and the ASC. As noted earlier, the formation of the ASC was a response to 'political' pressure. However, it presents its activities as politically neutral. Its willingness to listen to the concerns of interested parties, for example, is construed as evidence of a concern and ability to respond quickly and flexibly so as to improve the objectivity and effectiveness of its standards. Consultations with such parties are thus portrayed as a means of acquiring information about the problem for which the standard being developed is to provide the solution.

The ASC account of its activities has been questioned by a number of commentators (e.g. Lafferty, 1979; Ashton, 1983). For example, in his response to the ASC's consultative document on setting accounting standards, Stamp (1979) suggests that the ASC has contrived an illusion of neutrality and independence through the device of stressing how it has been criticized for being insufficiently responsive to its critics and also for buckling under pressure; for producing standards which are too detailed and also for developing standards which are insufficiently specific; for failing to create uniform standards and also for making standards inflexible, etc. Arguing for a more self-consciously political approach to standard setting, Stamp recommends the open recognition of a conflict of interests between the producers and users of financial statements.

Stamp notes how producers are generally resistant to tight or comprehensive standardization. This is because standards are widely regarded by producers of financial statements as 'an intrusion upon their right to manage the enterprise the way they think best' (ibid.: 10). Users, on the other hand, are seen to welcome greater uniformity and expect the ASC to resist pressures from the producers to slow down or water down the process of standardization. For this reason, Stamp suggests, 'the business of establishing accounting standards is a highly political process' (ibid.: 11). Instead of 'bleating' or 'crowing' about the conflicting evaluations of the work of the ASC made by producers and users, Stamp's advice is that the existence of conflicting points of view should be openly recognized and that the ASC should concentrate upon (i) defining its objectives with clarity and precision; and (ii) winning support for the proposals they define and the actions they take. In a grim warning to the profession, he advises that

> It is essential for the profession to demonstrate that it has the will and the means to establish standards and, equally important, to enforce them. Otherwise government intervention is inevitable, and once it occurs it will be irreversible (ibid).

Standard setting and the legitimation of authority. Other commentators have sought to place the setting of accounting standards in a wider historical and political context (e.g. Zeff, 1971; Moonitz, 1974; Hopwood, Berchell and Clubb, 1979; Hopwood, 1983). Hope (1979), for example, has argued that the critical issues in standard setting are political because the process of decision-making depends upon public confidence. This dependence, Hope suggests, places a heavy burden on those who set accounting standards, for the recognition of the role of public confidence

> suggests that accounting choices of measurement and reporting are *social* choices and that therefore accountants, and particularly accounting policy makers should concern themselves with such *social* choices (ibid.: 552).

Moreover, Hope argues that if the setters of standards are to successfully carry their heavy burden of responsibility to the public

> the ASC must firmly grasp the nettle of 'political' accounting; that the value-judgements and social trade-offs necessary to the formulation of acceptable standards *must be spelt out publicly* (ibid.: 562).

The ASC has itself stressed the importance of expanding the openness of standard setting, and claims that

> It is within the ASC's own powers to expand the openness of standard setting and much has already been done since the publication in 1978 of the consultative document on setting accounting standards (ASC 1981: 7–8).

The chief justification given for this concern to be responsive to the wider public is the need for effectiveness. For, as the ASC asserts in the report and recommendations that followed commentary on its consultative document,

> to be effective, accounting standards set in the private sector need to be set in the open after the widest possible public consideration and debate of all proposed standards (ibid.: 7).

In support of its basic belief that accounting standards should be set in the private sector, the report observes that 'very few commentators were in favour of accounting standards being set by the legislature, a government department or a government agency' (ibid.: 21–2). However, given the comparatively narrow interest range of the bodies consulted, this response is hardly surprising. Moreover, when presented with a stark and abstract choice between private and public control, it can be anticipated that the former will be preferred, if only because those consulted are, in the main, ideologically committed to the minimum of state intervention. When examined in this light, the ASC's concern to 'open up the debate' appears to be stimulated and restricted by the sectional interest of the profession, and especially the English Institute, in retaining formal control over the standard setting process. And the concern to safeguard the public interest seems to amount to little more than an exercise in defending the profession's privilege of self-regulation.

The issue of the legitimation of the process of accounting standard setting has been raised forcefully by Gerboth (1973). In doing so, he has argued that the test of a standard's legitimacy should not be its effectiveness but, rather, the *democratic* process of its setting. The key distinction between these criteria of legitimation is that whereas the effectiveness of a standard is mainly dependent upon its acceptability to the interests of the preparers and current users of accounts, the democratic setting of a standard depends upon the responsiveness of the standard setters to the interest groups who neither prepare nor currently use accounts but, nonetheless, are affected by their scope and content (cf. Hope, 1979).[9] The politicization of accounting rule-making, Gerboth (ibid.: 481) contends is 'just' because

> In a society committed to democratic legitimization of authority, only politically responsive institutions have the right to command others to obey their rules (ibid.).

Although the spirit of Gerboth's argument may be applauded, it rests upon two questionable assumptions. The first is that a commitment to 'the democratic legitimization of authority' actually exists in society. The second, and related, assumption is that the prevailing distribution of power in society can allow any such commitment to become a reality. These assumptions are questioned because, in the case of accounting standards regulation, at least, there is little or no historical evidence of the accountancy profession's concern to subject its authority to public scrutiny and debate. On the contrary, the profession has jealously defended its privilege of self-regulation against what has been perceived as threats (e.g. from the state) to this 'right'. Equally it must be said that potentially powerful organized interest groups in society (e.g. trade unions) seem to have accepted the received wisdom that accounts are basically 'technical' and 'neutral' and, therefore, have not made a political issue of the scope and content of standards or of the accountability of their setters. As a consequence, the setters' espoused, but democratically unaccountable, concern to act in the public interest appears to have amounted to little more than introducing marginal reforms to the process and content of standards, reforms that seem to be designed primarily to anticipate and appease the criticisms of the preparers and current users of accounts (including the state) and thereby reach a new equilibrium within the status quo (Schmitter, 1974; Crouch, 1979).

Understood in this way, the standard setting process is an example of (veiled) societal corporatism in which, to quote Schmitter (1977: 64), the accountancy profession is 'recognized or licensed by the state and granted a deliberate representation and monopoly within their respective categories (e.g. accounting standard setting) in exchange for observing certain controls on their selection of leaders and articulation of demands and supports'. More specifically, standard setting is an example of a process of public policy formation characterized by fully blown 'concertation' rather than 'pressure' (Schmitter, 1982). That is to say, the accountancy profession is not simply a consultant, or a combatant, with public authorities in respect of the scope, content and enforcement of accounting standards. Nor, indeed, is it even 'just' an indispensible negotiator or made jointly responsible for their determination. Rather, the profession is completely responsible for this area of policy-making so that its decisions 'take on a characteristically semi-public or para-state quality' (Schmitter, 1981: 263).

Discussion. In the light of the preceding observations on the political perspective, Solomon's 'professionalist' anxiety about the politicization of accountants can be seen to have some substance. In a perfectly competitive political market — which appears to be Gerboth's (1973) model of the democratic process — each member of the public would have an equal opportunity to shape accounting standards, given a rough equality of resources and access to the decision-making process. However, power is not symmetrically distributed in society. Gerboth (ibid.: 481) acknowledges as much when he observes how accountancy standards 'affect the economic well-being of ... millions of individuals, few of who had anything to do with the profession, its power, or have a significant say in its use'. However, instead of evaluating the process and output of standard setting in relation to the interests of these millions of individuals, Gerboth is seemingly content to assume that the politicization of accounting standards will ensure that accounting rules will conform more closely to the public interest. What he overlooks is how, in the real, neo-corporatist world of monopoly capitalism, most members of the general public are in effect excluded from representing their interests to a standard setting body. In this world, standards are designed for the groups with the greatest political clout and appeals to the sovereignty of the public interest are principally a means of obscuring and legitimizing the reality of monopoly control.

Concluding remarks
An underlying assumption of this paper has been that the organization and regulation of accounting practice must be seen in historical perspective. In particular, the efforts to attain and safeguard self-regulation should be understood in relation to the profession's dependence upon corporate patrons who, in general, have favoured the flexibility of rule-making by the profession over regulation by the state. Historically, the profession has sought to contrive and preserve an image of independence based upon the idea that its members are trained to prepare and present accounts that provide 'a true and fair view' of the financial situation (Chastney, 1975). By and large, this idea underpinned the authority of the profession until the late 1960s when public confidence was undermined by the failure of the major accountancy bodies to speak with one voice, a failure which was followed by a series of spectacular cases of accounting failure (Tinker, 1985). In making the process of setting accountancy standards the focus of the paper, attention has been directed at the efforts of the profession to defend its privilege of self-regulation of accounting standards in the face of pressure for reformsfrom the Department of Trade, the media and users of accounting information. In turn, this has led us to a critical examination of the professed independence of the profession (and, in particular, the Accounting Standards Committee) and its proclaimed capacity to represent the public interest.

The outcome of this investigation has been the revelation of an elite group that in effect is unaccountable to the general public, and which is constrained only by the fear of state intervention. This view of the accounting standards setting process is based upon a number of observations. First, the ASC has consistently ducked the issue of the conceptual foundations of accounting. As numerous commentators on the ASC's consultative document *Setting Accounting Standards* were noted to have observed, the ASC's ambivalence towards the identification or development of such a framework does not sit easily with its programme of standardization. Second, and relatedly, the ASC has virtually ignored the recommendations of *The Corporate Report*. Published by the ASSC in 1975, this discussion document was particularly critical of the scope of corporate reports in so far as their provision of measurements and information are mainly of use only to shareholder and creditors. Neglected, the document suggests, are the legitimate interests of a wider class of (potential) users of accounts, such as employees, consumers, environmental pressure groups (see also Parker, 1976; ICAEW, 1976). In particular, *The Corporate Report* contends that accounts should facilitate the social accountability of economic entities because 'they are involved in the maintenance of standards of life and the creation of wealth for and on behalf of the community' (ICAEW, 1976: 15). Yet, despite, its claims to represent the public interest, the ASC has virtually disregarded the general public as a (potential) user of accounts.[10] Third, there is considerable evidence that the process of standard setting has been influenced by pressures from the industry (see Moonitz, 1974; Watts and Zimmerman, 1979). One of the most blatant cases concerned revisions of the proposed standard on research and development expenditure.[11] In their detailed analysis of this case, Hope and Gray (1982) conclude that the position of the ASC changed on the issues of accounting treatment and disclosures of R and D as a result of pressures from industry and, in particular, because of representations from the aerospace industry. The 'dramatic (if unsurprising) implication of this', they note, is that the machinery of the ASC currently enables (indeed it invites!) companies partially to determine the terms of their own accountability by allowing them to influence the disclosure and measurement aspects of their financial reports. Fourth, there is the issue of the enforcement of standards. Clearly, standards are a hollow pretence if there is no mechanism to enforce them (Mumford, 1978). At present, accountants are required by the professional associations to ensure that financial statements comply with the standards and to disclose and explain significant departures from them. However, in practice, action from the accountancy bodies has been minimal. Furthermore the direct economic dependence of the auditor upon the audited organization promotes a situation in which corporate management rather than the users of accounts is regarded as the 'real' client. The main sanction against organizations that breach accounting standards has been a qualified audit report. But this is unaccompanied by any further legal or financial penalty.[12]. So, in effect, standards can be ignored with impunity.

In conclusion it is relevant to reflect further upon what this study may offer to the illumination and development of our theoretical understanding of private interests governments as agents of social order and public policy. Of the four models of social order identified in the introduction to this volume, professional accountancy bodies most closely resemble 'the Association' whose distinguishing principle of interaction and allocation is 'organisational allocation' (in contrast to the 'spontaneous solidarity' of Community, the 'dispersed competition' of the Market and the 'hierarchical coordination' of the State (Streeck and Schmitter, in this volume). Within the Associative model of social order 'the key actors are organizations defined by their common purpose of promoting and defending functionally defined interests' (ibid.). In the case of accountancy bodies, their primary interest, as professional associations, has been to secure and enhance the material and symbolic value of their members' labour. To this end, they have continuously negotiated amongst themselves, with other private interest governments and with the state, to achieve and maintain recognition of their privilege of self-regulation in respect of a coveted niche within the labour market.

More specifically, this study of accounting standards setting has illustrated how, in response to pressure from the state and the users of accounts, the English Institute acted to defend its self-regulatory powers by creating the Accounting Standards Steering Committee. This, together with the subsequent formation of the CCAB, represented the effort by the largest body to devise an organizational mechanism capable of enabling a profession fragmented into six bodies to speak with one voice. Similarly, the revisions in the constituency of the ASC and its creation of the advisory Consultative Group are both indicative of the ASC members' recognition of the contingent or strategic interdependence of the profession in relation to other organized interest groups as well as the state.

These observations serve as a useful reminder of the empirical possibility of a subordinate and submerged nature of the associative form of social order. For, in the context of advanced capitalist societies, at least, the market and the state may well continue to be the dominant institutions. Together with community they do indeed 'constitute important limiting and facilitating conditions for and inside any given associative arrangement, and without them such arrangements could not exist and function' (ibid.). In the case of accountancy bodies, it has been noted how these associations appeal to, and depend upon, the values of community: accountants profess their service to the community, and their guidance by the public interest. The market is also of great significance in so far as professionalization is perceived as a strategy for monopolizing control over the supply, and of influencing the demand for, accounting labour. Finally, the preparedness of the state to license the self-regulation of the accountancy profession has been critical in legitimizing their communitarian claims and in securing and expanding the market for their services (Willmott, 1983).

By attending, in the earlier sections of the paper, to the historical formation and segmented development of accountancy bodies it has also been possible to illustrate how the identification and pursuit of collective interests is shaped within, and constrained by, the organizational structure of the profession's private interest governments as well as by the composition of their membership. Then, when examining the establishment and reform of the Accounting Standards Committee, we were better able to appreciate the significance of the historical and organizational development of the profession for the *form* of associative regulation that emerged as an alternative to 'free market' or 'statutory' policy formulation and implementation in respect of the setting of accounting standards and the disclosure of accounting information. In addition, the study of the ASC has provided both an illustration of the preparedness of the state to accept, and indeed promote, voluntary collective self- regulation even though this 'implies a loss of direct control' *and* a confirmation of the idea that the existing mode of self-regulation 'would be impossible without the "Damocles sword" of threatened direct state intervention' (Streeck and Schmitter, in this volume).

This observation reinforces the view that, when exploring the potential of association arrangements for policy-making, it is necessary to be mindful of the institutional contexts in which private interest governments emerge and take shape. For, as Streeck and Schmitter (ibid.) rightly stress,

> Even where a large share of public policy is made by and implemented through intermediary associations, *these are always to some extent dependent on community values and cohesion, kept in check by economic and political market forces, and subject to hierarchical control* (ibid; emphasis added).

An appreciation of the dependence of intermediary associations upon the market and the state is critical because it begs the question of their organizational capacity and political power to devise and implement policy which better represents the public interest — in the sense of it being 'more socially adjusted and normatively acceptable' (ibid.). In turn, this raises the too easily overlooked issues of how meaningful references to 'the public interest' can be in a society that harbours an endemic conflict of interest between groups that are systematically more or less (dis)advantaged by it. In our examination of the standard setting process it was evident, especially in respect of the ASC's dismissal of the moderate recommendations contained within the Corporate Report, that accountants, as accounting policy setters, have equated 'the public interest' with 'preserving the health' of 'the capitalist system' in a way that secures the stake of accountants within it. If maintaining the status quo (and, in particular, the privileged position of policy setters within it) is what is meant by producing policy that is 'more socially adjusted and normatively acceptable', then the ASC can be judged a (qualified) success. Or, at the very least, it can be said to have played an important ideological role in providing an 'independent' legitimation of the illusion of a united public interest.[13] If, on the other hand, the notions of social adjustment and normative acceptability are understood to mean more than avoiding state regulation by (re)gaining the confidence of other, more powerful organized interest groups, there are rational grounds for questioning the ability of the profession to move policy-making in this direction in the absence of radical change in the dominant social order (cf. Burchell, Cooper and Sherer, 1982). For, as things stand, the profession is *institutionally* embedded in a structure of social and economic relations that systematically constrains and distorts its capacity to critically examine and reconstruct the conception of the public interest that it professes to serve.

The conclusion to be drawn from the preceding discussion is that, in the immediate future, the accounting profession is likely to continue conspicuously to display its concern to be responsive to 'the needs of society', as these are selectively represented to it by its members, its users and its patrons, including the state. However, in the longer term, a growing recognition of accounting standards setting as a critical area of public policy may promote debate on the role and legitimacy of accountants' private interests with government as the principal interpreter and guardian of the public interest. If this happens, then it is unlikely that the equation of the needs of society with the recommendations of professional accountants, corporate management, investors and creditors will maintain its precarious balance. For any such debate on the purpose and grounds of accounting standards is likely to foster an awareness that behind their imposing, impersonal authority there lies a series of contentious value-judgements about the proper scope of disclosure and the basis of measurement, value-judgements which are of no little social and economic consequence.[14]

68 Private interest government

Notes

1. The Privy Council is composed of 'worthy public figures' selected by a secretive and mysterious process. The Privy Council is justly described as a central pillar of the Establishment. Through a complex process of counter-petitioning and negotiation between the petitioning body and an ad hoc committee appointed by the Queen (advised by privy councillors), the royal charter is either granted or refused (without any explanation or right of appeal).

2. In 1957 the size of the membership of the seven major professional bodies was as follows. It can be seen that the combined totals of the Institute and the Society were substantially more than all the other five bodies put together (adapted from Garrett, 1961: 337).

Professional body	Date of formation	Size of membership in 1957
Institute of Accountants in England and Wales (ICAEW)	1880	20,124
Society of Incorporated Accountants (SIA)	1885	11.335
Institute of Chartered Accountants of Scotland (ICAS)	1854	6,187
Institute of Chartered Accountants of Ireland (ICAI)	1888	1,044
Association of Certified and and Corporate Accountants (ACCA). Now called the Association of Certified Accountants (ACA)	1905	10,103
Institute of Municipal Treasurers and Accountants (IMIA). Now called the Chartered Institute of Public and Finance Accountants (CIPFA)	1885	2,804
Institute of Cost and Works Accountants (ICWA). Now called the Institute of Cost and Management Accountants (ICMA)	1919	5,758

3. Before this time, many initiatives designed to achieve a unification had failed. These included the proposal, most strongly advocated by the less prestigious non-chartered bodies, to establish an Act of Parliament setting down the rights and responsibilities of bona fide accountants in a way directly comparable to that of the legal and medical professions. However, such intiatives have been consistently blocked by members of the chartered bodies, especially the English Institute, on the grounds that it devalues or 'levels down' their status (Watson, 1979: ch. 6). The current situation is that, in the absence of registration, anyone can call himself or herself an accountant. But members of the English Institute have managed to retain their monopoly over the use of the title Chartered Accountant.

4. In 1970, 80 per cent of all newly qualified chartered accountants ended up in industrial employment.

5. Although such inspections had been provided for by the 1862 Companies Acts,

few had been undertaken before the 1960s and of these even fewer were published. Under the Companies Acts of 1948 and 1967 the legal right of shareholders to request the Department of Trade (D of T) to make such an inspection was extended to members of the company and the courts. The powers of the D of T inspectorate were further strengthened in the 1976 Companies Act. To the considerable annoyance of companies that are subject to inspection, the D of T is obliged to provide no explanation of its interest. Inspections are generally undertaken jointly by an accountant and a legal expert appointed by the D of T.

6. The exchange between Stamp and Leach, the President of the Institute, is reproduced in Stamp and Marley, 1970. See also Stamp, 1981a.

7. Following its review of the standard setting process published in *Setting Accounting Standards*, the ASC has slightly modified its procedures in an effort to increase consultation and thereby increase the probability of acceptance of its standards. These modifications are detailed in 'Review of the Standard Setting Process' published in *Accountancy* in July 1983.

8. By May 1979 fifteen standards had been published. Of these, two — 'Accounting for changes in the purchasing power of money' (S.S.A.P. 7) and 'Accounting for deferred taxation' (SSAP 11) were withdrawn under pressure. The details of all EDs and SSAP that had been issued, accepted and withdrawn by 1979 are given in *Accounting Standards 1979*.

9. In his rather more perceptive and penetrating discussion of the political character of accounting standards setting, Hope (1979) contends that a fair and equitable procedure for developing standards can be achieved only by respecting the right of *every* group to make a case to the standard setting body in defence of its own interests and by taking full account of the *social choices* and *economic impacts* associated with each possible standard. Commentating on the workings of the ASC, Hope notes that it lacks the expertise necessary for assessing the economic impact of its standards. In doing so, he raises (but does not pursue) the question of whether a committee composed almost exclusively of accountants is compatible with democracy. Thus, in an aside he notes how 'one might indeed pose the question that if standard setting in a democracy is viewed as a social process, is it acceptable that accountants, with their 'necessarily' limited range of expertise should be the group to control the standardization process. One might in fact conclude that standards should be set by a Government agency, similar to the SEC.' (ibid.: 563). Disappointingly, Hope does not elaborate upon the tension between democracy and self-regulation. He does not address the political question of the public accountability of the ASC nor, relatedly, does he challenge the ASC's means of gauging and safeguarding the public interest. Failing to distinguish between formal and substantive democracy he looks upon the ASC as a deviation from the ideal of a substantive democracy rather than as an imperfect expression of the reality of formal democracy. Similarly, he appears to assume that this deviation can be corrected by drafting some experts on the economic impact of accounting standards onto the ASC. Instead of exploring the tension between the interest of every member of the public in the setting of accounting standards and the private interest of the accountancy profession (and the financial community) in maintaining self-regulation, Hope reaches the somewhat lame, technocratic conclusion that the economic impacts of accounting standards must be considered by members of the ASC if the elusiveness of standards that are acceptable to its many various constituents is to be overcome.

10. Commenting upon the ASC's disregard of *The Corporate Report*, Stamp (1979) has attributed this neglect to the 'profoundly anti-intellectual attitudes of the profession's leadership'. While this may be so, the deep-seated nature of these attitudes must be traced to the historical origins and development of a profession that continues

to depend upon corporate patronage. Arguably it is this dependence which makes problematical any recognition of the claims of a wider class of users of accounts.

11. Other examples are (i) the standard on deferred taxation where the ASC was pressured into allowing increased flexibility in accounting for taxes following threats from major companies that they would not comply with the proposed standards; and (ii) the standard on depreciation that was changed to grant property companies exemption following lobbying from property investment companies (Lafferty, 1979).

12. Following the comments on its consultative document, the ASC rejected the possibility of statutory enforcement of standards by a body similar to the Securities and Exchange Commission (SEC) in the USA. The SEC requires the registration of all significant financial statements and is empowered to refuse statements bearing a qualified audit report and to threaten withdrawal of a company's listing on the Stock Exchange. The recommendation of the ASC has been to reject such a procedure on the grounds that

> it would be more in keeping with the practice of private sector regulation in the UK and Ireland for the 'further action' (following a qualified audit report) to be an enquiry by a supervisory body of undoubted standing in the community (Accounting Standards Committee, 1981: 26).

The ASC's proposal was to establish a Panel 'guided by the need to act in the general interest' appointed jointly by the Council for the Securities Industry, the CCAB and the Stock Exchange to examine departure from accounting standards referred to them by the Quotations Department of the Stock Exchange, by any of the major accountancy bodies or by the general public. If non-compliance was found to be justified, the case would then be referred to the Stock Exchange to determine appropriate action. This proposal has not been accepted by the Stock Exchange which, traditionally, has been principally interested in protecting its members' interests, and not with 'the general interest' (Stamp, 1981b).

13. The idea that accountants and their standards are guardians of an unproblematical public interest underpins, and is taken as given, in the vast majority of commentaries. See, for example, Edwards, 1976; Shackleton, 1977; Edey, 1977; Weetman, 1977; Westwick, 1980; Lee, 1980; Watts, 1983. The embryo of an alternative framework for understanding accounting standards can be found in Tinker, 1980; Tinker, Merino and Niemark, 1982; and Cooper and Sherer, 1984).

14. A number of the issues relating to the accountability of the accountancy profession and its relationship to the state are the subject of a research project funded by the Economic and Social Research Council to be conducted by the author in collaboration with David Cooper (University of Manchester Institute of Science and Technology) and Tony Low and Tony Puxty (University of Sheffield).

List of abbreviations

ACA	Association of Certified Accountants
ACMA	Association of Cost and Management Accountants
AICPA	American Institute of Certified Public Accountants
ASC	Accounting Standards Committee
ASSC	Accounting Standards Steering Committee
CCAB	Consultative Committee of Accountancy Bodies
CIPFA	Chartered Institute of Public Finance and Accounting
CSI	Council for the Securities Industry
ED	Exposure Draft
FASB	Financial Accounting Standards Board
FAF	Financial Accounting Foundation
IASC	International Accounting Standards Committee
ICAEW	Institute of Chartered Accountants in England and Wales
ICAI	Institute of Chartered Accountants in Ireland
ICAS	Institute of Chartered Accountants of Scotland
SEC	Securities and Exchange Commission
SIA	Society of Incorporated Accountants
SSAP	Statement of Standard Accounting Practice

4

...tism in the British voluntary sector

David C. Wilson and Richard J. Butler

Introduction

This chapter examines the inter-organizational relationships which have developed between the state and voluntary organization in Britain. Statutory and voluntary collaboration has been of enduring concern in some organizational literature (see, for example, Leat, Smolka and Unell, 1981; Wolfenden, 1978; Hatch and Mocroft, 1979; Wilson and Butler, 1983) but much of this research has concentrated on the relative efficiency or the autonomy of voluntary organizations given variations in the contingencies they face, namely task complexity and dependence. For example, Leat, Smolka and Unell (1981) argued that as voluntary organizations became increasingly dependent upon the state for money and information, the state achieved commensurately more influence over decision-making. Further, Wilson and Butler (1983) demonstrated that the scope for strategic choice open to four leading British voluntary organizations was shaped *inter alia* by the nature of their central task and their varying dependence upon the state for both information and finance. Here too, external contingencies were seen to erode decisional autonomy.

This recent work provides the starting point for the present paper. Whilst a weakness of these approaches may be argued to be inherent in their emphasis on a contingency perspective to inter-organizational relations (the one organization is in the environment of the other; the focal organization seeks to achieve a congruence or 'fit' between itself and its environment) such contingent relationships also reveal a potential for the analysis of the voluntary sector as a whole and its relationships with the state. In particular, the contingency research highlighted the important role of associations and co-ordinating or mediating organizations which act as 'private' governments on behalf of voluntary organizations in their relationships with the state. In addition, the increasing concern of the state to re-allocate many areas of social and medical services to either the voluntary or the commercial sectors (known popularly as privatization) has increased the potential for voluntary organizations to operate in these areas, necessitating increased linkages between the state and 'private' associations which co-ordinate the potentially expanding voluntary activity (Wassenberg, 1982).

These relationships between the state, private associations and sectors of the economy (in this chapter, the voluntary sector) are the central focus of the corporatist paradigm (Schmitter, 1974). Such a paradigm is, therefore, appropriate to the concerns of the present chapter. It has also been argued by some authors that a 'pure' form of corporatism is unlikely to exist in practice for it is in the interests of the state to retain some degree of direct control over sectors of the economy and not risk devolving control to private associations. Of course, even a 'pure' form of corporatism involves the state retaining some degree of control, for it is the state which initially grants public status to the intermediary private associations. Nevertheless, such retained control remains indirect in the 'pure' corporatist system with the state acting largely in an administrative or procedural capacity. Where the state exercises control *directly* by means of substantive legislative or monitoring activities then this form of corporatism has been termed 'hybrid' (Wassenberg, 1982) or 'false corporatism' (Clegg, Dow and Boreham, 1983).

Self-regulation through associations in the voluntary sector
Examined in the light of increasing state reallocation of many services and the commensurate need for voluntary organizations to adapt to rapidly changing circumstances, the intermediary role of private national associations has become increasingly important. These national associations act as mediators between the state on the one hand and organizations in the voluntary sector on the other hand.

The most well-known national association is the National Council for Voluntary Organizations (NCVO) in which any voluntary organization may become a member. NCVO acts as both co-ordinator and, to some extent, a controller of voluntary activity, giving information and advice to voluntary organizations in the light of prevailing government policies. NCVO also liaises with the state in planning overall strategies aimed toward the voluntary sector, often acting as interlocutor between the state and voluntary organizations and vice versa. The history of NCVO can be traced back to 1919, when its predecessor — the first national association — was created. This was called the National Council of Social Service (NCSS) which later became re-named as NCVO on 1 April 1980.[1]

NCSS was to 'encourage, assist and safeguard voluntary action by acting in concert with existing state *services*' (Brasnett, 1969: 22 passim. By 1928, however, there was evidence of the incorporation of NCSS into state *policy-making*. Co-optation had begun, in particular concerning state policies over what were considered the appropriate fields of activity for voluntary organizations. With the increasing role of the state in providing social and welfare services, especially during the inter-war years, NCSS started to recommend which were the favoured areas of voluntary operation.

For example, in the early 1930s the policy of the NCSS was to encourage those voluntary organizations which were centrally concerned with finding work for the rapidly rising number of unemployed people. Encouragement was largely (but not solely) couched in fiscal incentives. Voluntary organizations operating in these earmarked areas were almost certain to receive some level of state funding for their activities (Rooff, 1957; Johnson, 1981). Following the Beveridge Report (1942), the state began the wholesale incorporation of what were previously disparate voluntary organizations into the statutory provision of social services. Finding jobs for the unemployed now became the concern of *the state*. Co-opting the NCSS into this expansion of the statutory manifesto meant that the Association was forced to face its constituency of voluntary organizations with very different recommendations. Voluntary activity was to concentrate upon the psychological and social consequences of unemployment. Finding jobs was not now a voluntary concern. Indeed, this period saw the genesis and the rapid proliferation of unemployment clubs which were to cater for the presumed psychological needs of the unemployed. The government, however, accepted responsibility for further finding or creating jobs for the unemployed.

Interest mediation from the voluntary sector toward the state has also developed strongly over the last sixty years or so. Whilst Lehmbruch (1982: 21) may view corporatism as fairly weak in evidence in Great Britain (from a government/industry perspective), the voluntary sector has, nevertheless, witnessed a number of successful co-operative policies between government and voluntary organizations which have been initiated by individual organizations and represented by the various associations. There are many such associations other than NCSS, a number of which represent the interests of voluntary organizations working in specific domains such as employment, youth care, housing and citizen's rights. The National Council of Voluntary Youth Services, the National Assocation for the Care and Resettlement of Offenders and the National Association of Citizens' Advice Bureaux are examples of such private associations which are also incorporated into the policy-making processes of the state and are empowered to exercise public authority in their various domains (Atkinson and Coleman, 1985).

These associations mediate state policies to their various constituencies rather than to the voluntary sector as a whole and, in this respect, mediate interests along similar lines to Lowi's (1979) 'sponsored pluralism' or what Wolfe (1977) has termed the 'franchise state'. Nevertheless, the majority of these sectoral associations are also represented on the National Council for Voluntary Organizations and in this respect they are, therefore, an integral part of the tripartite relationship between the state, NCVO and the voluntary sector.

Such was the proliferation after 1950 of voluntary activity, involving mutual help groups, pressure groups and 'alternative' organizations, that the Voluntary Services Unit (VSU) was established in the Home Office (in collaboration with the major national associations). The VSU is designed to incorporate suggestions for policy which emanate from the voluntary sector through the associations and, where appropriate, to provide financial assistance to those voluntary organizations which span the interests of several government departments (or are not the sole responsibility of any one department).

Co-operative policy-making throughout the tripartite system of national associations, voluntary organizations and the state's Voluntary Services Unit was instrumental in bringing into force the 1974 Housing Act. This meant that, for the first time, voluntary effort in the housing field was feasible on a large scheme. Previously housing association schemes had never been economically viable, as they could never be self-supporting. Following the Housing Act, voluntary organizations are now supported and encouraged by government to fill the gap for housing needs which lies between those provided by local authorities and private developers, especially to cater for those sections of society which have specific needs such as the aged, the handicapped or the poor.

The foregoing brief description of some of the corporatist elements of voluntary sector and state relations suggests that it may be viewed as essentially a collaborative system, evolved and consciously developed by both parties and mediated through a number of 'peak' associations (Wassenberg, 1982). At this meso level of analysis (Wassenberg, 1982: 85) the complementary and mutually supportive roles of voluntary and state activities may be viewed as co-existing in dynamic harmony, changing emphases and directions (mediated through the associations) when economic and social conditions demand new initiatives or roles from both the state and the voluntary sector. How far this apparently consensual corporatist system is fully realized in practice, or how far the descriptions of the *structure* of the corporatist system mask the more political *processes* of state-voluntary sector relations is the focus of the following analysis.

Sample and data
Data were collected from a total of seventy-two voluntary organizations, chosen to reflect the diversity of task and size of

organizations in the British voluntary sector. Data were collected both by structured interview schedules and by more detailed case-study methods.[2] The data presented in this chapter focus on the level of involvement and the relative influence of the state and private associations in the strategic decision making of voluntary organizations in the sample. These data are a part of a broader study of voluntary organizations concerned with other aspects of voluntary activity which are tangential to the present chapter.[3]

Data were collected from respondents who occupied senior managerial positions in each of the sample organizations. No interviews were conducted in either the national associations or in state agencies for these were neither the concern of the larger research project (see note 3) nor was this practicable given the limited time and resources at the authors' disposal. In all organizations in the sample, multiple respondents were asked to assess the relative influence of state agencies and private associations in strategic decision-making. Respondents were asked to specify which had been, in their opinion, strategic decision topics over the last ten years in their organization. Having listed a set of these topics (which, in all cases never was less than five strategic decisions) respondents were asked to identify which private associations and which state agencies were involved in each decision. In addition, respondents were asked to rate each interest on a five-point scale of influence, ranging from 'a little' to 'a very great deal'. In those few cases where respondents differed widely in their assessment of the influence of any specific interest (such as a state agency or a national association), then a single score was obtained by re-submitting the question to each respondent and, if disagreement still occurred, a single score of relative influence was obtained by discussion between the respondents and the researcher.

In four organizations, detailed case-studies were carried out. These focused on recent strategic decisions as well as current strategic problems. Examples of these decisions are to change the source of income in a welfare service organization, to alter radically the number and type of services offered by a poverty relief agency and to become a pressure group when previously the organization had been a supplier of services uncritical of governmental policies. In each case, multiple open-ended interviews with multiple respondents were carried out. Data collection spanned a period of approximately nine months, although this reflects only the 'formal' period of data collection. Contact is still maintained with each of the four intensive case study organizations in order to monitor their current (and potential) strategies.

In many cases, respondents wished to preserve anonymity for their organization and this has been respected here. Where respondents did not wish to keep the name of their organization anonymous then the actual name of the voluntary organization is used. The data, therefore, contain a mixture of pseudonyms and actual organization titles.

The relative involvement of private associations and state agencies in strategic decision making

One indication of the relationships developed in the tripartite system of the state, private associations and the voluntary sector is the extent to which state agencies are involved in strategic decision-making in relation to the associations. The word 'indication' is used deliberately in this context, for the relative level of involvement of associations and state agencies tell us little about the nature of that involvement (direct or indirect) and, equally, neither presupposes nor endows any power to those interests involved (Wilson et al., 1982). Nevertheless, the relative levels of involvement are a first step along the path toward a systematic empirical analysis of the inter-organizational relations sustained in the corporatist system of the British voluntary sector. This level of analysis clearly belongs to what Wassenberg (1982) and Cawson (1984) have termed 'meso'-level corporatism.

At this level of analysis, interests are not represented directly by individual organizations or actors, but are represented through 'private interest governments' (Schmitter and Streeck, 1981) which themselves operate within the aegis of the state. Analysis of the involvement of the state and private associations (which correspond to Schmitter and Streeck's private interest governments) facilitates a first step toward delineating a *pattern* in the mode of operation of the corporatist system. This pattern is presented in Table 1.

The data in Table 1 indicate that across the sample of 72 voluntary organizations state agencies are involved at least at the level of one department in the strategic decision-making of voluntary organizations. In all cases, agencies of the state are involved. On the other hand, only forty-one of the sample organizations indicated that private associations were involved in strategic decision-making. This leaves thirty-one organizations in which private associations are not involved at all. The state (represented by local and central government departments, the Charity Commission and the Inland Revenue), at least from a representational perspective, appears to be dominantly pervasive in comparison with the private associations.

Of course, such data do not explain or indicate the mechanism by which the state may or may not operate in the corporatist system (Beer, 1969). They only indicate the comparatively pervasive and seemingly direct involvement of the state in the decision-making of voluntary organizations in comparison to the private associations. It

TABLE 1
The pattern of involvement in decision-making in voluntary organizations: private associations and state agencies
(n = 72 organizations)

No of organizations in which the Charity Commission is involved in decision-making	55	
No of organizations in which the Inland Revenue (tax) is involved in decision-making	29	
Total number of local government departments involved in decision-making	31	
Total number of central government departments involved in decision-making	84	
Total number of *state agencies* involved	199[a]	in 72 voluntary organizations
Total number of *private* associations involved	61[b]	in 41 voluntary organizations

[a] minimum = 1, maximum = 5 state agencies involved per organization (average per organization = 2.8)
[b] minimum = 1, maximum = 5 private associations involved per organization (average per organization = 1.5)

would be hasty to conclude, on the strength of these data, that the tripartite system of interest intermediation through the associations was in any sense 'false' or 'hybrid'. For involvement tells us little about the nature of state activities in the decision-making arena (Astley et al., 1982). Of course, whilst corporatism cannot be defined without the presence of the state being assumed, the nature of state involvement must be specified in order to illustrate those processes that are corporatist and those that are not.

The following sections, therefore, examine the relative influence of state agencies and private associations over strategic decisions in the voluntary organizations in our sample. In addition, the data examine the *nature* of the exercise of any such influence in order to uncover whether the state agencies are acting as direct or indirect regulators of voluntary activity.

The relative influence of private associations and state agencies in strategic decision-making

Influence for both state agencies and private associations was assessed on a five-point scale ranging from a little to a very great deal. In an unstructured, open-ended question respondents were also asked to detail the nature of the influence of each interest and in what form it was primarily exercised. Influence was considered over a period of the last ten years in the strategic decision-making of each organization.

Following Wilson (1984), it was decided to split the state agencies into four separate categories, for the nature of state influence varies widely across these categories. The four categories are the Charity Commission, the Inland Revenue, local government departments and central government departments. The data in Table 1 are presented in this form, although it is only clear why such a categorization is employed once the nature of the *influence* of each state agency is known, rather than just its level of involvement.

The Charity Commission represents the enactment of *legislative control* of the state over organizations in the voluntary sector. The Commission comprises some 350 employees (chiefly civil servants and lawyers) and currently monitors the activities of some 145,000 voluntary organizations (Charities Digest, 1984). Legislative control is founded upon the laws of charitable trusts or, as it is more commonly known, charity law. These laws are designed to distinguish between which voluntary organizations may be termed charitable and which voluntary organizations may be deemed to be non-charitable. Once a voluntary organization is endowed with charitable status it enjoys exemption from income and corporation taxes. In addition, registration as a charity carries the less tangible but equally important benefit of legitimation (Wilson, 1984). Voluntary organizations can use their charitable status to convince potential donors that the organization is efficiently administered, is a worthwhile cause and carries a state seal of approval for its activities.

The Inland Revenue, on the other hand, exercise their influence in a different domain, although prior to 1960 the Charities Division of the Inland Revenue was the sole arbiter of charitable status. Today, however, the Inland Revenue administers all tax concessions for registered charities which, contrary to popular belief, are not necessarily automatic. The Inland Revenue effectively exert influence by constantly 'policing' the fiscal aspects of voluntary activity. Charities which are 'offenders' and break 'Revenue Law' are, thus, disallowed tax exemptions which, in many cases, are worth over £1 million per year.

Local governments (such as the Greater London Council and other regional metropolitan councils) and central government departments (such as the Department of Health and Social Security) act both as *funders* of and *competitors* to voluntary organizations (Wolfenden, 1978). Local and central government departments often provide a parallel service to those provided by voluntary organizations, particularly in the areas of medical and social welfare. In some cases, the voluntary organization is supplementary to state services, a good example of this being the Women's Royal Voluntary Service. In this respect, a client seeking services in these areas could choose either voluntary or statutory providers. There is competition between the two sectors. Financial support is also provided by central and local government departments either as one-off payments for specific projects, or as recurring support grants. It has been argued that commensurate with financial support is a great deal of direct state intervention in the decision-making of voluntary organizations (Leat, Smolka and Unell, 1981; Johnson, 1981; Wilson and Butler, 1983). Government departments that fund voluntary activity also expect to have a voice in their method of operation.

TABLE 2
The relative influence of state agencies and private associations in strategic decision-making[a]

Mean influence of the Charity Commission	3.0	(n = 55)
Mean influence of the Inland Revenue	1.5	(n = 29)
Mean influence of local government departments	1.5	(n = 31)
Mean influence of central government departments	4.5	(n = 84)
Total mean influence of state agencies in all four categories[b]	2.6	(n = 199)
Total mean influence of private associations	1.2	(n = 61)

[a]On the scale: 1 A little
2 Some
3 Quite a lot
4 A great deal
5 A very great deal

[b]Differences between the means significant at $p < .01$ using z- test for sample means

Table 2 reveals the relative influence of each category of state agency, the total mean influence of state agencies overall and the total mean influence of private associations.

Of the four categories of state agencies, central government departments score the highest relative mean influence score (4.5) with the Charity Commission slightly less influential overall ('quite a lot' on the rating scale). Both the Inland Revenue and local government departments appear to have only a 'little' influence over strategic decision-making. The results for local government are not surprising given the level of analysis of the research which focused on the national operation of voluntary organizations rather than the local level. It is to be expected, therefore, that central government rather than local government would be perceived to be both more influential and involved to a greater extent in decision-making (see Table 1). It would appear that, equally, the Inland Revenue do not exercise their 'policing' control very often. They are mentioned as being involved in decision making in only twenty-nine organizations and even in these their mean influence overall is only rated 'little' (1.5).

Private associations, whilst reported to be involved in decision-making in nearly two-thirds of the sample, have a total mean influence score of 1.2, whilst the state agencies' overall mean is 2.6 (see Table 2). The difference between the two means is statistically significant at $p<$ .01 (Freund and Williams, 1970: 236–40), although it should be noted that both mean scores fall below the middle point of the scale.[4] Nevertheless, the influence of private associations is relatively small indeed, adding support to the pattern of involvement previously indicated in Table 1. Of particular interest, however, are the highly influential ratings of central government departments and the Charity Commission. The nature of this influence is discussed in the next section.

The influence of central government and the charity commission

From the corporatist perspective, the key question is to what extent the influence of these interests is exercised in a direct manner (through intervention) or indirectly (through the granting of public status etc. to private associations). The activities of the Charity Commission have already been examined elsewhere in detail (see Wilson, 1984). The main thrust of the Commission's influence is exercised through monitoring the activities of voluntary organizations. The Commission decides which organizations are to be recognized as charitable and which are not. For example, political activities such as those espoused by campaigning or pressure groups (Amnesty International, Greenpeace, Shelter) are not considered charitable, whilst activities which replicate or augment state services are considered charitable (National Society for the Prevention of Cruelty to Children, Royal National Institute for the Blind) in so far as they remain 'non-political'.

As Lehmbruch (1977; 1982) and Streeck and Schmitter (in this volume) argue, the retention of regulatory influence by the Commission (as a state agency) does not *ipso facto* render the corporatist system hybrid, false or essentially pluralist. The private associations (such as the NCVO) are still empowered as private interest governments to administer terms of regulation for their members' behaviour. In this respect, private associations act both as policy formulators and policy implementers (in the macro perspective) for their constituent voluntary organizations. However, no private association has yet managed to negotiate with the state over the terms of eligibility for charitable status, although moves toward this facility are in evidence. In particular, NCVO has recently undertaken a programme of research to advise voluntary organizations that are seeking to become registered charities as well as to build up a collection of cases which could, in the future, act as legal precedents for applications to be a charity (NCVO, 1984). In this way, regulatory control will fall within the domain of the private associations, which will be endowed by the state with the power to enforce charitable status decisions.

At present, however, private associations do not have such control. On the one hand, the state has charged private associations with responsibility to manage their constituent voluntary organizations. On the other hand, the state has retained a very important element of direct control via the Charity Commission. In summary, direct legislative control is exercised by the Commission in three ways:
1. A desire to preserve the status quo;
2. Pressure to persuade future voluntary organizations to offer services modelled along existing lines of those performed by some state agencies and not to act as an alternative service;
3. Pressure to persuade voluntary organizations to adopt formalized, bureaucratic structures (adapted from Wilson, 1984).

It is with respect to central government departments that a picture of partial or hybrid corporatism begins to emerge. This is not because of the mere presence of the state (seemingly pervasive in Table 1) or because of the existence of pervasive 'procedural control' (Mayntz, 1983) as is evident in the sample of voluntary organizations. If the Charity Commission is viewed in addition to central government departments as controllers of procedure in the self-regulating system of private associations, then indeed *two-thirds of all state influence* is described in this way by respondents.

For example, whilst the Royal National Lifeboat Institution (RNLI) is unique in Britain as the only national lifesaving service for those in peril on the sea, the state nevertheless retains procedural control over many aspects of sea rescue from the use and abuse of drugs for urgent medical attention for those rescued, to the design and construction of lifeboats. RNLI is a member of NCVO and, because all income to RNLI is from voluntary donations, it is, therefore, arguably self-regulating and independent of the state. Yet, analysis of the data shows evidence of indirect procedural control whereby if it were felt that the rescue service was not being conducted in a manner congruent with the public interest, the state would take control by intervening directly in the RNLI and, ultimately, taking over provision of the service.

However, *one-third* of all state influence through central government departments was described by respondents in ways which were beyond the rather indirect exercise of potential procedural control. Whilst voluntary organizations are willing to comply (as constituents) with their various national associations, direct and, often, conflicting influences come from central government departments which act as substantial sources of funds for these organizations. Where the state directly funds individual voluntary organizations, then it also exercises direct influence over their strategy. Irrespective of self-regulation, private associations and monitoring, the state retains control over individual voluntary organizations through the funding mechanism. Membership of any national association does not seem to preclude the dominance of state influence where the relationship between a voluntary organization and the state is primarily financial.

The National Council for Voluntary Organizations was approached in November 1983 by many of its constituent voluntary organizations which expressed disquiet at the direct and interventionist influence of central government which was seen as a consequence of the funding relationship. Not only does the state determine how much money is allocated directly to each organization, it also has the power to decide the terms of the financial contract so produced (NCVO, 1983). However, neither the NCVO nor any other national association can regulate these conditions of financing although they continually lobby Whitehall for 'arms-length' funding which does not carry with it any consequential control or intervention by the funding body.

For example, respondents in voluntary organizations which provide and build housing for the needy and the poor expressed the view that the state had almost total control over decision-making, for all such organizations were almost wholly financially dependent on state funds. This meant that decisions of when, where and how to build were all subject to the direct influence of the state. Indeed, many voluntary organizations in these services have ceased to exist as central government policies have ceased to favour funding voluntary activity in housing schemes.

A further erosion of the autonomy inherent in self-regulation occurred where voluntary organizations could not restrict the amount of funds they received from the state, in relation to their total income. A number of educational and welfare organizations in the sample, whilst dependent upon state funding, still retained the power or the autonomy to restrict or control its level should it be felt that the state was trying to influence the organization in ways contrary to its members' interest. However, other organizations, particularly in the social welfare domain, were not in a position to decide how great a proportion of their income came from the state. These organizations were subject to direct state interference in their decision-making, often forced to take courses of action which would otherwise not have been pursued, under the ultimate threat of extinction from the drying up of state funding.

This picture of self-regulation through private interest governments on the one hand and an interventionist state on the other (where it acts as partial or sole financier) resembles Beer's (1969) theory of 'quasi-corporatism' later espoused by Jessop (1979), Ferraresi (1983) and Wassenberg (1982) as false or hybrid corporatism. Corporatism as a process of interest intermediation is allowed to operate only so long as it is broadly in line with the functional interests of the state (Offe, 1983: 59–62). Yet, the present research illustrates that, relatively, this kind of false corporatism occurs only in one-third of the sample of voluntary organizations. Two-thirds of the sample appear to operate within a broadly corporatist system with the state allocating all but procedural and legislative control to the private national associations.

Furthermore, the majority of voluntary organizations that do report direct influence of the state through the funding relationship fall into health or social welfare domains. As Cawson (1984) notes, these types of services in particular are organized centrally through agencies of the state and administered through local government. It is not surprising, therefore, that the state wishes to retain control over strategic decisions in these areas, particularly when they are taken by voluntary organizations entrusted with providing such services (for example, the National Society for the Prevention of Cruelty to Children, Alcohol Education Centre, Federation of Alcoholic Rehabilitation Establishments, Cancer Research Campaign and the Imperial Cancer Research Fund). Such organizations would not be able to achieve 'closure' over either technical or professional skills in these areas, given the existence of the state run National Health Service, so they would also be in a weak position to manage their services through a corporatist system. The a priori sectoral interests of the state in health and social welfare would preclude such autonomy.

Summary and conclusions
It has been argued in this paper that the tripartite relationships between the state, national associations and the voluntary sector may be examined fruitfully by employing a corporatist perspective on the mediation of interests between the parties. Voluntary sector and state inter-relationships lend themselves readily to the corporatist perspectives espoused by Schmitter (1974), Panitch (1980), Booth (1982) and Wassenberg (1982).

The data show that the voluntary sector overall appears to be characterized by high levels of state involvement in their policy-making processes. In particular, the Charity Commission and central government departments are perceived to exercise the greatest influence over strategic decision-making in comparison with private associations such as the National Councils. Such relatively high influence, however, does not necessarily mean that what may be viewed from a structural perspective as 'pure' corporatism is, in the enactment of interest intermediation, partial or 'false' (Clegg, Dow and Boreham, 1983). The relatively greater representation and influence of the state is focused largely on monitoring activities through either the Charity Commission or central government departments to ensure that certain standards of provision of services are upheld.

Partial corporatism does seem to occur when a voluntary organization either receives a substantial level of funding from the state and/or operates in the domain of health and social welfare. In these cases (a third of the total sample of seventy-two organizations) the state intervenes directly in decision-making processes and is the ultimate arbiter over what is and what is not to be on the agenda for decision (Bachrach and Baratz, 1970; Lukes, 1974). In these voluntary organizations, the state has the capacity to exert pressure to conform to particular modes of operation in selected domains. This analysis concurs with Olson's (1965) findings that the influence of the state will prevail over collective representation in domains that fall within areas which are in the political interest of the state.

In addition, the state will try to exercise some control over which organizations are eligible to operate in the provision of health and welfare services and which are not. This is largely achieved through the arbitration of the Charity Commission over eligibility for charitable status (Wilson, 1984) although this does not mean that total control is secured in this way. Non-charities do operate in these areas, but their continued operation is always open to question given their precarious financial situation. They pay all taxes and receive no exemption from any other liabilities usually incurred by commercial business organizations. In particular, the Commission legislates against pressure groups and single issue groups which do not wish to work alongside the state but seek to change the mode of state operation (Olson, 1982: ch. 3).

However, for those voluntary organizations that are not subject to direct state intervention (the majority, if the sample is representative) the tripartite system of the state, private associations and constituent organizations appears to conform closely to a relatively pure form of neo-corporatism (Lehmbruch and Schmitter, 1982). Self-regulation through the national associations, with the state taking a back-stage role, is particularly evident in voluntary organizations that are either unique in the services they provide or largely independent of any substantial state funding (RNLI and Oxfam are examples). Furthermore, whether or not a voluntary organization is deemed charitable by the state does not preclude representation on any of the national associations. Membership of associations is, therefore, not directly controlled by the state.

The picture from the present data is both pessimistic and optimistic from the corporatist perspective. It is optimistic because, largely, the voluntary sector does operate along the lines of a self-regulating system through private interest governments (associations) which are charged with public policy by the state. It is pessimistic because in particular sectoral or functional domains the process becomes largely one of 'false' or 'hybrid' corporatism. Given the inherent flexibility and potential contribution of voluntary organizations, particularly in health and social welfare, the reluctance of the state to rescind direct control may be viewed as a kind of 'institutional sclerosis' (Olson, 1982: 78) which precludes a potentially dynamic and possibly unique form of corporatism from adapting responsively and quickly to environmental, technological and social changes.

Notes

The research reported in this paper was supported by SSRC grant no. 7960/2.

1. Discussion of the National Association is restricted in this paper to England and Wales. Scottish voluntary organizations are represented and co-ordinated by the Scottish Council of Social Service. Discussion of the Scottish system, which differs in many respects from its English counterpart, lies outside the scope of this chapter.

2. The data presented in this paper have been adapted by the authors from information collected by S.K.E. Saxon-Harrold who is currently a doctoral student linked to the research project reported here. More detailed in-depth data on specific case studies were collected by the current authors.

3. The results of the wider study are forthcoming in a book by Butler and Wilson (1985) which compares the task and institutional environments of commercial, statutory and voluntary organizations.

4. Hickson et al. (1985) also examine the overall influence of state agencies in *non* voluntary organizations and, somewhat surprisingly, the overall means (on the same scale) are very similar, with 2.5 in state-owned businesses and 3.0 in private businesses. However, Hickson et al. (1985) also point out that where state agencies are interventionist (i.e. attempt to control organizational decision-making directly) then the mean influence of state agencies such as the Treasury, Department of Employment, Department of Environment is 4.4 in private business and 4.2 in state-owned business. These results bear comparison with the influence scores in the present data for central government departments which have a mean influence score of 4.5.

5
De-bureaucratization and private interest government: the British state and economic development policy

Michael Hughes

Introduction
The analysis of de-bureaucratization has received scant attention in comparison with the central role which the concept of bureaucracy plays in organization theory. However, recent policy initiatives taken by the state in Western Europe and North America have drawn attention to de-bureaucratization, particularly in the new substantial literature on corporatism (see Winkler, 1976; and 1977; Lehmbruch and Schmitter, 1982). This focus upon the state in the process of de-bureaucratization includes several broad themes relating to the dispersal of state functions and changes in policy concerning non-state interests.

Private interest government (PIG)
The state distributes authority, public *compétence* and legitimate coercion through a compartmentalized structure. It develops association-firm limits which effectively increase the power of incorporated private agents but withhold overall control. This is achieved via a hierarchical structure of linkages which strengthens vertical lines of authority whilst reducing the number of horizontal ones (expressing and articulating private interests). Thus PIGs are encouraged on the basis of a limited number of self-regulated associations within broad parameters of control which replace directives from central government institutions.

Policy and decision-making
The state promotes a compartmentalization of agencies overseeing policy and devolves its implementation to non-state organizations which mediate between policy-making and execution. Hence, regulation, control and monitoring of policy is achieved at 'non-bureaucratic' levels.

Off-loading
State functions and activities are off-loaded to voluntary organizations or non-state enterprises. This retains state coverage of

its interests but reduces direct involvement. Manipulation of interests is preferred to direct control of representational groups.

Size
The diminution of large-scale state bureaucracy is, in itself, commonly regarded as de-bureaucratization. Thus the sheer size of organization (whether measured in terms of number of employees, range of functions, geographical coverage or budget) is often, misguidedly, taken as an indicator of bureaucratic traits (*inter alia* centralization and formalization) which can be removed by making the state bureaucracy 'smaller', 'local' and more 'sensitive' or 'responsive' to change.

Budgeting
The impetus for proposing de-bureaucratizing measures is often that of redistributing and targeting resources with some, rarely achieved, objective to reduce overall state expenditure. This covers a range of possibilities including selective 'cuts' in expenditure and the reallocation of 'savings' to promote certain policy options. The effects of such policies are not infrequently a reduction in employment in the state's central administrative apparatus and selected institutions (for example, in the UK we might include the nationalized industries, health and social security, and education) with an increased financial support for 'economic' development programmes (for example, innovation in industry, new technology).

These themes concentrate upon state related changes in the 'bureaucratic phenomenon' whilst implying *organizational* levels of change. Both aspects are linked in the process of creating private interest governments as a possible means of de-bureaucratization but are often treated separately. So, this paper is an attempt to illustrate this process by examining certain aspects of state–civil society–economy relations manifested in neo-corporatist structures and strategies. De-bureaucratization is perceived as a change in both intra and inter-organizational relations of the state and interest associations. A discussion of Burns and Stalker's (1966) work, following Perry (1981), will illustrate the two analytical levels implicit in this consideration. These two levels of analysis closely resemble areas in organizational analysis following Weberian and political economy perspectives:

Organizational structure
In the context of bureaucracy, the focus upon structure adopts a Weberian emphasis on the rational exercise of authority, organizational control, and domination. From this standpoint, de-

bureaucratization involves the design of an alternative structure better suited to the attainment of goals that do not require the 'efficient' and 'manifest' execution of managerial authority, or state authority in the public domain (e.g. Rothschild-Whitt, 1979; Burns and Stalker, 1966). Rather, the structure will subsequently reflect a variety of features *opposed* to the rational–bureaucratic model such as participation, flexibility and competence, based upon the premise of trust and a commonality of cause.

Inter-organizational relations
This level of analysis rests on a concern with the political economy of organizations (see Benson, 1975; Clegg and Dunkerley, 1980). Thus bureaucracy can also be viewed, in a non-Weberian manner, as an institutionalized form of state activity. Instead of a focus on the growth of rational–legal domination, bureaucracy is embodied in the administrative apparatus of the state. De-bureaucratization and the creation of PIGs clearly involve a change in the relations between the state apparatus and the spheres over which it has direct, sovereign, *control* in civil society. More specifically, relations will shift from ones of 'command' to a more negotiated order of bargaining and mutual accommodation with initiatives coming from either side, provided that state imposed parameters to the process are observed.

By invoking the concept of corporatism I hope to demonstrate that these levels of analysis are conjoined. An emphasis upon the distinction between them is partly the result of the recent development of contingency theory which conceptualizes 'organization' and 'environment' separately without much attention to what precisely is the difference (see Lawrence and Lorsch, 1967; Aldrich, 1979). This theory suffers from a range of conceptual problems including boundary definition and maintenance, organizational goals, exchange, genesis and survival, which underly the endeavours of so much recent work in organizational analysis as Aldrich (1979) and Zey-Ferrell (1981) demonstrate. By examining state policy and action with respect to organizations in policy-directed social change, we can attempt to move toward a more adequate understanding of some of these deficiencies.

I would suggest that certain paradoxes may arise from disassociating the organizational and inter-organizational (or environmental) levels of analysis, briefly indicated as:

1. *De-bureaucratization in a social order based predominantly on a rational–bureaucratic structure of relations between organizations, interest associations and the state.* If analysis rests primarily at the macro level, *relational* aspects between the state and private interest

governments will be emphasized. Thus the state apparatus engages in some measure of de-bureaucratization and encourages PIGs, although both may retain or adopt bureaucratic structures within this looser framework of relations. Centralized decision-making and policy formulation can also be retained by the state whilst incorporating interest groups within these processes and then devolving a certain degree of implementation, thus appearing to decentralize important areas under its control. At an ideological level this may become a crucial arena of struggle between contending interest groups supporting (or opposing) various strategies to satisfy their demands for greater participation or democratization in the public domain. Moves to de-bureaucratize through PIGs still requires authority and legitimacy from the state as it is not a purely voluntaristic process despite its self-governing character. Thus the overview of a society experiencing state sponsored de-bureaucratization is one of devolution, grass-roots action by interest associations, and a 'destructuration' of certain areas of the state apparatus. However, these changes do not necessarily disturb the continued execution of state policy or centralized control of functions by *bureaucratic* state institutions.

2. *De-bureaucratization of bureaucratic organization.* Analysis with an organizational focus characteristically stresses changes in authority relations within an organization, 'improvement' in managerial communication systems and the development of participative styles, de-centralized decision-making and horizontal lines of information exchange. This de-bureaucratization generates group and team-building efforts, greater delegation of authority and informal social relations. However, these intra-organizational features, regarded as 'non-bureaucratic' or 'organic' (Burns and Stalker, 1966), remain within a structure which still retains organizational policy parameters, hierarchical goal-setting and managerial control systems. Even in overtly 'democratized' or 'self-governing' organizations, these factors may be imposed through inter-organizational relations outside its arena of influence. Thus, de-bureaucratization, and elements of destructuration, are constrained by meso and macro level considerations.

These paradoxes, at the inter-organizational level in particular, can be translated into features of a corporatist structure and strategy to illustrate a meso level analysis, by using Wassenberg's (1982) notion of a 'disassociation of levels':

Disassociation of levels in structure. The state reproduces itself by changing its *form*. Hence, legally and nominally, it divests itself of certain institutions and permits or creates links between it and 'non-state' organizations (for example, quangos, functional interest associations, and unions, employers). Structural links are relaxed, from direct to indirect, 'loosely coupling' each level.

Disassociation of levels of control. De-bureaucratization represents a 'push-down' effect of control in 'state' activities such as welfare services, employment opportunities, economic policy, etc., by establishing broad guidelines for decision-making and introducing financial support from incentives to 'private' agencies.

Disassociation of levels of policy making. Policy is initiated by the state but execution is performed by non-state organizations (for example, large corporations, unions, employers). Detailed implementation of state policy is made subject to a process of negotiation in which private interest associations participate and have an indispensable role (for example, wage levels, industrial recovery/change).

Disassociation of levels of decision-making. Fundamental decisions about civil society and the economy are taken at state level by government but details are left *not* to the state bureaucracy but to incorporated interests (for example, disbursement of funds for new industry by local and business interests).

These disassociated levels represent a *control* option by the state which projects an ideology of state withdrawal from the economy and civil society whilst retaining an effective presence through corporatist arrangements. It is a shift in state-associational relations which distances the state from civil society through dependence upon mediating organizations. Similarly, *within* organizations a 'disassociation of levels' may permit a degree of de-bureaucratization where this is compatible with the attainment of managerially desired outcomes. Often, this process relates not so much to the awareness of the benefits of structural changes but to the possibility of its implementation, based upon the organization's locus in the economy−state relation, as we shall see in the discussion of Burns and Stalker (1966).

Consequently, the emergence of private interest government between both levels requires a similar disarticulation and distancing of the bureaucratic apparatus from each sphere of activity or function, whilst retaining ultimate (sovereign) control over outcomes. This control is reproduced through the formation of indirect links between and within organizations, which are most evident when the state creates new agencies or devolves powers to existing agents in order to facilitate greater 'accountability and responsibility' within civil society. Within organizations this process is most frequently observed in efforts to cope with perceived instability and change affecting the performance of the association, or the relation between its members.

However, the concern here is with those aspects of de-bureaucratization which involve *both* state and organizational levels, and upon which a considerable tradition of organization theory has been based, although interpreting it solely from the perspective of the organization. Such interpretations focus on bounded organizational change which obscure the interaction between organization and the state in the analysis of 'management'. In the discussion of Burns and Stalker (1966), I hope to show that bureaucratic structure in itself is not the crux of the analysis. Rather, what they so dramatically demonstrate is the replacement of direct bureaucratic control by a hierarchically structured network of relations, the consequence of which is a failure in the achievement of state policy. The retention of bureaucratic links directly between the state and organizations had earlier proved successful without de-bureaucratization. However, orthodox interpretations of Burns and Stalker (1966) continue to view this in a quite different manner (for example, Aitken and Hage, 1971; Hull and Hage, 1982), as we all know firms failed because they did not develop 'organic' (non-bureaucratic) structures. I will suggest that success and failure in this study are determined not by particular changes or lack of change in organizational structure per se, but by the inter-organizational relations in which these changes may or may not occur.

Neo-corporatism and de-bureaucratization
Social science and, more particularly, organizational analysis has treated bureaucracy as a hardy perennial in its conceptual and research repertoire. A focus on de-bureaucratization and corporatism is a more recent item on our intellectual agenda (Eisenstadt, 1959; Panitch, 1980) but promises to become an equally flourishing 'growth industry'. Our attention has been drawn to both concepts by various contemporary events in Western European societies, the USA and to some extent in Eastern Europe (see Kostecki, 1981; Mrela, 1981; Chirot, 1980), which have experienced greater state intervention in the economy and subsequent pressure for its withdrawal. This underscores the need for organization theory to tackle these issues, previously relegated to other sub-fields and disciplines, since state policy bears directly upon organizational relations. Therefore, interest in phenomena related to the decentralization of state activity and function partially reflects a more widely perceived 'disenchantment' with the role of the state in civil society and seems to resonate with an established theoretical focus on centralization/decentralization in organizational analysis (for example, variations on the 'mechanistic-organic' theme).

Consequently, our range of concepts must be broadened in scope to include and integrate our understanding of state–organization relations specifically rather than considering this as an environmentally contingent interface. One such conceptual addition in an analysis of de-bureaucratization might be neo-corporatism. It brings together both 'inter and intra-organizational' levels and facilitates the analysis of both the form and content of state–association relations.

The fundamental changes in state strategy during the implementation of corporatist structures are those that alter the state–organization relation from a direct to a more indirect one. Thus, more comprehensive business and professional associations and trade unions may be co-opted while others are subordinated, forming a more elaborate hierarchy of control. This shift replaces the simpler dyadic relationship and exchange prevailing among individuals, firms and inter-personal groups, and between them and the state bureaucracy, with one with a more complex network of non-state (quasi-state or quango) institutions.

This hierarchy can be characterized by an association's relationship to the state:

Incorporated
An association is permanently recognized and accorded a distinctive status by the state in exchange for the performance of some activity or function. It assumes the role of mediator in state policy and application, and forms the core of a control network with the state.

Excluded
An association is not incorporated and is therefore subject to decisions and actions of those that are part of the state's control network. These associations form a constellation of excluded interests contending for recognition or opposing the status quo.

Marginalized
Smaller associations may be at the periphery of the new network and experience a 'turbulent (political) environment' over which they have little or no control. Their status, and relations within the network, is unstable, uncertain, and they are not part of the major activities or struggles taking place within and between the larger incorporated/ excluded elements. The outcome of such struggles of course may alter their status, as would a change in their own power-resources and future repertoire of strategies deployed in political arenas of struggle.

These features of a corporatist structure change and reroute the articulation of demands and pressures on the state within civil society, by restricting the respective political processes in which any element in the network engages.

Participation
Corporatized associations participate in aspects of agenda-building, decision-taking, and the state's implementation of subsequent changes, 'governing' their members' behaviour in turn. Other elements bear the burden of 'action' or 'fulfilment' of the goals/outcomes of such changes within predetermined parameters, set within the constitution, for example, which governs their actions.

Representation
Corporatist structures damp down the range of interest articulation conducted through representative institutions in the political system. The upward lines of communication to the state are truncated and superimposed by co-opted associations. These linkages are partly reversed to predominantly downward lines of authority whereby associations impose standards and responsibilities on the behaviour of their members.

Access
Excluded and marginalized communities, social groups, individual citizens and production–distribution organizations in civil society have reduced access to representative channels and are limited in their capacity to articulate demands effectively or to form new or alternative interest groups. A corporatist structure fundamentally alters the vertical and horizontal linkages between elements, reducing access to and formation of means of interest articulation.

Thus, the rise of private interest governments and de-bureaucratization by the state, using a corporatist structure, does not necessarily enhance participation, representation, or access by individuals, social groups or economic units. Rather it involves a distancing of the state from the basic constituents of civil society by developing a baffle of intermediation. The immediate cause of such structures is not infrequently a crisis of state legitimacy or of the economy, where the state attempts to solve problems of decline, stagnation, or rapid development programmes (Booth, 1982; Hammergren, 1977; Hughes, 1982; Pike and Stritch, 1974; Wiarda, 1981).

Organization and structure
In addition to the analysis of 'de-bureaucratization by the state' there is a more traditional focus on organizational structure which is now extended to consider the conditions under which it takes bureaucratic/non-bureaucratic form, or some intermediate variant/composite of these types (*inter alia* Walker and Guest, 1952; Gouldner, 1954; Blau, 1955; Woodward, 1958, 1965; Burns and

Stalker, 1966; Udy, 1959; Lawrence and Lorsch, 1967; Thompson, 1967; Hall, 1972; Pugh and Hickson, 1976). This field has now become characteristically based on a contingency approach which treats the organization essentially as an actor responding to environmental exigencies. Success, efficiency or survival are the primary criteria for evaluating changes in or the suitability of organizational structures. These criteria are specifically related to a set of prevailing conditions projected on to a rather amorphous, under-conceptualized 'environment'. Characteristics of the environment, which the organizational structure is 'expected' to match, are essentially reformulations of managerial perceptions about environmental stability–instability, the relative importance of certain inputs, etc. The analysis is particularistic without specifying or adequately conceptualizing historical features of organizational relations at the macro level of analysis. In this way de-bureaucratization, or shifting towards a non-bureaucratic structure, means re-assessing structure in response to perceived environmentally determined 'needs'. Hence, *qualifications* of this type of analysis turn on discussions of strategic choice, managerial discretion and organizational slack, 'ecological' factors, etc.

In Weberian terms what happens is that de-bureaucratization, whatever the cause for the change, constitutes an attempt to shift from *formal* rationality to *substantive* rationality. A new organizational design takes certain selected areas and submits them to a re-evaluation of goals–away from rational mechanisms or administration and towards action guided without unambiguous rules, oriented to some more highly valued end such as innovation. This realignment bears more upon a set of 'cultural' attributes for the organizations decision-makers than authority relations, which are for the most part left intact.

Burns and Stalker's (1966) study of structural change in the UK electronics industry provides a key reference work for most discussions of de-bureaucratization at the level of organizational analysis. However, *interpretations* of this work are deficient in a number of respects.

What I intend to suggest in the next section is that work based on an organizationally-bounded and ahistorical view, following Burns and Stalker's research, is inadequate and that their study can be better located within a broader analysis of inter-organizational relations at the very least, and political economy would provide a more promising perspective on their study.

Simply put, Burns and Stalker's book did not really support early development of the contingency approach which viewed organizations as passive respondents to environmental pressures with success or failure depending on the organization's capacity or willingness to change. Rather, their material dramatically illustrates state penetration through a deliberate policy toward the firms studied by using an intermediary association to co-ordinate a network of firms expressly set up to implement state economic development plans. The state operated a 'hands-off' scheme through substituting a co-opted association in place of a previous system of direct controls via its bureaucratic apparatus.

Thus, this discussion will endeavour to demonstrate that the failure of firms in this case, rather than being purely a result of lack of changes in organizational structure, is more likely to have resulted from intermediation between firms. The economic and political arenas of initiative and execution were controlled by the state and its agent. The internal problems of firms subject to this system of control, therefore, were primarily a result of their location in an organizational political economy.

The political economy of Burns and Stalker
Despite the status accorded to Burns and Stalker's (1966) study, there is a small but significant critical literature (see Perry, 1981; Wood, 1979) which suggests a way forward from the sort of analysis so much influenced by Burns and Stalker, Woodward (1958) and others, i.e., the contingency approach.

> A major weakness of the contingency writings is their rather limited reading of the work in which they purpose to be rooted. Thus, for example, almost total emphasis is given in accounts of Burns and Stalker's work to its dichotomous classification of formal organisations ... (Wood, 1977: 353)

The much quoted analysis of mechanistic and organic organization structure comes only on pages 119–22 of *The Management of Innovation*, and it may not be the most important or most powerful element in the work. Most interpretations of their research give primary emphasis to the internal managerial political system rather than the considerable amount of data and discussion of the 'environment' which was to become so important (despite being under-conceptualized) in subsequent theoretical developments in contingency approaches. Instead, the organization became the focus of analytical attention and was seen as an adaptive entity, responding and changing according to managerially mediated influences on it from the 'outside' world.

> Mechanistic management corresponds rather closely to those aspects of Weber's account of bureaucracy which the specialism emphasises and is identified as an organisational form appropriate to enterprises operating in stable technical and commercial milieu. Successful accommodation to

rapid change in these environmental factors is associated with the alternate, organic system, which is characterised by a much more fluid role structure, a network structure of communication and control and emphasis on cosmopolitan expertise. (Perry, 1981: 45)

The main thrust of the discussion will be that a passive view of organizational change and latter variations on this theme are inadequate. Burns and Stalker can be revived in a more suitable generic guise as a political economy of organizations (and, more specifically perhaps, as an analysis of organizations within neo-corporatist structures) rather than as an orthodox systems theory.

> Modern organisational forms, governmental and industrial, represent the application of rational thought to social institutions in the same way that technology is the product of the rational manipulation of nature. In the same way, too, it congeals the processes of human affairs — 'fixing' them so that they become susceptible to control by large-scale organisations. The reverse aspect of this tendency is the increasing subjection of the individual to the psychological and material domination of the social order, a domination increasingly objective and universal as civilisation advances technically. (Burns and Stalker, 1966: 12)

The two main studies

Two important studies were conducted by Burns and Stalker in the 1950s concerning small to medium sized Scottish firms participating in a government-sponsored, indirectly controlled, electronics development scheme, and eight established English electronics companies which had successfully developed and grown before, during and since 1946. In other words, the Scottish firms were part of a state development programme and were completely new to electronics research, development and manufacture; whereas the English firms were already established and had been nurtured throughout the Second World War on defence contracts coming directly from the state.

The conceptual context in which Burns and Stalker place their research is interesting in itself, and they state this before discussing their findings.

> The first part of this book is directly concerned with identifying industrial organisations as the product of the actually developing change processes in society and of the purpose and commitment of entrepreneurs and managers. What I have called the technological system itself is treated in the same way. And not only the 'dysfunctional' but also the two ideal types of management system are presented as the outcome of responses of managers to their commercial and technical situation and the definitions of tasks and relationships which they accepted or rejected. (Burns and Stalker, 1966: xvi)

So here we have the basic contingency approach principle but it is embedded in a view of industrialism and technology which pervaded the UK at least in the late 1950s and 1960s and shares some of the features outlined by Kerr et al. (1971) in the USA.

> The industrialism we now have, or are getting, is a new industrialism; its effects on people inside and outside the immediate world of industry is substantially different from what we, in the oldest industrial country in the world, have to accept as customary, maximal and acceptable. The electronics industry is itself one of the first creatures of the new combination of science and industry, one of the earliest manifestations of new industrialism. (Burns and Stalker, 1966: xxi)

Therefore, it is somewhat surprising to read in the first seventy-three pages of Burns and Stalker (1966) an account of state intervention, and failure based on macro level socio-political structures; especially given their emphasis and optimism about the role of technology and professional managers.

Success and 'environment':
bureaucratic control and innovation
The success element of the study is based on the English companies which had started before the Second World War and developed under favourable conditions of a stable market and close, direct contact with user needs (i.e., government defence contracts in wartime). The process of successful innovation identified by Burns and Stalker consists of the important close contact between scientist and user, between need and design. The case of radar development in the UK is cited to show how well the process worked through close co-operation between industry, government and science.

The early English electronics firms were small or subordinate units of larger firms. They developed a wide potential for commercial operations under the secure and lucrative defence contract system which enabled them to build up their research and development capacity to use later when moving into harsher market conditions after the War.

These eight English firms all grew rapidly after the Second World War. By 1958 one firm had sixteen times its 1946 capacity; another increased its number of employees from 150 to 3000 in eight years; and another doubled its turnover in seven years. The reasons for this expansion were given as:
1. There was a market demand for the products that these companies could produce and in which they had a technological lead (for example, television, laboratory instruments, radar, navigation, computers, semi-conductors, guided weapons).

2. They had diversified horizontally and vertically.
3. They had developed new product ranges based on known techniques and systematic surveys of customer needs and commercial opportunities (for example, through data-processing)
4. They had entered into joint ventures and penetrated new markets to use existing resources.

This picture is one of firms that had grown and been innovative in a sheltered environment. The state had effectively and directly regulated the development of new products, supplies of materials and the market. This overarching control by the state 'standardized' the production and marketing role of these firms. The firms stored their capacity to tackle a commercial market after the War, when they avoided dependency on state contracts and become intimately related to commercial and industrial organizations and technological needs. There is little analysis of the role of professional management or the firm's internal organizational structure by Burns and Stalker other than the acknowledgement that the managers developed a 'code of conduct', 'subject the intellectual, emotional, and moral content of [the individual's] ... life to the ends presented by the working organisations of the society...' and that management involves everybody at some time in the company. No need here for a *specific* response to unstable environments or development of organic systems. As they say:

> The centre of interest for us lay in the management itself. If by 'management' is meant a special category of individual in a concern, it has extremely ill-defined limits, but we have not sought to introduce any more precise connotations. We have rather used the word in its other sense of directing, co-ordinating and controlling the operations of a working community; and, as we try to make clear, this kind of activity can involve everybody in a concern at different times and in different respects. (Burns and Stalker, 1966: 13).

So, I would suggest that this is not so much about organic structure within a firm as it is about the political economy of organization—state relations and organizational 'culture'. This point is implicitly recognized by Burns and Stalker when they refer to the need for managers to become 'electronically-minded', i.e., everyone is engaged in the research and development effort at some point and managers must 'turn-on' to this.

A case of failed de-bureaucratization?
A very different situation applied to the Scottish firms studied — which, in the orthodox interpretation, failed to become successful electronic innovators because their managers could not change from mechanistic to organic management systems. However, the first

section of Burns and Stalker's analysis hints that these firms were more or less doomed to failure because of external administrative and power structures; whereas a different structure had given the English firms a sporting chance of success.

The Scottish firms were locked into a peripheral position in the UK economy and in relation to the state. At the outset of the scheme in which they were invited to participate, this became reinforced. During the immediate post-war period, technological developments, such as the ones illustrated by the English electronics firms, were an important and dynamic part of the economy, but it became quite apparent that Scotland had no share in this new technology. It still relied on declining heavy industries based on iron and steel and coal. The Scottish Council, an association founded in 1947 to encourage industry in Scotland, in co-operation with (the then) Scottish Home Department and Board of Trade, successfully negotiated the placement of government defence contracts in Scotland, although it was now peacetime and the pressure on government to intervene directly and develop advanced defence technology was minimal. In fact, as a result of the successes of the English firms, there was, as far as the state's requirements were concerned, an excess of capacity in research and development. The state was prepared to allocate contracts to large research and development units, but these were all in England. There were no Scottish firms of this type, only an English company plant in Edinburgh (Ferranti). In addition, all the Scottish operations were too distant from London to keep in close contact if the state was to supervise development directly. Without the state defence contracts the Scottish Council scheme for introducing electronics could not begin — the firms wishing to join the programme needed guaranteed work before they could hire expensive research and development personnel.

Therefore a strategy was developed whereby there would be a degree of devolution and delegation in the scheme, replacing direct links between the state and small Scottish firms by using the Scottish Council and Ferranti as 'mediating agents'. A number of small Scottish companies would join the Scottish Council scheme and would be considered as a single association by the state. The Scottish Council would co-ordinate these embryonic ventures, Ferranti acting as the technical information centre, and negotiate with authorities for research and development contracts which Ferranti would then break down and dispense as sub-contracts to the new firms under its supervision. Thus Ferranti acted as the state's intermediary for technological training and information which was to be based at new government-sponsored laboratories located at Ferranti's site in Edinburgh.

Immediately, we can see fundamental differences in the conditions under which the Scottish firms had to develop. They were distant from the user of their eventual products (i.e. the state), and dependent for an assessment of its needs, both geographically and commercially, upon the Scottish Council and Ferranti who became a monopolistic 'broker' between them and the state (Perry, 1981). These Scottish firms were effectively 'marginalized' under this arrangement. During the scheme the state reduced spending on new buildings so that the training laboratories were delayed until 1954. This point illustrates the notion of 'disassociation of levels' and the role of the state in the saga very well. It wanted to achieve broad political objectives in helping an an underdeveloped and declining region of the British economy, but used an association of private interests to effect the means to achieve it.

As the electronic scheme progressed, the state contracts proved to be rather infrequent. Ferranti took the lead in sub-contracting the work, directing, monitoring, and processing the contracts in accordance with the scheme's overall policy, but at a distance from the state. As a result the new small firms took on far too many development contracts, *hoping* for more profitable production contracts later, regarding this as investment for the future. This work had a low rate of return and Ferranti diverted it to the small Scottish firms whilst retaining the more lucrative contracts for itself. The firms in this scheme had wanted to improve their position in the market by developing new technology with a view to exploiting the commercial market. Instead they bore the brunt of the development work without establishing a manufacturing capacity. Ferranti became the main beneficiary of the scheme and had a set of new laboratories to prove it. The Scottish firms expected to acquire what Burns and Stalker call 'electronic mindedness' from the Scottish Council scheme. All they got was an advanced lesson in corporate power and strategy from the state and Ferranti.

Corporatist structure or mechanistic mismanagement?
A crucial element in this analysis is the small Scottish firms themselves. Even if the conditions surrounding the implementation of the Scottish Council's scheme had not prevailed, the nature of the firms themselves was hardly conducive to success.

The firms had elected to join the scheme for a variety of desperate reasons. Most of them were facing a shrinking or closing markets for their existing products, something of which they were aware even before the war. Burns and Stalker give several examples, including one of a company which manufactured rolling-stock for the railways and a mechanical engineering firm which made high precision products. All the Scottish companies that joined the scheme were seeking redemption from almost certain decline if not closure. They mistakenly anticipated that they would leap into the electronic boom by acquiring a research and development team, to be trained and apprenticed by Ferranti under the auspices of the state. Most of these Scottish firms fared very badly and withdrew from the scheme at a loss without acquiring sufficient expertise to survive in the commercial market. Some of the firms produced obsolete products because they did not have enough contact with commercial users. Half the companies disbanded the research teams or converted into separate testing units.

No doubt this study tells us a great deal about changing conditions in the organizational environment, but most interpretations of Burns and Stalker do not take this into account. Having accepted the thesis of the new industrialism, they stress the rise of managerial control (as a separate phenomenon from ownership in capitalism) and, hence, over-emphasized the role played by internal managerial machinations in the fate of these small firms.

It is precisely the role of the state and the monopolistic allocation of resources and services by non-state associations, presumably acting in the public interest, empowered by the state, which needs to be adequately conceptualized fully to understand Burns and Stalker's study. One can see the system of relations which emerged between the state, the Scottish Council, Ferranti and the Scottish firms in which the small firms were marginal. The principal economic and political advantages were enjoyed by those in control of the state-association network, and they were fully prepared to exploit their strategic position to maximize their own rewards.

An important point which this raises is the financial and political resource base which a business corporation has at its disposal. In the Scottish case, Ferranti, together with the Scottish Council, had considerable amounts of both and could manipulate the subordinate firms and its 'environment' effectively (up to a point) in their guise as state agents. The small Scottish firms had neither set of resources and consequently were exploited and marginalized. Whether the association in question is large or small, an incorporated member of a network (the 'electronics club' in this case) or financially powerful may in fact tell us more about the survival prospects of firms and their potential for success than looking at managerial attitudes. De-bureaucratization within the small firms participating in this scheme failed partly because of the 'successful' devolution of public authority by the state to a self-regulated association of private organizations.

Organic and mechanistic structure

From Burns and Stalker's own writing we can see that organic management systems are elaborate working cultures which are expensive and depend on the continuous development of ideas rather than structure. Mechanistic systems on the other hand refer to the whole enterprise and depict behaviour patterns, as well as a structure of authority.

The 'transition' from one mode to the other involves an addition to the power system. A shift from 'mechanistic' to 'organic' involves the power of an enterprise's management, which has invested its efforts in production oriented structures, being supplemented by a managerial ideology of change centred on the innovative and marketing function, thereby developing a substantive rationality.

Burns and Stalker do provide excellent grounds for developing a more detailed analysis of inter-organizational networks, particularly enterprise–state relations, and call our attention to the fact that change is a process requiring detailed historical knowledge of various parties involved (see Perry, 1981). Furthermore, they demonstrate how large, secure corporations can afford to sponsor the creation of 'organic'/innovation ideologies for managers in sub-sections of the organization to exploit the corporation's financial advantage and location in a political economy. It is not a general or universal principle stating that mechanistic is bad and organic is good, since it is not a necessary condition for survival.

Conclusion

The failure of the Scottish firms to become successful innovators was more a problem of their position within an association of private interests than a failed management system.[1] Their isolation from contact with the market and user (i.e. the state) was compounded by Ferranti's intermediary role and exploitative action in the scheme.

Given this analysis, I would suggest in conclusion that to apply a contingency model — i.e. uncritically accepting the parameters of a particular systems framework — in societies advocating the development of 'private government' and an ideology of de-bureaucratization is unsatisfactory. Contingency approaches undervalue the need to revise one's notions of environment, power, the political system and corporate networks. Child (1976) has indicated the choice which is open to corporate managers (and owners) at the strategic levels of decision-making, so why develop and apply a theory which virtually reduces them to puppets at the mercy of 'environmental' pressures or ignore the very active role which corporations and the state play in determining and manipulating 'environments', whether the organizations be large industrial corporations or cultural institutions. Particularly in societies where state intervention or withdrawal is advocated, it is a prime analytical error to ignore the totality in which the organization is situated in order to apply a technically sophisticated methodology to change management systems, which promises effectiveness in theory but not in practice. The methodology cannot create successful organizations, which can then indulge in de-bureaucratization/'culture-experiments' with their managers and engage in market exploitation. De-bureaucratization, at the inter-organizational level of analysis, may only be an expedient for the state and, within organizations, only a limited option.

Note

An earlier draft of this paper was delivered at the Sixth EGOS Colloquium in Florence, November 1983. I am grateful to the participants in Wolfgang Streeck's sessions for their comments, particularly Hugh Willmott who acted as discussant, and for Philippe Schmitter's subsequent editorial advice. Finally, I am indebted to my ex-colleague, Nick Perry, with whom I worked for several years at the University of Strathclyde where we exchanged ideas on certain issues examined in this chapter; some of the results of these discussions have been incorporated here. Of course, I alone am responsible for the end product of these inputs.

1. It is ironic that Scotland in the 1980s does have a thriving electronics industry in 'Silicon Glen', a forty-mile long corridor between Greenock, near Glasgow, and Livingston, close to Edinburgh. There are now about 300 firms in the information technology industry there. Many of the smaller ones are Scottish-owned, but the most substantial presence is formed by multinational corporations (for example, IBM, Motorola, National Semiconductor). Approximately 70 percent of recent investment has come from US firms which began moving into the West of Scotland in the late 1960s and early 1970s, after the failure of the Scottish Council Scheme. A second phase of state involvement and a new determined effort to implement a development strategy began in 1976 when the Labour Government formed the Scottish Development Agency (SDA), following the exploitation of North Sea Oil, in a bid to fend off a political challenge from the revitalised Scottish Nationalist Party. In terms of creating employment opportunities and encouraging economic development, the SDA's success has been founded on attracting investment from successful foreign firms operating in global commercial markets. In addition to dominating North Sea Oil production, multinational corporations now form an 'electronics club' in Scotland of which indigenous firms are only junior members.

6
The politics of the pharmaceutical price regulation scheme
Jane A. Sargent

Despite its name the Pharmaceutical Price Regulation Scheme (PPRS) aims to control the profits the UK prescription medicine industry receives on its sales to the National Health Service (NHS). All versions of the scheme have been operated on the basis of the assumption shared by successive British governments that a reasonable level of overall profit on sales to the NHS will produce a reasonable level of overall prices for the medicines supplied.

The scheme has been in operation in various forms since 1958. Until 1978 it was known as the Voluntary Price Regulation Scheme (VPRS), and the change to its name reflects the lack of voluntarism with which members of the prescription medicine industry agreed to and applied price regulation measures.

The object of the scheme is not to achieve the lowest possible price for medicines supplied to the NHS but to produce a 'fair and reasonable' drug bill for the Service. Until 1969 this was the only object specified in the scheme. Thereafter the preamble to the scheme has emphasized wider objectives. These objectives are to secure:

> not only that safe and effective medicines are available on reasonable terms to the National Health Service, but also that a strong, efficient and profitable pharmaceutical industry in the United Kingdom is capable of such sustained research and development expenditure as should lead to the future availability of new and improved medicines, both for the National Health Service and for export.[1]

No definition of reasonable is provided in any version of the scheme, neither does any include a negotiated profit formula. Yet, it is upon the requirement that the scheme produce a 'fair and reasonable' drug bill that it is assessed by the industry and by the government and upon which negotiation of successive versions of the scheme has been based.

The shape of the PPRS and its predecessors has been the subject of negotiation and agreement between the government (currently represented by the Department of Health and Social Security (DHSS), the Scottish Home and Health Department, the Ministry of Health and Social Services for Northern Ireland and the Welsh Office), and the British prescription medicine industry's trade association, the

Association of the British Pharmaceutical Industry (ABPI). The scheme provides a framework within which individual companies supplying medicines to the NHS can negotiate with the state agency the level of their profit return on these sales and the range of prices they can charge the NHS for their products. Agreement and implementation of the PPRS are thus the outcome of two separate negotiating processes. The agreement process first involves the ABPI as a mediator between the interests of the government and the industry, whereas during operation of the scheme neither the state agency nor the industry have chosen to conduct their negotiations through an intermediary.

During the first decade of the NHS's life after the Second World War the Committee of Public Accounts frequently claimed that the prescription medicine industry earned excessively high profits and that these reflected the high prices the industry was charging for its products. To amend this, the government could have encouraged the industry to establish a system of self-regulation through its trade association, or it could have sought separate agreements with individual manufacturers on the prices they charged for their NHS sales, or both.

This case study analyses under what conditions and to what extent the relationship between the government and the British prescription medicine industry has been mediated by the industry's trade association, the ABPI. Attention is focused on the dual relationship of the ABPI on the one hand with the government and on the other with its members and the prescription medicine industry as a whole. Of particular interest are the functions the Association has performed on behalf of the government and on behalf of its members and the industry as a whole, and the mechanisms of mutual control which have developed between the Assocation and its two 'environments' during negotiation and operation of each version of the price regulation scheme. Of principal interest in the account that follows of the history of the PPRS is the extent to which the ABPI has acted as a lobby (spokesman for its members and/or the industry) or as a private interest government (capable of enforcing its decisions and agreements upon its members even against their resistance) during successive renegotiations of the scheme and during the period of operation of each revision of the PPRS.

The background to the scheme
In 1954 the Minister of Health and what was then the Joint Committee on Prescribing joined with the Committee of Public Accounts to demand government control over the cost of classification 2, 3 and 4 proprietaries supplied to the NHS. These proprietaries were human

medical and dental specialities — medicines not advertised to the public and sold under a brand name — which were not regarded as therapeutically superior to standard drugs.[2] Thus, on 10 May 1954 the Minister announced to the House of Commons during a debate on the NHS 'that doctors would soon be advised not to prescribe . . . [this] group of preparations for which agreement could not be reached with the manufacturers on what the Ministry considered a reasonable level of profit'.[3]

The government's justification for this measure was that as the Exchequer was ultimately the main purchaser of these preparations, in effect a monopsonistic buyer, it should be able to have a say in the level of profit return the industry received on the sale of these products to the NHS. Hence, the Minister proposed that the level of profit on these products should fall within the range generally accepted as appropriate in other fields of government trading. At the time this range was 7.5 to 15 per cent on 'capital employed', the capital being calculated on an historical basis.

The manufacturers of these preparations feared that the Minister's proposals would have a damaging effect on their home sales, research, productivity and export trade. These fears were based upon the facts that classification 2, 3 and 4 proprietaries constituted the major part of the medicines supplied to the NHS in 1954 — they accounted for approximately 90 per cent of the cost of all proprietaries prescribed under the NHS and thus also accounted for the main part of the prescription medicine industry's total output. In addition, it was in the form of medical specialities in particular that products of research and development were, and still are, introduced into both the home and export markets. Moreover, because of the rapid obsolescence of prescription medicines the industry's future prosperity is largely dependent upon its ability to produce a level of profitability on its medical specialities which is sufficient to fund its costly investment programme.

The Minister's proposal of 10 May had been to negotiate price agreements with individual manufacturers. Whilst it did not reflect an intention to fix these prices under a system of state control, neither did it imply a willingness to involve an intermediary, even though a large number of companies were involved. On 14 May 1954 the Ministry of Health formally informed the ABPI of its proposals, however, and in response the ABPI's Council set up a negotiating committee and empowered it to conduct negotiations on the proposed policy with Whitehall.

The Negotiating Committee was composed of members of Division B of the ABPI. This division then included manufacturers of medical, veterinary and dental speciality products for home and export trades, the advertising of such products being confined to members of the professions concerned.[4] Amongst the members of the Negotiating Committee were representatives of leading pharmaceutical companies such as ICI, May and Baker, Glaxo Laboratories, the Wellcome Foundation and the British Drug Houses.

These and other leading members of the UK pharmaceutical industry decided to participate collectively in discussions with the Ministry of Health on the subject of the Minister's proposals for a number of reasons. Firstly, of course, they recognized that they would have a stronger voice if they presented their case collectively rather than individually. They also recognized the determination of the state to restrict the level of the NHS drug bill to 'fair and reasonable' limits. Furthermore they believed that they should be prepared with a more suitable set of measures in the event of being unable to persuade the Ministry officials of the undesirability of the Minister's scheme. If there was to be a pricing policy it should be as acceptable as possible to manufacturers and not prejudice the future prosperity of either the prescription medicine industry or the pharmaceutical industry as a whole.

It is important to note that the manufacturers acknowledged the government's claim that there were excesses in the pricing and profitability of certain prescription medicines and were willing, therefore, to accept an external check on payments made for their products out of public funds. But they argued that generally the prices for their products were 'fair and reasonable', and that the savings to be gained from a pricing policy would be low in relation to total expenditure. This view contrasted sharply to that of the Minister of Health, the Treasury and the Committee of Public Accounts, all of which anticipated large savings from the policy (approximately £1.75 million per annum). It was largely upon the strength of this difference of opinion that the first Voluntary Price Regulation Scheme was born. The following account of the history of the price regulation scheme illustrates how and why participation in a system of price regulation came to conflict with manufacturers' commercial interests. It also shows the effect of this tension upon their relationship with the state during operation of the scheme and with the ABPI as their mediator during negotiation of successive versions of the scheme.

The first price regulation scheme
The ABPI's Negotiating Committee met for the first time on 26 May 1954 and after two further meetings completed a memorandum which was sent to the Ministry of Health on 1 July. In this memorandum the Committee explained why the criterion for assessing prices under government contracts was considered inappropriate to the

circumstances under which drugs were provided to the NHS and reasons were given why any attempt to apply the criterion would have a prejudicial effect on the industry's research, productivity and export trade.[5] In a covering letter, the ABPI expressed its willingness to cooperate in securing all reasonable economies in expenditure on the NHS and stated that the Negotiating Committee had already begun to formulate alternative proposals for arriving at mutually satisfactory prices for classification 2, 3 and 4 proprietaries.[6] These alternative proposals were later to become the Voluntary Price Regulation Scheme.

Having agreed upon the essentials of the alternative scheme the Negotiating Committee appointed a sub-committee of pricing and cost experts from the companies represented on the main committee to work out certain details of the alternative scheme. At a meeting on 9 August 1954 ABPI representatives and officials from the health departments discussed the principles of the alternative scheme and agreed that the ABPI should continue to work on the scheme and that it should be submitted to the Ministry upon completion.

After further meetings of the main and sub-committees and further contacts and discussions with the relevant ministry divisions the scheme was finalized and submitted to the departments of health on 2 December 1954.

The Association's scheme was later revised in order to meet the objections raised by the departments and was tested by applying it to a sample of 200 products of 28 firms selected by the departments. Although modified during the course of the negotiations, it did not lose its essential features. The negotiations had comprised some fourteen meetings of the Negotiating Committee between May 1954 and January 1957, on two occasions the Committee met with officials at the Ministry of Health, in addition the Committee's chairman and secretary met with officials at the health departments several times and in the concluding stages of the negotiations held two lengthy meetings with the Minister of Health and the Joint Under-Secretary of State for Scotland.[7] Governmental satisfaction with the ABPI's intermediary role during these negotiations was expressed in the letter informing the Association of the Minister's decision to implement the scheme: 'I should like to express the appreciation of the Minister and the Secretary of State for Scotland at the co-operation which the Association has afforded in this matter. The Ministers are confident that they may rely upon the Association's continued assistance in this field.[8]

The ABPI's brief had been to formulate a scheme which was reasonably satisfactory to both the departments of health and the manufacturers and this had proved 'a most difficult and formidable task'.[9] Largely because of the difficulties involved, the VPRS was not entirely to the satisfaction of either of the interested parties. Whilst hopeful of large savings from the scheme and pleased that the manufacturers had accepted the need for price restraint the Treasury, at least, had misgivings about the scheme on the government's side: 'It is one which has been accepted ... as being in advance of anything we have so far been able to do ... But it does not follow from that that we will necessarily go on with this arrangement.'[10] For the manufacturers' part fears remained about the potentially harmful effects of any price restraint scheme on the industry's productivity, research and export trade.

The main provisions of the scheme were as follows:

A part (A) which gave three alternative general formulae for determining maximum prices.
The first of these (A.1), the 'Export Criterion', was to apply where more than 20 per cent of the output of a given medicine was exported, and in this case the home price was not to exceed the weighted average export price.
The second (A.2), the 'standard equivalent' provision, laid down that where the export criterion was inapplicable, the price of a medicine with an exact equivalent was not to exceed that of the equivalent.
The third (A.3), provided a 'trade price formula' to be used where neither A.1 nor A.2 was applicable, and which gave a method of calculating the maximum price using an allowance related to the basic ingredient cost, with added allowances for oncost, processing and packaging.
A part (B) which allowed for direct negotiations between manufacturer and the Ministry if the manufacturer so desired, or if none of the formulae were applicable.
Certain other provisions, including particularly an undertaking by the ABPI that if in any cases formulae prices should prove higher than current prices, current prices would not be increased except where an increase was justified by an increase in costs, and a provision that for the first three years during which a medicine was on the market its price was left entirely to the manufacturer's discretion, and the scheme did not apply (the 'Freedom Period').[11]

The formulae given were intended for use by the departments of health and individual manufacturers during negotiations on the price to be paid for classification 2, 3 and 4 proprietaries by the NHS. No role was intended for the ABPI either as an intermediary during these negotiations or as a lobby on behalf of the manufacturers collectively or on behalf of individual manufacturers. The ABPI's functions during the period the scheme was in operation were to supply the Minister of Health periodically with information needed for the scheme to be applied and to fulfil its undertaking to prevent price increases unless these were justified by increased costs in cases where formulae prices were higher than current prices.

Both these functions were of central importance to the ultimate success or failure of the scheme. They depended upon the ABPI's representativeness of manufacturers of classification 2, 3 and 4 proprietaries, upon its ability to ensure their compliance with the scheme, and upon its ability to provide the state with the information required. Partly in response to these requirements, the Association's constitution and rules were amended on 28 February 1958 to secure a more balanced representation on the Association's governing body, the Council, of the different interests within the Association (Lang, 1974: 64). Moreover, in 1958 a recommendation was made by the Association's finance committee for a streamlining of the ABPI's financial arrangements and for a review to be undertaken of 'the practicability of adopting an alternative method of assessing subscriptions which could produce a higher income and would remove anomalies'.[12] These anomalies had been caused by the burden placed on the ABPI's resources because of the increased workload it had undertaken on behalf of Division B. The same development had also prompted the Association to appoint an additional assistant secretary the previous year.

On the other hand, the changes to the Association's constitution and rules did not include measures which invested in the ABPI the ability to make its agreement with the state on a pricing policy binding upon its members — regardless of the fact that manufacturers had just agreed to a scheme of price regulation whose success largely depended upon the ability of their representative association, the ABPI, to ensure their compliance with the scheme. This was in line with the British non-interventionist tradition that trade associations should be voluntary organizations. The government, whilst sharing this attitude, hoped that the ABPI's decision-making procedures during negotiation of the VPRS had entailed a sufficiently high level of participation by Division B members to ensure their compliance with the final agreement. It also hoped that the Association was representative of all the companies to which the VPRS applied.

The inadequacy of the ABPI's decision-making procedures and/or its representativeness quickly became apparent, however. Not all the relevant companies were willing to abide by the scheme. Much of the problem centred on the British subsidiaries of the large Swiss corporations which, among other things, did not until 1960 agree to be bound by the VPRS. This and similar incidents highlighted the ABPI's organizational weakness and prompted the Committee of Public Accounts to press for more stringent controls when the second VPRS came up for negotiation: 'Your Committee recommend that the Ministry should discuss with the pharmaceutical industry the implications and failures by members of the industry, whether or not they subscribe formally to the terms of the Voluntary Price Regulation Scheme, to co-operate in the negotiation of fair and reasonable prices for proprietary products'.[13]

The second VPRS

During the period of operation of the first VPRS the ABPI was pleased with how smoothly the scheme ran and that problems of interpretation and implementation were isolated and solved without difficulty.[14] Not surprisingly, therefore, its Division B members were willing to continue with the scheme after the end of its three year trial period subject to certain amendments which they felt were necessary in the light of experience. The ABPI's Negotiating Committee was therefore reconstituted in 1959. It was very similar to its predecessor but, in keeping with the expansion of foreign manufacturers into Britain in the 1950s, representation of the Swiss and US corporations was strengthened with the addition of representatives of Ciba Laboratories Ltd and Pfizer Corporation Ltd.

The government also felt the need for the scheme to be continued, despite the Treasury's scepticism of its benefits, although subject to certain modifications. The Treasury and the Committee of Public Accounts had expressed dissatisfaction at the savings the first VPRS produced. In its Second Report for the year 1959 – 60 the Committee stated that the Ministry of Health had estimated that the VPRS would save up to £750,000 on an annual expenditure of £20 million but in fact the scheme had produced a price reduction estimated to save only £412,000 on an annual expenditure of £28 million.[15]

Negotiations began in early 1960 after the Ministry of Health sent a memorandum to the ABPI setting out the government's proposals for changes. Prior to commencement of the negotiations the Association had issued a questionnaire to all members of Division B inviting them to give their views on the Ministry's memorandum and information on their experiences of operating the VPRS. The replies received were considered by the Negotiating Committee and arrangements were then made for the committee's chairman and secretary to begin exploratory discussions with officials at the health departments. Agreement was reached on a revised scheme on 14 December 1960 to become effective from 1 January 1961.

Although it now applied to proprietaries classified under category S by the Committee on Classification of Proprietary Preparations, the revised scheme was broadly similar to its predecessor. Category S merely represented a combination of classification 2, 3 and 4 proprietaries but avoided the phrase 'not therapeutically superior to standard preparations'. The main modifications to the scheme were that henceforth patented products with sales to the NHS in excess of £0.5 millions per annum could be made the subject of direct negotiations between the Ministry of Health and the relevant firms at the option of the Ministry, even if their prices could be regarded as satisfactory on the weighted export criterion. In addition, the qualification for the export criterion was raised to 25 per cent of output and direct price negotiations on major products could be based, at the request of the firm, either on the profitability of individual products or on their overall profitability.

During negotiation of the second VPRS the Council of the ABPI had conducted another review of the constitution and rules of the Association and agreed to changes which became effective in April 1961. These changes were intended to enable the ABPI 'to respond to the developing needs of the industry and to improve its services to its members'.[16] They comprised, among other things, the replacement of the council as the Association's governing body with a Board of Management. The board consisted of only twelve members (as compared with the old council of thirty-one members) and was responsible for 'general administration of finance, for the co-ordination of divisional policies and for the appointment and general supervision of specialist committees serving the membership as a whole' (Lang, 1974: 72). Each division was to elect its own Council which was to report to the Board. The Councils were to be composed of a chairman, vice-chairman and the immediate past president of the Division and a number of elected members. Division B decided upon nine elected members. Under these arrangements, negotiation of the VPRS became increasingly the concern of Division B and henceforth, the Negotiating Committee reported to the Council of Division B which reported to the governing body.

Once again these changes did not bring with them the authority for the ABPI to enforce its agreement with the state agency upon its members. Interestingly, however, in 1958 the Association had published the first edition of its Code of Advertising Practice and compliance with the code became a condition of ABPI membership. The prescription medicine industry, and by implication the government because the code was not regarded as a restrictive practice, seem to have accepted that non-interventionist values can be compromised in the interest of the safety of medicines but not as regards their prices and profitability.

Almost immediately after the new scheme was introduced the industry's anxieties about its restrictive effects on their activities began to be realized. In 1961 there was a disagreement and ultimately a legal battle between the US company Pfizer and the NHS over the price to be paid for the antibiotic Terramycin. This incident once again highlighted the lack of control the ABPI had over its members and that participation in the negotiating committee's activities was not always sufficient to ensure a company's compliance with the VPRS. The dispute arose when a number of companies offered to supply Terramycin to the NHS at a considerably lower price than charged by Pfizer. In an attempt to force Pfizer to reduce its price when agreement could not be reached within the framework of the VPRS, the Minister authorised the importation of Terramycin for use in the hospital services of NHS. Pfizer challenged the importers' right to supply the product but the Minister invoked section 46 of the Patents Act by claiming that the hospital services were Crown users. The House of Lords upheld this claim and thereby permitted the Ministry and any other government department or agent of the government to work any patent 'for the services of the Crown'.

In 1963 the ABPI's inablity to ensure the compliance of its members with the VPRS was revealed once again. Two of the Swiss corporations involved in the first incident, Ciba and Geigy (the former of which was the other new member of the ABPI's Negotiating Committee), relying upon the indispensability of their products refused to negotiate any price reductions with the Ministry on their entire range of products. This elicited the following remarkable response from the Treasury: 'Whatever form or forms of voluntary price restraint are agreed upon with the Association of the British Pharmaceutical Industry, they must be clearly understood to be binding on all its members'.[17]

By the time the second VPRS was due to be renegotiated, it was the market power of the large, and in particular foreign-owned, corporations rather than the mediating role of the ABPI that was beginning to shape if not the details of the VPRS then the way in which it was interpreted and implemented. Largely in retaliation, the government seems to have become increasingly willing to use its various statutory powers to keep the prices of these corporations within 'fair and reasonable' limits. As the ABPI had never had nor been intended to have a mediating role during implementation of the VPRS, a failure of the Ministry of Health and individual companies to reach agreement on prices did not, of itself, undermine the ABPI's role. It did, however, highlight to the Ministry the disadvantages inherent in a voluntary scheme. Consequently, the ABPI's ability to control its members became a matter for discussion during negotiation of the third VPRS. 'The Ministry argued that it was the Association's responsibility to bring to bear its influence 'in the corporate sense' upon any reluctant members'.[18] Clearly, the government was anxious by this time that certain compulsory characteristics should be introduced into what was meant to be a purely voluntary scheme. Yet, not surprisingly, this was unacceptable for Division B members. Hence, the third VPRS contained no undertaking by the ABPI on behalf of its membership. The Association merely agreed to use its 'best endeavours' where there was delay or difficulty in negotiations between companies and the Ministry.[19]

The third VPRS

The third version of the scheme came into operation in July 1964. It was to run for an indefinite period which could be terminated on six months' notice by the Ministry or by the industry, such notice not to be given earlier than July 1967.

There were four important modifications to the 1961 scheme in the third VPRS. Firstly, the scheme was extended to all medical speciality products prescribed by general practitioners. Secondly, the 'freedom period' was increased from three to four years for products resulting from substantial and original research. At the same time pharmaceuticals whose active ingredients had been known for five or more years were to be denied any period of freedom. In addition, specific allowance was granted for research expenditure in the calculation of prices under the formulae criteria. Thirdly, the scope for direct negotiations was extended to about half of all medicines purchased by the NHS as the new scheme allowed for direct negotiations for patented products with sales over £400,000 per annum and unpatented products with sales over £100,000 per annum. Finally, arrangements were included for price agreements to be back-dated.

Renegotiation of the scheme had commenced with replacement by the ABPI of its Negotiating Committee with a National Health Service Affairs Committee the terms of reference of which were wider than the former's. The President of the ABPI was appointed for the first time as the chairman of the committee, and the ABPI's vice-president was appointed as vice-chairman with special responsibility for VPRS matters. These appointments reflected the importance of the VPRS to the ABPI's status both vis-à-vis the state and vis-à-vis its members.

The committee met for the first time in September 1963 and a further six times before the end of that year. During this period members of Division B were asked to suggest amendments to the 1961 scheme. These suggestions were later considered by the VPRS sub-committee together with the amendments the Association understood the Ministry to be proposing. On the basis of these two sets of amendments the sub-committee prepared a revised scheme which first gained the approval of the full committee and then the approval of the Council of Division B. The revised scheme was then circulated to Division B members and in the light of criticisms received from them was amended and then submitted to a special meeting of the Division which was held on 30 January 1964. Formal negotiations with the Ministry of Health commenced on 17 February. Lang commented on these negotiations:

Interestingly enough although both sides in the issue fully realised that the scheme was a voluntary one, each set about the task as if it were otherwise — which perhaps it was becoming. With each successive year, and each successfully negotiated VPRS, the fortunes of the one were becoming more and more dependent upon the success of both. And whether the ABPI and the Swiss group [of members] appreciated it or not, the pharmaceutical industry was becoming progressively entwined in government administration as was the reverse. (Lang, 1974: 74)

The industry's perception of the need to unite behind the ABPI was reflected in the appointment of top ABPI representatives to head the NHS Affairs Committee and its VPRS sub-committee. This move came too late, however, to prevent the government from increasing its statutory powers to enforce compliance with the scheme. In 1964 the government extended its wartime powers to require suppliers of medicines to the NHS to keep accounts and records in a specified form and to provide such estimates, returns or information as might be necessary for its negotiations with the firms. This Act also empowered the state to control the maximum prices of medicines supplied to the NHS. The government clearly endorsed the Committee of Public Account's view that the principle of voluntary price restraint is acceptable only so long as it is universally observed'.[20]

In 1967 the Report of the Committee of Enquiry into the Relationship of the Pharmaceutical Industry with the National Health Service,[21] The Sainsbury Committee, added its backing for this view. The Committee attacked the industry for making excessive profits and recommended that standard cost returns should be introduced which would involve stricter scrutiny of companies' costs, prices, profits and capital employed. The Committee also recommended that the Minister must have recourse when the negotiations with a company failed to section 46 of the Patent Act 1949. The Committee added that 'the services of the Crown' should be extended not only to hospital services but also to the much larger drug market of the General Medical and Practitioners Services. The Health Services and Public Health Act 1968 implemented this recommendation.

Against this background of growing pressure on the state to acquire more statutory powers to ensure compliance with the VPRS, negotiation of the fourth version of the scheme commenced with a warning from the ABPI:

The great danger of course, is that a new and stricter price regulation scheme would depress the overall profitability of the industry to such an extent as to bring it below the level necessary for the support of innovation and growth. Even more, it might well selectively cut down the high rewards which *should* be earned for exceptionally successful innovation. The result would be to create a mediocre industry rather than one with outstanding peaks of excellence.[22]

The fourth VPRS

The new scheme, which took effect in September 1969, differed substantially from its predecessors. It included an introductory preamble — to which the ABPI attached great importance — which for the first time stressed the objective to promote a strong, efficient and profitable pharmaceutical industry in the UK together with the intention to agree a 'fair and reasonable' drug bill for the NHS. Price negotiations were no longer based upon the export criterion, nor upon the standard cost return as proposed by the Sainsbury Committee, but upon the company's total sales of NHS products in the UK and on its profitability from these sales. Companies were required to supply the Department of Health and Social Security (as the Ministry of Health had then become) with an Annual Financial Return (AFR) in an agreed form giving details of their sales, cost and capital employed for the preceding financial year. Negotiations between companies and the Department on the prices of products sold to the NHS were, henceforth, to take place on the basis of these returns. Two supplementary tests were made available to the Department by the scheme should the Department require them. Firstly, comparison with prices in 'similar' overseas markets and, secondly, where this was practical, comparison with the prices of any close substitute in the UK market.

Thus, the 1969 version of the VPRS represented the first attempt by the government to monitor and influence both the industry's prices and its profits. It allowed for no period of price freedom, no restriction on the range of products subject to direct negotiations, permitted price changes to be backdated to eight months after the end of the accounting year covered by the last AFR and required that firms give the Department early warning of any home sales which they expected to rise by 20 per cent per annum or more.

Negotiation of the scheme had been difficult. Many companies had become fearful of the combined effects of the state exercising direct restraint on profits through a price regulation scheme and at the same time stimulating price competition to an extent which they felt would be absent in a free market situation. Although the scheme was still the cause of much concern to members of the prescription medicine industry 'a substantial majority of [ABPI] members felt satisfied that the proposed agreement was in all the circumstances the best that could be secured'.[23]

Yet the new scheme further undermined the ABPI's role during implementation of its provisions. It specifically required companies to provide the type of information proposed by the Sainsbury Committee to the Department in the form of annual financial returns. Moreover, the information provided in the AFRs was to be confidential, available not even to the ABPI. The government had previously relied on the ABPI to provide information necessary to operate the VPRS and upon the Association's pledge 'to use its good offices with its members to ensure the prompt submission of all relevant information necessary for the purposes of negotiations under the Scheme'.[24]

Lang has suggested that a relationship of mutual dependency was established between the ABPI and the Ministry, and later Department of Health, through the VPRS:

> Having assumed the responsibility for the payment of drugs distributed to the people in 1948, the British government over the next twenty years became intimately involved with the pharmaceutical manufacturers. The VPRS, as a negotiating instrument between the ministry and the ABPI, created a common bond between the two upon which they both came to rely heavily.... Likewise, for the ABPI, the VPRS was a protection against radical government action and criticism as long as it could be seen to be bargaining in good faith... (Lang, 1974: 172 – 3).

According to Lang, the strength of the ABPI's negotiating position was that successive governments wanted both a competitive situation in the UK pharmaceutical industry and a bargain with the ABPI to supply drugs at a negotiated price. For the success of such a bargain the government was obviously dependent upon the representativeness of the ABPI and upon its ability to ensure that its members would abide by any agreement reached with the government by the Association.

However, the ABPI's decision-making procedures do not seem to have been sufficient. Ten years after the VPRS was introduced the industry's main incentive for agreeing to and complying with the scheme was its fear that the government might impose far more restrictive and interventionary measures on the industry than those embodied in the VPRS. The strength of this fear is evident from the fact that the 1969 version of the VPRS employed the criteria for controlling the prices of medicines supplied to the NHS which had first been proposed by the Minister of Health in 1954 and which the manufacturers were then able to dissuade the Minister from implementing. The relationship between the industry and the state agency had clearly altered over the decade 1958 – 68. During that time the balance of power which had been tilted initially in favour of the manufacturers had shifted in favour of the government. The history of the scheme from 1968 to the present day will show that this shift has not been reversed.

Satisfaction with the fourth VPRS was short-lived for many companies. In 1971 the attitude of companies which had accepted the scheme 'was one of increasing concern and dissatisfaction'.[25] This attitude was due, in part, to their experience of operating the scheme which they found to be cumbersome and onerous, and partly due to a realization that the scheme was inappropriate to the economic circumstances of the early 1970s. In a period of rapid cost inflation and growing international competition a scheme designed not to keep prices stable but to reduce them was seen as 'increasingly irksome and unsuitable'. This concern was reinforced by analyses of data emerging from the figures supplied to the Department of Health in companies' AFRs for the three years 1967 – 9. The data showed that in contrast to the period covered by the Sainsbury Committee the industry's performance and profitability on sales to the NHS had dropped sharply and profitability on export sales had also fallen — according to the industry because of the undue pressure put on home sales by the VPRS. Consequently, in May 1971 the ABPI prepared a paper for the Secretary of State outlining these arguments and advocating radical simplification of the scheme.

The fifth VPRS
The version which came into operation in October 1972 did not reflect this demand. Nevertheless, there were some important changes. The scheme was to run for a period of not less than five years until October 1977. The earlier provision that criteria should be devised for taking a company's sales promotion expenditure into account when assessing its profitability was omitted. At the same time, the industry's important contribution to the economy through its rapidly increasing exports and its investment in research and manufacturing was given more explicit recognition. Small companies with annual sales of less than £100,000 were exempted from supplying AFRs unless these were specifically asked for, while companies with sales between £100,000 and £750,000 per annum were requested only to present a copy of their audited accounts and a breakdown of their sales. Finally, price restraint clauses were modified for products of minor importance. Outside the scheme, the Department agreed that at the request of a company, officers of the Industrial and Export Branch of the DHSS would, where practicable, be present at negotiations between the company and the Department.

The industry's fears that the government was seeking a means to control prices unilaterally rather than reach agreement with the industry was finally realized for a short period at the end of 1972. Early in November 1972 the VPRS provisions for minor price increases were overriden when the government imposed a standstill on wages and prices. This situation continued for medicines until the end of February 1973 when the government announced that prices of NHS medicines would continue to be governed by the VPRS. The industry welcomed this decision as a sensible one.[26] But in 1973 the government used yet another of its statutory powers in order to ensure price reductions on certain medicines supplied to the NHS.

The issue arose when Roche Products Ltd — the British subsidiary of the Swiss multinational Hoffman-La Roche — was required to reduce the prices it charged for its two main products: librium and valium. When Roche resisted, the government permitted other firms to manufacture and distribute equivalents of these preparations under section 41 of the Patents Act 1949. The result was that Roche Products Ltd withdrew from the VPRS and was then referred to the Monopolies Commission. The Commission's Report revealed that in 1970 the Swiss parent of Roche Products Ltd had charged its British subsidiary £570 and £922 per kilo for librium and valium respectively, whilst the active ingredients of these products were available from various manufacturers at £9 and £20 respectively.[27] In the light of these findings the Monopolies Commission notionally adjusted the firm's international transfer price, recalculated the firm's financial statement and declared Roche's profits as 'quite unjustified' and the result of 'excessive prices'. Consequently, the company was ordered to cut the 1970 prices for librium and valium by 60 and 75 per cent respectively. The report became the subject of almost continuous proceedings either before the Special Orders Committee of the House of Lords or the Courts.

Eventually Roche Products Ltd rejoined the VPRS and the government repaid it £8.25 million as a consequence of profits forgone by the company in the two and a half years during which the price cutting orders were in effect. Nevertheless, the incident had caused the prescription medicine industry as a whole much concern and had raised doubts about the effectiveness of the VPRS as an instrument of control over the prices of NHS medicines.[28]

Election of a Labour Government in October 1974 served to heighten the industry's concern as this brought with it the threat of nationalization of parts of the industry. As a result, the industry became increasingly aware of the merits of the VPRS and was even ready to acknowledge 'the helpful and sympathetic approach of the Department of Health to questions of price revisions under the VPRS procedures'.[29] This is not to say, however, that the industry did not become more anxious about the effect of the VPRS upon its productivity, research and export trade and the government's interpretation of this effect. This anxiety is reflected, among other things, in the fact that the ABPI commissioned a study on the impact the VPRS was having and its likely influence on the future of the industry. Speaking to *ABPI News* before his retirement in 1976, Mr Teesdale, the ABPI's director observed that:

Future historians of the UK pharmaceutical industry may argue endlessly over whether the ABPI should ever have accepted the Voluntary Price Regulation Scheme and particularly the AFR [Annual Financial Returns] system. It could be said that it got us into a system of control from which we may never be able to escape. It might be argued that it saved us from something worse.[30]

Worse was to come, however. Regardless of the industry's wishes to the contrary, section 46 of the Patents Act 1949 was incorporated into the 1977 Patents Act (in section 55). The good news for the industry was that section 41 of the 1949 Act was excluded from the 1977 Act. But, the greatest defeat for the industry, and the ABPI, came in the form of the Health Act 1977. Under provisions of this Act the Secretary of State for the Social Services acquired the power to fix the price of medicines by Order if necessary — in other words, if agreement could not be reached with a manufacturer within the framework provided by the VPRS.

The pharmaceutical price regulation scheme

During negotiation of the present version of the VPRS the ABPI and the state agreed to remove the word voluntary from the scheme's title. The scheme was renamed, equally inappropriately, the Pharmaceutical Price Regulation Scheme. It came into operation in April 1978 and is intended to continue subject to six months notice of termination by either party. A new scheme is currently under negotiation (September 1984). An interim revised agreement was announced in December 1983 which took effect from 1 April 1984.

Under the PPRS companies consent to provide the Department with forecasts of their expected profit levels in the first three months of the financial year. Companies with sales of less than £200,000 per annum to the NHS are exempted from supplying any financial information to the Department of Health. The Department is now able to establish limits on a company's sales promotion expenditure. Of greatest significance to the industry, however, are the interpretive aspects of the scheme which give most benefit to those companies that contribute most to the nation's economy in terms of investment in plant and job opportunities.

Under the present scheme, as under the 1969 and 1972 versions, the Department of Health sets target profitability levels for the pharmaceutical industry as a whole on the basis of the Treasury's guidelines that suppliers of goods to government departments should earn profits which are in line with the average for British industry. On the basis of the profitability target for the industry as a whole, the Department constructs a 'merit league table' of profitability targets for individual companies. These are calculated on the basis of information provided in the companies' financial returns. The Department may make book adjustments to a company's profit statement after considering, for example, the level of the company's sales promotion expenditure, its reported stock levels and capital, the exchange rates and the inflation rates it has used in its calculations. Under the PPRS, unlike its predecessor, rebates on excessive profits can be agreed.

In keeping with its role as the sponsor of the UK pharmaceutical industry — in addition to its role as its chief regulator and main customer — the Department operates a tolerance level on a company's profitability record. This is done in order to avoid penalizing companies for effort and thus reducing the industry's incentive to increase its productivity and returns. Consequently, if a company's profit level is over target one year this will be allowed if it is regarded as due to the company's efforts rather than to incorrect or misleading data having been included in the company's financial returns. In addition, the Department permits companies to offset deficiencies in their profit levels one year with proportionate excesses the next.[31]

Negotiations between the Department and individual companies also cover the prices the companies charge for their products. If the Department finds a company's profitability record or estimated profitability unacceptable, or a company regards its profitability target as unacceptable, the company and the Department will meet to discuss proposed price changes. When the company's overall range of price increases or decreases has been agreed, the Department will often ask for a statement giving details of how the company expects to distribute the price rises or cuts amongst its products. The Department's criterion for assessing the acceptability of price increases for individual products is their relation to the retail price index. If the Department is not satisfied with a change a company seeks, it may encourage it to adopt alternative measures. If necessary, the Department can coerce the company. It will be recalled that the Minister can fix the price of individual medicines if agreement is not reached between the company and the Department, under the Health Act 1977.

The PPRS committee of the ABPI — the successor to the Negotiating Committee — is currently composed of leading members of approximately ten major British and foreign pharmaceutical concerns, including the Swiss corporations which have refused to abide by the VPRS in the past: Roche Products Ltd and Ciba-Geigy Pharmaceuticals Ltd. Members of the PPRS committee are elected by the ABPI's Board of Management to which they report directly, the old system of councils having been abolished. During negotiation of the price regulation scheme the PPRS Committee has a great deal of autonomy. In practice, a few of its members, including the chairman together with the ABPI's Director, conduct the negotiations with officials at the Pharmaceutical Products Branch of the Industries and Export Division of the DHSS up to and including the Under Secretary for the Division.

Towards the development of private interest government?
As the ABPI's role during negotiation and implementation of successive versions of the price regulation scheme have changed, the Association has altered its internal procedures in order to suit the demands made upon it by the scheme. The intention was to equip those of the Association's members which were subject to the scheme (initially Division B) with the most appropriate decision-making procedures and committee structure to enable them to develop and maintain a close relationship with Whitehall. Not surprisingly, therefore, changes often involved a strengthening of the status of Division B on the ABPI's governing body and an increase in the decision-making autonomy of the Division, and later its Council and the price regulation negotiating committees, in matters arising from the scheme. The fact that alterations were so frequent and that the composition and name of the negotiating committee was altered several times reflects the ABPI's continuing effort to improve the compliance of its members with the scheme.

However, whatever changes were made to the ABPI's internal procedures, they were never accompanied by an increase in its 'governing properties' — its ability to ensure that its agreement with the state was binding upon its members. Largely because of this the voluntary nature of the scheme was eroded, and the scope of the scheme was extended from direct price regulation to control over the level of profit. Initially, the state relied upon both the ABPI's representativeness of all the companies to which the scheme applied and upon the Association's 'good offices' with these companies in order to ensure the success of the VPRS. As the ABPI's inability to make its members comply became increasingly apparent and the ABPI's representativeness was not as comprehensive as the DHSS would have wished, the government made use of its statutory powers under which it could supplement the VPRS or, if necessary, replace it in order to enforce price reductions. The government also increased the number and scope of the statutory powers at its disposal for these purposes and thereby became able to guarantee that all companies whether ABPI members or not would abide by the scheme. Today, officials at the DHSS monitor advertisements appearing in the trade and professional journals of the British pharmaceutical industry and other forms of the industry's promotional literature to see which products are advertised to doctors and by which companies. If a company is identified through this procedure that is not already included in the PPRS the Department will send it a copy of the scheme and invite it to submit the relevant financial information. A target profitability will then be set for the company on the basis of the information provided and a range of prices it intends to charge the NHS for its medicines will be negotiated between the company and the Department.

Yet, the government still relies upon the ABPI to act as an intermediary during negotiation of the price regulation scheme even though the Association is now the weaker party to the negotiations. This is because, in practice, the government is still dependent upon the good will of the prescription medicine industry for the successful operation of the NHS. It therefore relies on the ABPI to keep the industry informed of the DHSS's proposals for changes to the price regulation scheme, the DHSS's reasons for proposing such changes and the Department's willingness and efforts to reach agreement with the industry. The government also relies upon the ABPI to impart similar information on behalf of the industry to the state and to help the two sides reach agreement.

Not surprisingly, the relationship between the ABPI and its members during negotiation of the price regulation scheme has changed as the government has increased the statutory powers which stand behind the scheme. Whereas initially many of the largest and foreign-owned pharmaceutical companies were not prepared to comply with the scheme even though they had participated in its negotiation, as the Government increased its ability and willingness to coerce individual companies to comply, their reliance on the ABPI as their spokesman vis-à-vis the state increased. They realized that unless they were represented by a single spokesman during negotiation of the scheme the government might introduce price restraint inequitably. Thus, the head of the ABPI's professional staff, the Director, is a leading member of the negotiating team which invariably includes the Association's president and sometimes also the vice-president who are members of major pharmaceutical companies.

During implementation of the scheme, however, the companies' reliance on the ABPI decreased. Following introduction of the 1964 Emergency (re-enactment and Repeal) Act and the third (1969) VPRS companies were obliged to provide more information than had previously been required of them, direct to the state agency rather than to the ABPI. Moreover, the acquisition and use of statutory powers by the government rendered the DHSS capable of determining prices without the agreement of either the ABPI or the manufacturers. Yet, agreement is still sought. The Government has never used its powers under the Health Act 1977. Thus a non-statutory scheme of price and profit control is still operated which requires agreement between the state and the manufacturers.

This approach is obviously preferred by manufacturers to a system of state control. It is preferred by the government because it represents the best arrangement whereby the government can balance its divergent interests as the industry's regulator, main customer and sponsor. This balance is required because the market power of the manufacturers is still capable of ruining the NHS. Manufacturers are still free to choose not to supply the NHS with medicines. Today, the success or failure of the price regulation scheme rests no longer on the representativeness of the ABPI and its capability to deliver the compliance of its members; rather, it rests directly upon the maintenance of a balance between the market power of manufacturers against the statutory powers of the government.

The history of the PPRS would seem to be one of frustrated and incomplete development of private interest government. The role of the ABPI remained limited by the market power of its large members and the inclination of successive governments to direct intervention. In addition, the ABPI's preference not to become too closely involved in controlling its members in order to protect its own organizational stability seems to have had a limited effect. In its turn, this reflects the emphasis in Britain on the liberal tradition and thus preference for voluntary organizations and voluntary agreements between the state agency and manufacturers. Ironically, the inherent weaknesses of voluntarism have resulted over the years in a system of state control which is perhaps more unsatisfactory to the prescription medicine industry than that which would have developed had the industry's spokesman, the ABPI, been invested with authority to make its agreements with the government binding.

This outcome was not beyond the bounds of possibility, despite the prevalence of the non-interventionist tradition. It will be recalled that the year the first VPRS came into effect (1958), prescription medicine manufacturers conferred on the ABPI the authority to expel members for non-compliance with the Association's then new Code of Advertising Practice. Restrictions on manufacturers' advertising activities affect their competitiveness in much the same way, although not perhaps to the same extent, as restrictions on their prices and profits. Yet ABPI member companies were not prepared to delegate to the Association a corresponding power when they agreed to the first and subsequent versions of the VPRS.

This reluctance on the part of ABPI members was probably because advertising controls could operate in the commercial interests of manufacturers if they improved doctors' image of their products. Conversely, price and profit controls are usually inimical to manufacturers' commercial interests. Moreover, in 1958 manufacturers of classification 2, 3 and 4 proprietaries had sufficient confidence that the government would not refuse to purchase their products if they remained outside the ABPI or if they refused to abide by the VPRS. As the government increased its statutory powers in order to offset manufacturers' market power the opportunity for manufacturers to unite behind the ABPI was lost. Hence, today, the system of control that operates on the profits earned by prescription medicines manufacturers is more restrictive than manufacturers envisaged in 1958. At the same time it is less restrictive than it might be given the statutory powers the government has.

For much of the data presented in this paper and for comments on earlier versions I am especially grateful to Mr A.G. Shaw, former General Secretary of the ABPI. I am also grateful to Wolfgang Streeck, Manfred Groser and Wyn Grant for their comments on earlier drafts and to an official at the Pharmaceutical Products Branch of the Industries and Exports Division at the DHSS. The chapter is based on research funded by the Volkswagen Foundation and conducted in the market of the 'Organization of Business Interests' project.

Notes

1. The Pharmaceutical Price Regulation Scheme, April 1978, section 1:1.
2. Unbranded standard drugs are those listed in standard works of reference such as the *British Pharmacopoeia*.
3. Pharmaceutical Society of Great Britain 'NHS Debate', *Pharmaceutical Journal*, 15 May 1954, p. 391.
4. The ABPI comprised three other Divisions at the time: (i) Division A — manufacturers and wholesalers of pharmaceutical preparations for the home retail hospital trade; (ii) Division C — manufacturers of pharmaceutical materials and preparations for the home wholesale and export trades; and (iii) Division D — members of associate members of the ABPI engaged in export trade.
5. ABPI *Annual Report* 1954 – 5, p. 15.
6. Ibid.
7. ABPI *Annual Report* 1956 – 7, p. 15.
8. Ibid.
9. ABPI *Annual Report* 1954 – 5, p. 17.
10. *Special Report and First, Second and Third Reports of the Committee of Public Accounts* (London: HMSO) session 1956 – 7, question 3426, pp. 310 – 11.
11. This account is taken from the *Report of the Committee of Enquiry into the Relationship of the Pharmaceutical Industry with the National Health Service 1965 – 67* (London: HMSO, September 1967), Cmnd 3410 66/67, pp. 27 – 8.
12. R.W. Lang *The Politics of Drugs: A Comparative Pressure-Group Study of the Canadian Pharmaceutical Manufacturers Associaton and the Association of the British Pharmaceutical Industry 1930– 70* (Farnborough: Saxon House, 1974, p. 68).
13. *Third Report from the Committee of Public Accounts* (London: HMSO), session 1962 – 3, question 1696, p. 18.
14. ABPI *Annual Report* 1958 – 9, p. 17.
15. *Second Report from the Committee of Public Accounts* (London: HMSO), session 1959 – 60, paras 9 – 19.

16. ABPI *Annual Report* 1960 – 1, p. 13.
17. Minute published by the Treasury in a *Special Report from the Committee of Public Accounts* on 3 December 1963 quoted in Lang (1974: 167).
18. *Special Report from the Committee of Public Accounts* (London: HMSO), Session 1963 – 4, question 1513, pp. 161 – 2, quoted in Lang (1974: 168).
19. *Third Report from the Committee of Public Accounts* (London: HMSO), Session 1964 – 5, question 1457, p. 197
20. *Third Report from the Committee of Public Accounts* (London: HMSO), Session 1962 – 3, para 54.
21. (London: HMSO, September 1967), Cmnd 3410, session 1966 – 7.
22. ABPI *Annual Report* 1967 – 8, p. 14.
23. ABPI *Annual Report* 1969 – 70, p. 7.
24. ABPI *Annual Report* 1964 – 5, p. 8.
25. ABPI *Annual Report* 1971 – 2, p. 11.
26. ABPI *Annual Report* 1973 – 4, p. 16.
27. Monopolies Commission Report *Chlordiazepoxide and Diazepan*, HC, 197, 1973 (London: HMSO, 1973).
28. ABPI *Annual Report* 1973 – 4, p. 16.
29. Ibid.
30. *ABPI News*, December 1976, p. 6.
31. In December 1983 both the level of profit from NHS sales and the level of sales promotion allowed as an expense under the scheme were reduced. The target rate of profit for individual companies was reduced by an average of four percentage points and the discretion which the DHSS allows in certain cases when companies exceed the target profit rates was tightened and related more closely to the company's particular circumstances.

7
Quality regulation in the Dutch pharmaceutical industry: conditions for private regulation by business interest associations

Bert de Vroom

Introduction

State regulation and private regulation
Regulation — the creation and enforcement of rules, norms and sanctions to direct the behaviour of (a group of) actors in order to attain an intended outcome — is one of the main functions of a developed state which disposes over the necessary resources such as power, authority, bureaucratic apparatus and money. At the same time, we do find in many Western industrial societies private organizations involved in private or (semi-)public regulation, often with facilitation by the state.

Why should a modern state facilitate regulation by private organizations, and why should functional interest groups prefer self regulation over state regulation? From the point of view of the state different answers are possible. The subject of self regulation may not be related to a general public interest; in this case, there would be no (political) need for the state to intervene. Or the matter in question may be too complex (in a technical sense) for pure state regulation, making it necessary to rely on the professional know-how of private organizations. Also, it may be too controversial and state regulation would be likely to meet strong resistance resulting in high costs of control. Another explanation for private regulation might be ideological pressure for 'deregulation'. As far as functional groups are concerned, they may get involved in private regulation because they perceive a need to regulate the behaviour of their members in the interest of long-term interests of the group (for example, reduction of 'unfair competition' between firms in the same sector). Another motive might be to avoid state intervention threatening the freedom and flexibility of members, or to correct failing state regulation.

Conditions for private government in quality regulation
The central question of this chapter is under what conditions self-regulation of an industry becomes possible. For empirical reference, the chapter will take the case of quality regulation of drugs in the Dutch pharmaceutical industry. Quality, for the purposes of this

chapter, includes both the quality of the products and that of the advertisements for these products.

I propose to distinguish between three clusters of conditions for private regulation: (i) *features of the functional group* (in the present case, the pharmaceutical firms that produce and/or import drugs for the Dutch market); (ii) *features of the private organization* involved in quality regulation (or trying to be so); and (iii) *features of the state*.

A basic condition for the functional group I suspect is a minimal degree of homogeneity and a *collective interest* in regulating quality. When there is unfair or cut-throat competition with negative results for many firms in the functional group and no state intervention (or unsuccessful state intervention), firms may have a collective interest in regulating this competition. They could press the state for (effective) intervention. But since quality competition and advertising practices are important aspects of the market strategy of free enterprises, we might suspect that firms are not in favour of state regulation since this might easily 'go too far' in limiting their freedom and flexibility. From this perspective I suppose firms will be in favour of self-regulation, especially if they command the necessary resources and organizational capacity (see the second cluster of conditions). For the same reasons existing or growing state intervention may also result in a collective interest in self-regulation. Moreover, public controversies as the result of bad quality, or scandals may affect the consumption of industrial drugs (consumers may for example change to herbal medicines) and lead to state intervention. So consumer criticism might also lead to a collective interest in private regulation.

Self-regulation seems possible only if a functional group is able to establish an effective organization that could fulfil the regulatory tasks. In this respect I will distinguish three basic conditions. First, the *capacity to bind* members of the functional group to the regulatory policy of the organization. This capacity can be based on sanctions based on selective or monopoly and authoritative goods (Schmitter and Streeck, 1981). Without it the private organization will not be able to control free ridership and the competition along the original lines will probably continue. On the other hand, a highly developed capacity to bind might even be a substitute for a lack of collective interest. A second condition is the *resources* to carry out the regulatory activities — such as money, know-how, professional staff. The third condition I suspect is a certain *autonomy* of the organization from both the state and the functional group. This condition seems to pose a problem particularly to voluntary interest groups, also referred to by Dahl (1982). On the one hand, autonomy from the state might offer an opportunity to cater to the narrow egoism of members at the expense of broader public goods (for instance a required quality level of the products), so the state would probably replace the private regulation by state regulation. To avoid this, private organizations must acquire a corresponding autonomy (neutrality) in relation to the narrowly defined interests of their members in order to become accepted by the state. But this autonomy might go too far, and the originally private organization might develop into a kind of state agency. As a result, members would no longer recognize their interests in the association's policy and might leave it or refuse to accept its regulatory measures (unless the organization possesses a strong binding capacity).

The basic conditions for private regulation concerning the state I suppose are *lacking or unsuccessful state intervention* and *state facilitation* of private regulation. If there is strong state regulation in a certain area private regulation seems hardly possible. In general I suggest that it is only in a situation of minimal or failing state regulation that private regulation will become possible. It also acquires a degree of state facilitation. For instance private regulation in the form of cartels must be legally accepted or at least not be forbidden by the state. In order to attain sufficient resources, binding capacity and autonomy in relation to the members the private organization might also need other state facilities in addition to the legal acceptance. I suppose that a certain delegation of authority or power and the provision of subsidies are important conditions for effective private government.

In Table 1 the different hypothetical conditions for private regulation are summarized.

TABLE 1
Six basic conditions of private quality regulation

I. Features of the functional group
　1. A collective interest in quality regulation. This can be the result of
　　a. 'unfair', cut-throat competition;
　　b. (a threat of) state intervention, a lack of state intervention, unsuccessful state intervention; and
　　c. criticism by the public (consumers).
II. Features of the private organization
　2. Capacity to bind members of the functional group to the regulatory policy of the organization
　3. Resources to perform regulatory activities (know-how, professional staff, financial resources)
　4. Relative autonomy from the state and the functional group
III. Features of the state
　5. Minimal or unsuccessful state intervention
　6. State facilitation for private regulation, e.g.
　　a. legal acceptance;
　　b. delegation of authority/power to the private organization; and
　　c. subsidies, etc.

Aspects of quality regulation
A distinction can be made between the substantive content of quality regulations (the regulation of the *product*) and the regulation of *procedures* to get the required quality. Different degrees of state or private involvement can be distinguished on the basis of these and other subfunctions. With respect to product regulation I distinguish three functions: (i) formulation (for example, through legislation) of quality standards in general; (2) formulation of standards about the quality of a specific group of products (for example, drugs); (iii) operationalization of quality norms for specific products (for example, the therapeutical quality of anodynes). My hypothesis is that private associational involvement in the regulation of this category of consumer products will only become possible and perhaps necessary in moving from the first to the third function. In general the state will be responsible for at least the first two functions. As pointed out by Wilson (1974) and others, public attention and public criticism of products consumed directly by the public has formed an important stimulus for state intervention. Examples are food acts, environmental acts, consumer protection acts etc. With respect to the regulation of procedures I distinguish four different functions.

1. the actual implementation and administration of quality standards and norms,
2. control of the observation of these standards and norms;
3. supervision over implementation and control. and
4. sanctioning of transgressors.

Here again I suggest that private involvement in this area of consumer products will only be possible (if at all) within an overall state involvement. Especially the third and fourth function I suppose are likely to be the exclusive domain of the state.

TABLE 2
Seven aspects of quality regulation

I. Regulation of the *product*
   1. Formulation of a central framework (legislation) concerning quality in general;
   2. Formulation of standards concerning quality of specific products; and
   3. Operationalization of quality norms for specific products.

II. Regulations of *procedures*
   4. Implementation and administration of standards and norms;
   5. Control of the observation of the quality standards and norms;
   6. Supervision over implementation and control; and
   7. Sanctioning of transgressors.

The Dutch pharmaceutical industry

Some characteristics of the sector

Since the beginning of this century the industrial manufacture of drugs has increased strongly. Especially after the Second World War industrial drugs have taken over the market. Around 1980 the production of industrial drugs amounted to 90 – 95 per cent of total drug production. The remaining 5 – 10 per cent are produced by chemists and physicians. With the increased use of industrial drugs quality regulation has become both necessary and possible.

The pharmaceutical industry in the Netherlands consists of a heterogeneous group of 70 firms with 11,600 employees and an output of Hfl. 2062 million (1980). Among them are about 25 small and 42 medium-sized firms. Five firms are large multinationals which account for 90 per cent of production capacity and 80 per cent of total employment. These five multinationals are also engaged in research and development of new (branded) drugs.

The market for drugs consists of different sub-markets. An important distinction must be made between drugs for *human* use and for *animal* use which tend to be produced by different firms.

The distribution of the two kinds of drugs is organized differently. One can only get drugs for human use at the chemist's or druggist's, or on prescription. Some popular drugs ('over-the-counter-drugs') are also available in supermarkets and other shops. Drugs for animal use are for sale at petshops or on prescription by the veterinary surgeon.

There are two different ministries responsible for the two sub-sectors of the pharmaceutical industry. The Ministry of Public Health is responsible for human drugs and also for the regulation of the respective producers. The Ministry of Agriculture is responsible for animal drugs, and this responsibility also includes regulatory powers. As will be seen below, this division of administrative responsibilities is one important explanation for the different regulatory systems in the two sub-sectors.

The bulk of the output of the pharmaceutical industry is realized on the market for prescription drugs. This market is characterized by the fact that the consumption of prescription drugs is more or less monopolized by the health insurance organizations (*Ziekenfondsen*). At the same time, the market is strongly regulated by the state and semi-state organizations. About 70 per cent of the Dutch population is covered by the Health Insurance Act (*Ziekenfondswet*). Its implementation is delegated to private organizations (*Ziekenfondsen*) with delegated state authority and under supervision of the Health Insurance Council (*Ziekenfondsraad*) established by the state. The Council has the right to advise the Minister of Public health on which drugs should be accepted for prescription. In doing this it takes both quality (therapeutic effectiveness) and price into account. If the therapeutic effect is more or less the same, drugs with a lower price will usually be preferred by the Council. The great importance of this body for the interests of the industry is easy to imagine. Pharmaceutical firms will normally try to prove that their drugs are therapeutically superior. There also is growing competition between manufacturers and importers of 'specialties' (branded drugs) and of 'generics' (white labels) and 'parallel imports'.[1]

In the sector of animal drugs there is also competition between two groups of manufacturers. Some firms produce branded drugs using modern technologies and keeping to quality norms (such as 'good manufacturing practices' and 'good laboratory practices'). Other firms, usually smaller ones, produce drugs of low quality but also of a low price. They are sometimes referred to by the first group as 'bathtub-mixers' (*badkuipmengers*). Additional lines of competition involve 'white labels', parallel imports, and trading practices on the black market.

Since the early 1950s, the share of foreign producers of the Dutch home market has grown from about 50 to no less than 80 per cent. Imports are mainly 'specialties'; they are in the hands of a small number of multinationals which have their own import organizations. Competition between domestic producers and importers does not give rise to conflicts given the various monopolies on therapeutic submarkets and the fact that domestic producers export most of their products. There is however a growing conflict between the importers and domestic producers of specialties on the one hand and the so-called 'parallel importers' on the other. Parallel importers are not subsidiaries of multinationals but, in most cases, wholesalers. They import and sell attractive branded drugs at lower prices, taking advantage of price differences between different countries which are due to different registration costs, public subsidies, etc. The conflict between parallel importers who accuse their opponents of abusing monopolistic power, and manufacturers or importers of branded drugs who accuse the parallel importers of infringement on property rights has resulted in a great number of courtcases (Verkade, 1981).

The structure of the functional group in question (pharmaceutical manufacturers and importers) can thus be characterized as rather heterogeneous and competitive. These are not optimal conditions to start collective action for quality regulation. Nonetheless, the industry managed to establish more or less effective interest organizations and also effective private regulation, as will be seen shortly.

134 Private interest government

The associated pattern of the pharmaceutical industry
The different sub-sectors of the industry that we have identified are organized separately. Until 1975, the producers and importers of specialties had two different business associations: BIPA for the importers and NEPROPHARM for the manufacturers.[2] Both associations were organized, together with business associations from other industrial sectors, in a legally registered cartel named PHC.[3] This cartel was a clear example of 'private government', as will be seen in more detail further below. The PHC was responsible for the approval of drugs and for the regulation of drug use as far as quality aspects were involved. It also regulated price margins for wholesale trade and advertisement. This form of private government dated back to 1925. It emerged as a result of a lack of state regulation in the beginning of the century when the industry found itself in need of some degree of intervention: 'There were no norms for the lay-out of factories and for manufacturing standards, there was no control of manufacturing processes and no control of the chemical and therapeutical quality of drugs' (Beudeker, 1963: 814). According to its president, the PHC was founded 'to put an end to the chaos in the pharmaceutical sector. Everybody was trading all kinds of drugs and there was strong price competition. The illegal import of drugs from Belgium was one of the causes of this competition' (Pharmaceutisch Weekblad, 1977: 1226). In 1975 BIPA and NEPROPHARM merged into a new association called NEFARMA.[4] Two years later the PHC was dismantled. To substitute for the cartel, a new 'code of behaviour' was developed by NEFARMA.

NEFARMA, too, is integrated in a more extended associational system, being a member of the peak association of the chemical industry in the Netherlands (VNCI) and both a direct and an indirect member of the national peak association of industry (VNO). It also belongs to international business associations such as the International Federation of Pharmaceutical Manufacturers Associations (IFPMA), the European Federation of Pharmaceutical Industries' Associations, (EFPMA), and the Association Européene des Specialtés Grand Public (AESGP). For representation of their interests as employers the members of NEFARMA are organized in a separate employers' association (AWV). NEFARMA is an indirect member of this association, via the VNCI.

Producers of generics and parallel importers are not organized in formal interest associations and are not involved in private quality regulation. Due to their conflicting interests and competitive behaviour, they are not permitted to join the above mentioned interest organizations. At the moment of writing, there are however informal meetings of these groups to find an organizational form to defend their interests against the producers and importers of specialties.

The associational pattern at the 'animal side' is much more heterogeneous and much less developed. In this sub-sector, there are four different interest associations reflecting different interests of manufacturers of animal drugs: FIDIN organizes the manufacturers of prescription drugs for animal use; FAGROVET represents the manufacturers of popular ('over-the-counter') drugs used by cattle farmers (for their cattle!); DIBEVO includes manufacturers of popular medicines for domestic animals; and NEFATO comprises manufacturers of drugs used as additives to cattle fodder.[5] These different interest associations are however not integrated at a higher level in the associational system.

FIGURE 1
Associational pattern of the pharmaceutical industry in the Netherlands 1980 (simplified)

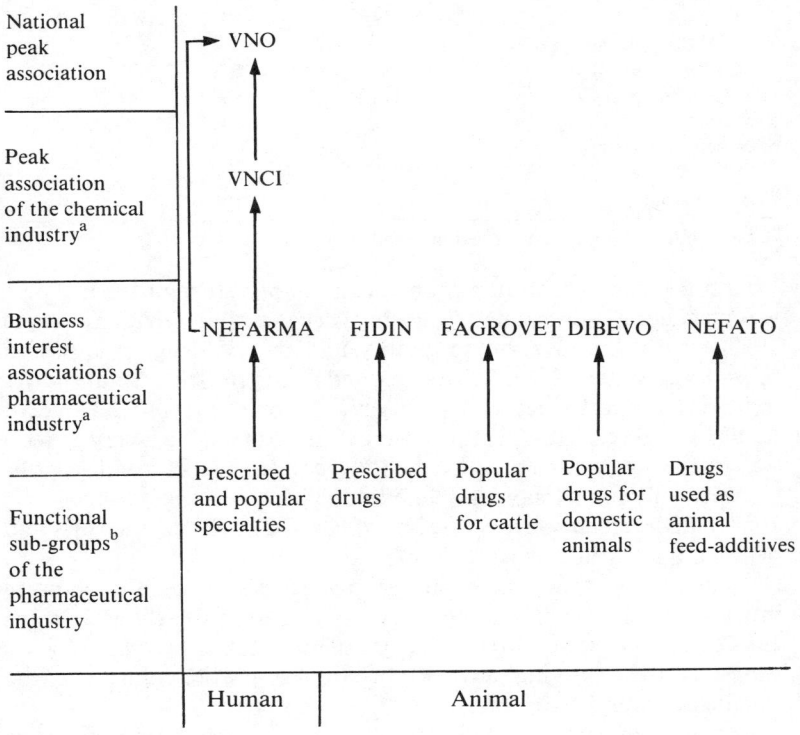

National peak association	→ VNO				
Peak association of the chemical industry[a]	↑ VNCI ↑				
Business interest associations of pharmaceutical industry[a]	⌐NEFARMA ↑	FIDIN ↑	FAGROVET ↑	DIBEVO ↑	NEFATO ↑
Functional sub-groups[b] of the pharmaceutical industry	Prescribed and popular specialties	Prescribed drugs	Popular drugs for cattle	Popular drugs for domestic animals	Drugs used as animal feed-additives
	Human		Animal		

[a] Only trade associations
[b] Manufacturers and importers

Case 1: the regulation of product quality — from private to state regulation

The development of quality regulation of industrial drugs for human use is characterized by a fundamental change from pure private to pure state regulation. This is illustated in Table 3.

TABLE 3

The relative involvement of the Pharmaceutische Handels Conventie (PHC) and the state (S) in regulating the quality of industrial drugs for human use in the Netherlands 1925–83

Aspects of quality regulation	Involvement of PHC and/or the state in quality regulation		
	1925-58	1958-63	1963-83
1. Formulation of a central framework (Act)	(PHC)	S (PHC)	
2. Formulation of specific standards	PHC	PHC	S (PHC)
3. Operationalization of specific norms	PHC	PHC	S
4. Implementation	PHC	PHC	S
5. Control	PHC	PHC	S
6. Supervision over 4 and 5	PHC[a]	S	S
7. Sanctioning	PHC	S (PHC)	S

[a]Carried out by the business interest associations involved in the PHC.

Until 1958 the situation was one of strong private regulation. There was no general legislation for industrial drugs at that time. However in 1958 a first Act to regulate quality and use of drugs was passed providing a general legal framework and giving the state the authority to intervene in all aspects of quality regulation (cf. level 1., Table 3). Until 1963, levels 2 to 5 (Table 3) were dealt with only in a very general way by the Act, and in practice the PHC continued its activities in this respect. Only supervision and sanctioning became a state affair. After 1963 state intervention increased further as various specific rules and detailed quality norms were developed.

At the same time, rules on the procedures of regulation were introduced and facilitation for private regulation (by the PHC) was cut down. The PHC (after 1975, its role was taken by NEFARMA) was left only a marginal advisory task in a bi-partite committee, the 'medicine committee'.[6]

This fundamental change from private to state regulation cannot be explained by changes in the structure of the industry or in the regulating organizations. There was still a collective interest in self-regulation, especially given the presence of an effective regulatory body which, from the point of view of the industry, made tight state regulation expendable.[7]

Growing state intervention and the disappearance of state facilitation for private government must be explained by other developments. One was the comparatively restrictive policy of the European Community on cartels; another, the already mentioned increase in the industrial production of drugs since the 1950s. The third factor was the emergence of a public system of health care, as one aspect of the rise of the 'welfare state'. The latter two developments moved the regulation of industrial drugs for human use to the centre of public and political attention. A number of critical incidents accelerated the trend towards state intervention. The most notorious one was the 'Softenon scandal'.[8] These incidents had strong effects on the mass media and public opinion. Questions were raised in the Dutch Parliament about the control of the pharmaceutical industry. The neutrality of the PHC was contested. As in other countries, the events resulted in stronger state intervention in the pharmaceutical industry.

In 1963 the state introduced the 'Besluit Verpakte Geneesmiddelen' (rules regarding the quality of pre-packed drugs for human use). In the same year a government committee ('College ter beoordeling van Geneesmiddelen') was established to register and evaluate industrial drugs for human use. Finally a new Bureau was set up by the state ('Bureau Bijwerkingen van Geneesmiddelen') in 1964 to which doctors can report harmful side effects of medicines and from which they get information on possible side effects.

All these new initiatives were based on the general Act of 1958. They severely reduced the scope for the activities of the PHC. The final death blow came in the early 1970s when the European Commission ruled that the existence of the PHC was in violation of the Treaty of Rome.

The response of the industry: NEFARMA
The end of the PHC, state intervention and public criticism created a new collective interest of manufacturers and importers of pharmaceutical specialties in reducing state intervention (both on the national level and the EC level) and defending their products against public criticism. This proved to be an effective condition for the foundation in 1975 of a new association — NEFARMA — to replace both the separate importers (BIPA) and manufacturers (NEPROPHARM) as well as the PHC.

Since 1975 NEFARMA has developed into a strong, centralized and united interest association with an ever more increasing influence on public opinion and state intervention. NEFARMA also succeeded in continuing some of the self-regulatory activities of the PHC, and even in introducing self-regulation in new areas, thereby preventing state intervention.

In 1980, 92 manufacturers and importers of industrial drugs were organized in NEFARMA. Compared to other business interest associations NEFARMA is well-resourced. The association had a professional staff of 11 persons in 1980, and since 1982 it also has a full-time paid president. Its budget in 1980 amounted to about 2.5 milion Hfl (US$1.25 million at 1980 exchange rate).

The need for strong collective action is reflected in the internal structure of NEFARMA. For instance, institutionalized sub-units for different sub-interests (manufacturers and importers) were abolished a few years after foundation, indicating that unity is more important for this association than giving recognition to sub-interests in the associational structure. The strength of the association is also reflected in a number of binding rules regulating the business behaviour of its members (see below).

As far as 'features of the functional group' and 'features of the private organization' (Table 1) are concerned, all the necessary conditions for private regulation seem to be present. The problems arise in relation to the state. But perhaps in the near future, when the present 'deregulation' trend continues, the pharmaceutical industry will get the possibility to win back some of the regulating functions that are presently performed by the state.

Case 2: the regulation of advertisement —
still a private affair

Advertising is an important element of quality competition in the market for (new) branded products. According to Wolffers (1984: 28), the pharmaceutical industry spends twice as much for promotion as for research and development. Promotion can be important in a situation where only small differences exist between different labels or between new and old products of the same label. In such cases, advertising emphasizes the superior quality of the respective product. It is also central to the ideology of free enterprise: 'Advertisement is a "cornerstone" of a society based on free enterprise and competition; so the pharmaceutical industry has also the right to advertise its products' (NEFARMA, 1978: 16).

But advertising can also have negative effects, even for the industry itself. 'Misleading advertisement' is a form of 'unfair competition'. This may lead the industry to regulate advertising or to press the state to intervene. Moreover, advertising may pose a threat to public health. Too much or misleading advertising might lead to overconsumption or misuse of drugs. For this reason, too, there is need for regulating advertising either by the state or by private organizations.

'Voluntary self-censorship'
Since 1926 advertising for over-the-counter-drugs — i.e. 'consumer advertising' as opposed to advertising to professionals — is regulated in the Netherlands by business interest associations rather than by the state. The interest associations of the manufacturers and importers of drugs, of advertising firms and of publishers of periodicals and newspapers agreed on an advertising code for popular drugs.[9] A private organization named KOAG[10] was established for implementation and control. This form of private regulation was, and still is, based on self-disciplinary *preventive* control (voluntary self-censorship). Every manufacturer or importer of drugs (including non-members of the business associations involved) who wants to advertise has to present a copy beforehand to the KOAG. Without approval of the KOAG it is practically impossible to place the advertisement since the other business associations participating in the KOAG have obliged their members not to accept advertisements without KOAG approval.

This successful form of regulation is however circumvented by a group of outsiders, the manufacturers and suppliers of 'alternative' drugs (for example, herbal medicines), which advertise, without KOAG approval, their products as drugs with positive therapeutic effects. A great number of these drugs seem to have hardly any or no therapeutic effect at all.[11] The KOAG is not able to prevent these advertisements because herbal medicine producers are not members of the interest associations of the pharmaceutical industry, and their advertisements are published in small local advertising papers which are not in the interest organizations forming the KOAG. The state also has no ability to control these advertisements since alternative drugs are not legally recognized as drugs. For these reasons, the pharmaceutical industry is in favour of more state intervention in this area.[12]

Together with the regulation of product quality in 1958, the state also intervened in advertising. Article 3 of the 1958 Act outlawed misleading advertising of drugs, and Article 30 provided for the establishment of a state inspection board. But the board was never actually set up, and KOAG could continue its activities.

There were several reasons why the inspection board was not established. First there was a constitutional problem. Preventive control by the state of advertisements can be considered a form of censorship and is as such contrary to the 'freedom of press' as guaranteed by the constitution (Beudeker, 1963: 825).[13] Secondly, the European Community was at the time trying to harmonize the different national regulations on advertising, and the Dutch government was waiting for this. But in 1980 this project had to be abandoned because a number of national governments (especially the UK and Germany) could not agree. Thirdly the KOAG was considered to function well, and satisfaction with private regulation increased even more when NEFARMA introduced in 1978 a new 'Code of Behaviour' with more disciplinary rules for the industry.

Self-regulation instead of state regulation
In 1973 manufacturers and importers of specialties (organized at that time in NEPROPHARM and BIPA) introduced a new form of private regulation of advertising: a 'Code of Behaviour'. [14] The code was based on two fundamental rules, a prohibition of misleading advertising and an obligation to ensure that advertisements were in conformity with prevailing standards of good taste and propriety. These rules were elaborated in a number of specific norms. To implement the Code, a specific institution, the 'Council for Medicines Communication' (RGA), was created.

This RGA regulation differed on several points from the KOAG regulation. In the first place, it was an initiative of only the manufacturers and importers organized in BIPA and NEPROPHARM, whereas the KOAG regulation was a joint venture of four different interest groups.[15] As a result, the RGA regulation system was fully paid for by the importers and manufacturers while the KOAG regulation system was covered by only 25 per cent. Every year the RGA delivered a report to the Ministries of Economic Affairs and of Public Health, as well as to NEFARMA (the successor of BIPA and NEPROPHARM). NEFARMA published the complaints and 'recommendations' of RGA in its annual report. The associations have made the Code binding on their members:

> a document has been submitted to (the members) for their signature, by which they expressly declare that they will respect the new Code and not to object to their medical communication being controlled by the RGA. Further NEPROPHARM and BIPA will leave no stone unturned to ensure that their members will comply with the new rules of behaviour (RGA, 1974: 25).

In the second place the RGA regulation did not only concern popular drugs and consumer advertising, but also prescribed drugs and advertising to professionals. Finally the RGA regulation did not involve preventive control, like the KOAG, but it adjudicated complaints in consequence of written or verbal advertisements.[16]

The main reasons for the establishment of the RGA regulation system in the early 1970s were increased state intervention in the pharmaceutical industry, growing public criticism of the pharmaceutical industry and the dismantling of the PHC. In 1973 the state developed specific rules for the advertising of drugs. BIPA and NEPROPHARM started their private regulation activities in the same year. This might be interpreted as a defence against 'threatening' state-intervention.

The RGA regulation system was a good example of the way voluntary interest associations try to find forms of regulation that can be accepted both by the state and by the members. One of the two fundamental rules in the 'code of behaviour' was identical with the legal prohibition of misleading advertising introduced by the government. At the same time the voluntary character of regulation was preserved. The second fundamental rule was not based on a legal obligation but on the 'ethics of the industry'. To this extent, the code was not band on legal rules but was a voluntarily initiative of the industry: 'A rule like this can hardly be laid down in a legal form' (RGA, 1974: 23). For the same reason the further elaboration of these rules had the character of 'criteria': 'Intentionally the term "criteria" has been used in this connection and also the interrogative form in which these criteria have been framed. The intention being to express distinctly that each of the criteria mentioned ought not to be regarded as a separate injunction or prohibition order....' (RGA, 1974: 24). The attempt to escape from severe state control was also evident in the element of sanctioning. The only sanction the private regulatory body had at its disposal was negative publicity. Nevertheless, in last instance the association could refer to state support:

> should any company therefore disregard a recommendation of the council..., there will be always the possibility of a lawsuit on the grounds of infringement of the rules in question. So the state regulation ought to be regarded as the last resort of the self-disciplinary supervision of medical communication by the pharmaceutical industry (RGA, 1974: 24).

On balance the voluntary character was more important than the etatist elements. The voluntary character was however reduced when NEFARMA introduced a new code of behaviour.

The extension of self-regulation
In 1978 NEFARMA introduced a new 'Code of Behaviour' combining all the different self-regulatory measures of the industry (like the KOAG regulation, RGA regulation, etc.) in one set of rules. This was followed five years later (1983) by the establishment of a 'Code Committee' to handle all complaints about pharmaceutical industry.

The introduction of the 1978 Code can be seen as a continuation of the tradition of self-regulation of the pharmaceutical industry and is a response to the dismantling of the PHC cartel: '...there is a fear that the complete freedom of trade nowadays might lead to undesirable developments in the future' (NEFARMA, 1978: 5), NEFARMA has put much effort in formulating the Code in such a way as to make it compatible with cartel legislation of the European Community.[17]

The new Code was also a response to public criticism of the pharmaceutical industry, especially of its marketing practices in the Third World. Notorious examples of such practices have been provided by Ciba-Geigy and Organon. Multinationals frequently sell their specialties (such as dianabol, durabolin, orabolin) in the Third World directly to the public whereas in Western countries they are only available on prescription. In the approach to the general public they tend to use simple advertisements which may be misleading (for example, negative side-effects are not mentioned: Wolffers, 1983; Van der Geest, 1984).

Criticism of such marketing practices has been formulated, among others, by the international consumer organization, IOCU. This has prompted the World Health Organization (WHO) to develop an international code for the pharmaceutical industry, to be adopted and elaborated by the national governments. One of the governments which at first responded positively was the Dutch government. But it was stopped short by the industry.

The industry too reacted to the public criticism and the threat of a binding regulation of the WHO. The International Federation of Pharmaceutical Manufacturers Associations, IFPMA, developed a voluntary code of its own, the 'IFPMA Code of Pharmaceutical Marketing Practices'. NEFARMA's new Code of Behaviour replicated the IFPMA Code. NEFARMA also successfully pressed the Dutch government not to take over the WHO code but to wait for self-regulation of the industry. When the President of WHO asked the Dutch government in December 1982 about its progress with the WHO Code, it answered that 'we have a strong impression that the industry is in favour of self-regulation, and so are we'.[18] In 1983, the new private regulation system of the industry was put to its first test. A complaint was filed against the marketing practices of Organon (one of the most important members of NEFARMA). If Organon was found in violation of the Code by its own peers, the case of self-regulation was strengthened. An 'acquittal', on the other hand, might have resulted in a negative image for self-regulation. And indeed Organon was censured by the Code Committee for misleading advertisement of drugs in the Third World. What for one major firm and member of the association was a defect amounted to a victory for the industry as a whole since the practice of self-regulation was legitimized.[19]

Case 2 and Case 1 compared

In Table 4 the involvement of private organizations and the state in advertisement regulation is summarized. Until 1958, both quality regulation (Case 1) and the regulation of advertising for drugs (Case 2) were a purely private affair. Since then private regulation is completely replaced by pure state regulation in Case 1. In Case 2, state intervention increases after 1958 with the formulation of a general framework and (in the 1960s) of various specific rules. But private involvement remains important, especially in implementation and control. Private inspection boards with their own rules, like the KOAG and the RGA, are accepted by the state. This acceptance is not only a passive one as the state itself uses these boards to file complaints against advertising practices. For NEFARMA this is proof of the legitimacy of private regulation. Also opposition groups use the private regulatory bodies to challenge the market practices of the industry.[20]

TABLE 4
The involvement of private organizations (P) and the state (S) in regulating advertisement for industrial drugs, 1926–84

Aspects of regulation	Involvement of private organizations and state		
	1926–58	Popular drugs 1958–84	All drugs 1974–84
1. Formulation of central framework	P	P/S	P/S
2. Formulation of specific standards	P	P/S	P/S
3. Operationalization of specific norms	P	P	P
4. Implementation	P	P	P
5. Control	P	P	P
6. Supervision over 4 and 5	P	P/S	P/S
7. Sanctioning	P	P/S	P/S

The difference in state involvement between Cases 1 and 2 cannot be explained by features of the industry or of the involved interest organizations. In both cases, the industry has an interest in regulation, a preference for self-regulation, and the organizational capacity to regulate. Increased state involvement in the registration of medicines (Case 1) has not come about on request of the industry. Therefore the difference must be explained by different attitudes on the part of the state while in Case 1 the state did not entrust regulation to the industry, in Case 2 it accepted private regulation.

One explanation is the problem of censorship mentioned before. Secondly, state intervention is more likely in matters of general public interest. The quality and price of drugs may seem to be of more importance with respect to public health and the public health care system than the quality of advertisement. If there is high direct state involvement in quality control and if most drugs are paid for by the public health care system, state regulation of advertisement practices may be of minor importance. Thirdly, existing private regulation of advertisement seems to function to the satisfaction of the state and the industry. Acceptance by the state is due, for one thing, to the 'neutral image' of private regulatory bodies. The industry appoints professional 'outsiders' to these bodies. For another thing, the state, after the introduction of a general legal framework and various specific rules does have the possibility to control private regulation. Acceptance by the industry is based on the voluntary and flexible character of private regulation and the possibility to participate in its operation. It also appears that being controlled by one's own peers is preferable to being regulated by a state bureaucracy. Finally there have been no scandals in advertisement of as serious a nature as the Softenon scandal in Case 1.

Case 3: the regulation of animal drugs — pressure for state intervention

The sub-sectors of industrial drugs for human use and animal use differ very much in the degree to which they are subject to regulation. With a few exceptions, there was hardly any regulation — neither state nor private — for animal drugs until 1976. In particular, product quality, quality of advertisement and the quality of manufacturing practices were entirely unregulated. This came to an end in 1976 when a legal framework for animal drugs was presented in the form of the 'Animal drugs Bill' (*Diergeneesmiddelenwet*). In the future, the Act could conceivably become a tool for quality regulation, and in this respect it may be comparable with the 1958 legislation on human drugs.

Why was there no regulation for animal drugs, and why were animal drugs not regulated in the same laws as human drugs? Why did the state intervene only in 1976? And why was and is there no private regulation in this area?

The failure of the 1958 Act to regulate animal drugs as well is due to the fact that responsibility for the two kinds of drugs lies with different state agencies. While the Ministry of Public Health is in charge of human drugs, animal drugs are under the jurisdiction of the Ministry of Agriculture. But this does not explain the complete absence of state regulation for animal drugs.

One explanation can be found in the characteristics of the sector. The manufacturing of *industrial* drugs for animal use has only started in the 1950s. Human drugs however have been industrially manufactured since the beginning of this century (Reynders and Van Winden, 1976: 9).

Animal drugs were made for a long time by the veterinary surgeon. He was (and still is) responsible for prescribed drugs both as a doctor and as a chemist and he also sells popular drugs. The manufacturing of drugs, including the control of quality, was considered part of his profession which is regulated by specific legislation.

The growth of large-scale cattle farming has changed medical care for animals from curative treatment of individual animals to preventive health protection for all animals (Ministerie van Landbouw, 1983: 18). This development not only changed the role of the veterinary surgeon but made industrial manufacturing of animal drugs economically feasible.

Another explanation for the lack of regulation are the characteristics of the product. Animal drugs have not been at the centre of public attention and criticism and for this reason there was no stimulus for state intervention, as was the case with human drugs. However, the recent large-scale 'preventive' use of pharmaceuticals and other chemicals in agriculture and cattle breeding has had consequences for the quality of foodstuffs such as meat and milk. As a result, pressure has arisen from consumer organizations for more (restrictive) regulation also in this area. A number of 'scandals' have served to heighten public concern.

The absence of state intervention is explained by the late development of industrial production and by scant public attention. But the question remains why there was and is no private regulation of animal drugs. An important condition for private regulation is the existence of a functional group with a minimal degree of homogeneity, a collective interest in regulation, and the organizational capacity to regulate. The sector of animal drugs is however very heterogeneous and competitive, as described above. This relatively small sub-sector is divided into a number of specific manufacturer-consumer relations, which are reflected in the associational pattern. Heterogeneity in firm size is also considerable. Next to very small and medium-sized manufacturers, there are a few large multinational firms in the industry. In addition there is competition between industrial manufacturers and veterinary surgeons. The sub-sector has to contend with 'unfair' quality competition, 'black market' practices, chaotic trade practices and, as in the sector of human drugs, with the competition of 'white labels' and parallel importers.

These conditions, together with the lack of state intervention, might be sufficient motives for self-regulation. The problem is, however, that there is no uniform need for regulation. The manufacturers of branded drugs seem to have a general interest in regulation. But the producers of white labels and those who engage in black market practices are not in favour of regulation.

In addition, there is a fragmented associational pattern which reflects the heterogeneity and the competitiveness of the sector. While the human branch of the industry has a highly developed associational system (one single, powerful interest association, affiliated to important sectoral and national peak associations) the system at the animal side shows a low degree of development. There are four small interest associations with overlapping activities and hardly any resources to regulate.[21] Some of these associations have tried to regulate the behaviour of their members, but without success. For instance FIDIN, the interest organization of manufacturers and importers of branded drugs for prescription, has agreed on a number of binding rules about fair competition, quality of manufacturing practices, etc. But it does not have the capacity to control and sanction them, and it is confronted with non-members as well as members who undermine these rules. The only possibility seems state sanction.

The inability of these associations to regulate the market themselves was an important motive for them to press the state for intervention. As a matter of fact, three of these four associations were founded with the objective to lobby for state-intervention. For years they have requested a central legal framework and some specific rules for the animal drugs industry. Up till now, the 'Animals Drug Bill' is not yet legally introduced. In 1983 the elaboration was further postponed by the government since new state regulation is not in line with its policy of 'deregulation'.

Conclusion

The central question of this chapter was under what conditions private self-regulation of industry becomes possible. The three empirical examples analysed in this chapter cannot give a general answer. More cases in other sectors and countries have to be compared.

What these three cases illustrate is the complexity of self-regulation. There is not a simple, single condition for the existence and persistence of self-regulation by business interest associations. For instance, a lack of state intervention on the one side and a collective interest of industry in regulation on the other are not sufficient conditions for successful private government, as illustrated by the case of animal drugs. Here we found a weakly developed associational system with weak interest associations incapable of self-regulation. The need for recognizing sub-interests inside the associational structure seems stronger in this sector than the need for unity. Compared with the producers of human drugs the external pressure — public criticism or unfair state intervention — to form a strong collective interest is absent. To the extent that there is in the animal drugs industry a collective interest in regulation, it is the result of internal 'unfair' competition, and this seems to be a problematic condition for unity.

Even a highly developed interest association cannot guarantee successful self-regulation — as was illustrated in the case of human drugs. Here a well-developed private regulation system was undermined by state intervention, and the presence of a strong collective interest in self-regulation and of a private organization with capacities to regulate were not sufficient to prevent this. Private regulation — especially in areas close to the public interest — is hardly possible without state acceptance. The importance of public health care on the one side and the strong public criticism of the pharmaceutical industry on the other worked against state facilitation of private government and in favour of pure state regulation.

Only when there is a collective interest in self-regulation, a highly developed interest association with sufficient resources to enforce a self-regulatory system and when the issue at stake is not too closely linked to the public interest, does self-regulation seem possible. This is illustated by the case of advertising regulation (Case 2).

Notes

This chapter is an outcome of the research project 'Organization of Business Interests in the Netherlands'. The project is part of an international research project on the organization of business interests in advanced industrial societies, co-ordinated by Phillipe C. Schmitter and Wolfgang Streeck. The Dutch research project is supported by the Netherlands' Organization for Basic Scientific Research (ZWO).

1. The competition between 'specialties' and 'generics' involves on the one side firms engaged in research and in the development of new branded drugs, and on the other side firms that manufacture the same drugs under their generic name and sell them at lower prices. This is possible after expiration of the patent of the branded drug. The manufacturers of generics can sell at lower prices because they do not have to incur the costs of research and development.

2. BIPA is the 'Bond van Importeurs van Pharmaceutische Artikelen' (Union of Importers of Pharmaceutical Products). NEPROPHARM means 'Nederlandse Vereniging van Fabrikanten van Pharmaceutische Producten' (Dutch Association of Manufacturers of Pharmaceutical Products).

3. PHC is the acronym of 'Pharmaceutische Handels Conventie' (Pharmaceutical Wholesale Trade Union). This cartel was one of the few cartels which was registered with the Dutch Government as well as with the EC in Brussels. It was in operation until 1977 (Pharmaceutisch Weekblad, 1977: 1225).

4. 'Nederlandse Associatie van de Farmaceutische Industrie' (Netherlands Association of the Pharmaceutical Industry).

5. FIDIN: Association of Manufacturers and Importers of Animal Pharmaceuticals in the Netherlands; FAGROVET: Association of Manufacturers and Wholesalers in

Veterinary Products; DIBEVO: National Association of Producers, Wholesalers and Retailers of Pet Articles; NEFATO: Association of Dutch Manufacturers of Animal Feed Additives.

6. 'Geneesmiddelen Commissie'. One important task of this committee is to advise the Minister of Public Health on the admission of drugs for prescription. The committee has twelve members, one of which comes from the pharmaceutical industry.

7. Private government through the PHC was so strongly developed that in some respects it had assumed the characteristics of a real government. This at least was the feeling of the industry itself, reflected in a retrospective comment by NEFARMA in 1978: 'For years manufacturers and importers of drugs had a growing uneasy feeling about the tight and partially outdated instructions of the PHO.' But rather than dismantling self-regulation, the industry would have preferred to continue it in a different form: 'There were already concrete plans to replace this system by more flexible regulation' (NEFARMA, 1978: 5).

8. Softenon is the branded name for 'Thalidomide'. Between 1959 and 1962 the Softenon affair was front-page news. Consumption of this narcotic sedative by pregnant women resulted in a great number of misshaped babies in different countries (in Germany about 10,000, in other countries between 1000 and 2000, in the Netherlands about 80).

9. The pharmaceutical industry was represented by the PHC cartel which in turn represented the interest associations of manufacturers and importers of specialties, NEPROPHARM and BIPA. In 1975 the PHC was replaced by NEFARMA.

10. Keuringsraad Openlijke Aanprijzing Geneesmiddelen (Inspection Board for the Public Advertisement of Drugs).

11. This is at least the conclusion of a government committee and also of consumer organizations (Commissie Alternatieve Geneeswijzen, 1981; Consumentenbond, 1983).

12. The industry expects that the introduction of the new Act on Misleading Advertisement will probably give the state a tool to control this 'unfair competition' (NEFARMA, 1979: 18).

13. Under the New Constitution, Article 1.7. (freedom of speech) is no longer related to commercial advertising, so the old legal argument against a state inspection board is no longer valid (WRR, 1983: 668).

14. 'Nederlandse Code voor de Aanprijzing van Geneesmiddelen' (Dutch Code on Medicines Communication). This code succeeded an agreement dating from 1962 which was made with an interest association of physicians (Kon. Ned. Maatchapij tot bevordering van de Geneeskunst KNMG). They did not participate in the 1973 code.

15. BIPA and NEPROPHARM have also considered the possibility of bringing this regulation under the supervision of the Enforcement Board of the Dutch Advertising Code (Commissie voor de Handhaving van de Nederlandse Code voor het Reclamewezen). But they decided that 'medical communication is such a specialized field of activity that a separate body to enforce this code ought to be created' (RGA, 1974: 22).

16. Since 1978 NEFARMA can also take the initiative itself of asking the RGA to rule on specific advertisements. An additional complaint by someone else is no longer necessarily required (NEFARMA, 1978: 18). By assuming the role of prosecutor, NEFARMA strengthens its role of private government.

17. The Code was presented by NEFARMA to the European Committee for approval and also to the Dutch Minister of Economic Affairs. The latter encouraged the association to start using this Code, and approval would be given if it proved to work well (interview NEFARMA).

18. Information based on interview with officials of NEFARMA.

19. Self-regulation is still criticized by various authors. The main argument is that it

does not dispose of real sanctions (for instance, a prohibition on selling certain drugs) and is not based on law but just on the 'ethics of industry' (Van der Geest, 1984; De Wildt, 1984).

20. The complaint against advertising practices in Third World countries was filed by WEMOS ('Werkgroep Medische Ontwikkelings Samenwerking'), a group which had for years been criticizing the practices of pharmaceutical multinationals.

21. DIBEVO, one of the four associations, is to some degree an exception. It is not exclusively an association of manufacturers but mainly organizes the retail trade. This association is well developed and does engage in private regulations, but only with respect to the retail trade. The interests of manufacturers are of minor importance for DIBEVO.

8
Prerequisites, problem-solving capacity and limits of neo-corporatist regulation: a case study of private interest governance and economic performance in Austria

Franz Traxler

Introduction
Although contemporary conceptualizations of neo-corporatism differ considerably with respect to their theoretical presuppositions and empirical content,[1] there is one fundamental idea which is common to nearly all of them. It is widely suspected that corporatism may have a specific stabilizing effect on Western societies by ensuring a co-operative form of interest intermediation and by integrating interest associations into the process of policy formation. In the recent literature, private interest governance is conceived as the most advanced form of neo-corporatism and as capable of making a unique contribution to social order which should be distinguished from 'conventional' mechanisms of societal guidance. Where interest associations acquire public policy functions and manage them autonomously, they replace state intervention and establish a kind of regulation which lies 'between' or even 'beyond' the market and the state (see Streeck, 1983a and the contribution by Streeck and Schmitter in this volume). In Streecks's words, this mode of corporatism 'may offer a "third way" between the market and the state that is free of both "market failure" and "state failure"'.

Classifying such an advanced form of corporatism as an arrangement peculiarly appropriate for societal guidance draws attention to its *genuine* problem-solving capacity. It implies that these arrangements do not only fulfil a general and latent function by controlling the working class,[2] but also an instrumental and intentional one with respect to specific economic problems. From an analytical point of view this raises two questions:

1. In what way can corporatist self-regulation be mobilized as a strategic alternative to state intervention or the market? To the extent that special and unusual conditions are prerequisites for the viability of such arrangements, they may not be available as a real choice for politicians or 'policy designers'. This would reduce considerably their practical relevance as a means for overcoming the present economic crisis.

2. What are the subsequent economic effects of private interest governance in diverse arenas of public policy? It is possible that its problem-solving capacity varies a great deal according to subject matter and surrounding interests. If a real problem-solving capacity does exist, are there any structural limits to it?

Dealing with both these questions requires an empirical investigation. This will be attempted by means of an analysis of the private interest governance prevalent in the Austrian dairy industry. In respect to our questions, the political economy of this industry in Austria is interesting for several reasons, not the least of which is that the sector is, from the point of view of national safety, health and social welfare, an extremely sensitive area.

This suggests a paradoxical context in which, on the one hand, a manifest and substantial need for political regulation has arisen but, on the other hand, any regulatory measures taken are particularly likely to cause conflict because they are bound to affect the interests of extensive and powerful groups in society. From the standpoint of state decision-makers, it may be especially tempting to devolve these regulatory functions to interest groups through a process known as *Staatsentlastung*.[3] Therefore, such a sector is particularly susceptible to corporatist arrangements. Within the Austrian economy the dairy sector is characterized by the highest degree of corporatist regulation. Virtually all parameters of management decision-making are under the concerted control of regulating interest associations. As a consequence of this, the sector's economic situation is nearly exclusively the result of regulations decided, monitored and implemented by the interest associations involved. Because market mechanisms and state intervention are practically eliminated, it is possible to observe the problem-solving capacity of this 'third way' of societal guidance in an isolated and exemplary manner. An attempt will be made in this chapter to develop some general hypotheses in response to the questions posed above based on the empirical findings from the Austrian example. Therefore, it is divided into the following sections:

1. An overview of how the system functions;.
2. An analysis of the preconditions necessary for the assumption of public regulatory functions by interest associations; and
3. A discussion of the possibilities and limits of off-loading the burden of state activities through private interest governance.

Private interest governance in the Austrian dairy industry

The Austrian system of regulation in the dairy industry is an example of a transference of public policy functions by deliberate state decision. The system rests on a specific law, known as the *Marktord-*

nungsgesetz (MOG). In it, the aims of the regulation and the means provided for its implementation are exactly defined.

According to section 3 of the MOG, the following are its economic-political goals:
1. Protection of the domestic dairy sector;
2. Secure producer and consumer-prices at as unified a level as possible;
3. Secure and economically viable delivery, processing and distribution;
4. Balanced and adequate supply to outlets;
5. Preparation of milk and milk products of faultless quality; and
6. Suitability of production and marketing methods to the possibilities in markets at home and abroad.

To attain these goals, the following regulatory measures are provided by law:
1. The fixing of countervailing duties (*Importausgleichsbeiträge*) to protect the domestic dairy sector against foreign competition.
2. The payment of price-compensatory and transport-compensatory contributions. These are collected from highly profitable processing firms and are then given as subsidies to less profitable firms.
3. The fixing of procurement and sales-markets for individual processing firms. Within the procurement-markets fixed for them, the processing firms are obliged to buy *all* the milk from designated farmers (in so far as quality standards have been maintained). Within their fixed sales areas, the processing firms are obliged to deliver to their purchasers. On the other hand, the farmers are only allowed to deliver their milk to those processing firms to whose procurement area they belong and the purchasers to buy only from the designated processing firm, according to an established territorial division of markets.
4. The fixing of quality standards and the implementation of regular quality controls.
5. The obligation of paying deliveries for export promotion. These deliveries are paid for by the farmers and the consumer through the retail price.

A special board (*Milchwirtschaftsfonds* — MWF) is set up to carry out these guidance measures. Four interest associations have the exclusive right to send delegates and to be represented on the decision-making bodies of the board.
1. The *Conference of the Presidents of Chambers of Agriculture* (PKLWK), which is the interest organization of the farmers;
2. The *Federal Chamber of Trade and Industry* (BWK), which functions as the interest organization for business firms;

3. The *Austrian Trade Union Federation* (ÖGB); and
4. The *Austrian Association of Chambers of Labor* (ÖAKT), both of which represent the interest of employees in the MWF.

Each association sends the same number of representatives. In practice, although their interests may conflict, they are under a very strong pressure to consensus within the MWF because decisions must be reached, according to the decision rules of the MOG, either unanimously or by a four-fifths majority. For this reason, no association can be overruled by the others. The administration of MWF measures is handled by a specific office, staffed by permanent employees and financed by proceeds from the sale of milk and milk products.

This comprehensive regulatory system means that, de facto, all parameters pertaining to the firms' decisions are subject to the political control of the interest associations involved:

1. The milk prices are political prices. This is true of the price paid to the farmers, as of the price charged to the final consumer. Both prices are fixed by the Federal Ministry of Business, Trade and Industry, and the four interest associations play a central role in their determination. The prices for milk products are fixed directly by the four interest associations within the framework of their co-operation in the 'Parity Commission for Wage and Price-Matters' (*Paritätische Kommission für Lohn-und Preisfragen*).[4] The fixing of all these prices depends upon political considerations. For example, the price of butter is substantially lower than the price of its production. Because the financing of the milk-processing sector has to be secured from the turnover of all products, the deficits that result from lower priced products are compensated for by the higher prices for other products.

2. The production and the sale of all milk and most milk products are also regulated. The MWF regulates which firms may produce which products and also fixes their sources of supply and sales outlets.

3. For the processing firms, these regulatory measures mean that their profitability is politically pre-established and guaranteed. The realization of profit or loss has a direct connection with the decisions of the MWF with respect to the production programme and markets allotted to individual firms. If, for example, a particular firm is allowed to produce only low-priced products, then the sales cannot cover the costs. In order to remove these economic disparities, a system of compensatory payments is provided. As has already been mentioned above, profitable firms producing high-priced goods have to make payments, which deficit firms receive as subsidies. The necessary clearing system is operated by the MWF. The actual profits or losses realized by the individual enterprises are corrected with the

help of co-called 'standard costs'. These are oriented by general principles of economic efficiency and are also calculated by the MWF. If the actual costs for a firm exceed the standard costs, its outcome deteriorates. The amount of difference is not taken into consideration by the MWF as costs. Conversely, profitability will be greater for those firms whose real costs remain under the standard costs. An incentive to increased productivity is thus generated by this clearing system. The firm's net result, corrected on the basis of standard costs, is then set against a profit limit also established by the MWF. If the profit realized by the firm exceeds this limit, the amount of the difference is levied. If the real profit remains under the profit limit, the firm receives a subsidy representing the amount of the difference. Standard costs and limit of total profits are, therefore, the criteria for the payment of both compensatory payments and/or subsidies.

4. Enterprises may also not make investments with complete autonomy. Investments are only recognized as costs within the clearing system if they have been approved by the MWF. As a guideline for the approval of investments, sectoral targets (*Strukturplan*) have been determined (again by the MWF) by means of which the rationalization and modernization of the Austrian dairy industry is supposed to be promoted.

This brief overview of the way in which the system of self-regulation functions in this sector should already have made clear that the interest associations have to manage tasks which have an extremely high potentiality for conflict. Their implementation demands an exceptionally high capacity for controlling the behaviour of their members. Although the problems are quite controversial, the system has obtained the consensus of the four interest associations involved and of the parties represented in parliament. On the one hand, each of the interest associations could block the system with its power of veto; on the other hand, the existence of the MOG has to be prolonged every two years by a two-thirds majority in parliament on grounds of constitutional law. Thus, the continuance of the system comes regularly under political review. In spite of this, the existence of the MOG — albeit with certain modifications — has been repeatedly and regularly sustained. In the following paragraphs, the reasons for this high degree of policy stability will be examined.

The conditions of stability

All four interest associations are characterized by an organizational structure which is particularly favourable for the assumption of public regulatory functions. The relevant organizational characteristics are, above all, (i) the domains covered by associational representation; (ii) the allocation of decision-making competence; and (iii) the high degree of professionalized management within each association.

Domain of representation

All four interest associations are not limited in their scope of representation to the dairy industry but cover a wide range of concerns. Their potential membership embraces members of all economic sectors and groups. The territorial organizations (*Landwirtschaftskammern*) of the PKLWK organize all independent and gainfully occupied owners or leaseholders in agriculture and forestry whether they are principally or secondarily involved in such production. The PKLWK, therefore, represents all Austrian farmers. The domain of the BWK embraces almost all industrial and commercial enterprises in Austria. Among its members are also all publicly owned enterprises. Through the individual trade unions which are attached to the ÖGB, all worker and employee groups are organizationally covered. In the territorial sub-organizations of the ÖAKT are organized all employees (with the exception of the top managers, the majority of agricultural and forestry workers and civil servants). The employees are, therefore, doubly represented in the MWF, as they are on most other corporatist boards. The reason for this is that only in this way can the symmetry of the political camps (*Lager*) which characterize Austria be ensured. The PKLWK and the BWK are, in turn, dominated politically by the Conservative Party (ÖVP). The Social Democratic Party (SPÖ) dominates in the ÖGB and the ÖAKT. The result of these all-embracing domains is that each association organizes extremely heterogeneous interests. The farmers of all specific product areas are covered by the PKLWK. In the dairy sector, it is important that the associations have to represent farmers both in the plains and the mountainous areas where conditions of production and costs of production differ considerably. Furthermore, the Raiffeisen Co-operatives (*Raiffeisengenossenschaften*) are organized within the territorial sub-organizations of the PKLWK. These co-operatives arose as self-help organizations for farmers during the last century. Their members and functionaries are also recruited primarily from this group. In addition to their membership in the territorial units of the PKLWK, the Raiffeisen Co-operatives have at their disposal a specific interest organization (*Österreichischer Raiffeisenverband* — ÖRV). The ÖRV is also a member of the PKLWK, as the *Landwirtschaftskammern*. These co-operatives have, since their inception, developed into large, professionally-run concerns of great significance in the dairy industry. At present, their market share of all milk and milk products represents almost 90 per cent. The largest of these co-operatives was thirteenth on the list of Austria's biggest industrial enterprises in 1980. It goes without saying that the interests of these agro-businesses are in no way identical with those of the farmers who supply milk to them.

Both producer and business as well as service firms are organized within the BWK. The BWK is, therefore, confronted with both the interests of the processing and commercial firms and with those of the co-operative and private processing firms. The ÖGB and the ÖAKT represent, within the MWF, the interests of the employees of this sector. Additionally, both workers' interest associations are to be reckoned as representatives of the consumer, so that divergent interests are also present within their organizational structures.

As a result of this heterogeneity of interests, each of the associations is subject to strong pressures towards internal compromise. A given association can only act vis-à-vis opposing associations within the MWF if an internal unification of its various interest positions has been successfully established. The ability to forge such compromises depends on an internally established decision procedure which is specially designed to cope with this problem (see below). In this connection, it is important that the existence of this procedure at the same time also increases the ability of the association to establish compromises with the other associations.

The overlap inherent in the comprehensiveness of their domains promotes the ability of the associations to reach a compromise because it leads to an interpenetration of interest positions and also of problem perspectives. For example, Raiffeisen co-operatives belong both to the domain of the PKLWK and to that of the BWK. This manifests itself in representatives of these co-operatives sitting in the MWF on behalf of both associations. Furthermore, a representative of another type of co-operative society (*Konsumgenossenschaft*) also occupies a seat designated for the ÖGB in the MWF, because this co-operative business concern is closely connected with social democracy and the workers' movement. In this way, business interests are represented in three of the four interest associations, albeit with variable weight and content. In spite of the overlapping of domains, no competition exists between the associations. This is because the PKLWK, the ÖAKT and the BWK are interest organizations which are based upon the principle of legally guaranteed compulsory membership. Members are legally obliged to pay the prescribed dues to their interest organizations. There is, between the ÖAKT and the ÖGB whose domains are practically identical, a close co-operative relationship which rests upon the principle of work-sharing. Essentially, the ÖAKT and its territorial sub-organizations function as a brain trust for the ÖGB. Both are connected to one another through numerous *Personalunionen* (shared leadership positions) and pursue a common political line within the MWF. One further effect of these comprehensive domains is that the interest associations have always to take into consideration criteria pertaining to the *whole* economy in the regulation of the dairy sector. The associations cannot indulge in any consistent or blatant sectoral protectionism because such a policy would disadvantage their members in other economic sectors. The more comprehensive domain of an association is, the less it is possible for it to externalize the costs of a protection-oriented policy and the more it is under pressure to orient itself to problems of the whole economy (Olson, 1982).

As a result of the comprehensiveness of their domains, the selected participating associations are not just occupied with problems of the dairy sector but are authoritatively involved in all economic and social policy decisions. All other systems of private interest governance that exist in Austria depend upon the co-operation of the PKLWK, BWK, ÖGB and the ÖAKT. The majority of public boards which serve to represent functional interests are composed entirely of representatives of the 'Big Four', as they are called in Austria. The multiplicity of public policy functions which the associations fulfill raises their total control capacity and makes it possible for them to increase the effectiveness of their regulatory measures in individual policy areas.

For the specific regulation of the dairy sector, the interest associations make use, not only of policies which are available to them through the MOG, but they can also bring to bear guidance measures from outside the system. As was mentioned above, the fixing of prices for milk and milk products takes place outside the MWF. The producer price for the farmers and the retail price for milk are fixed by the Federal Ministry for Business, Trade and Industry. In this way, the Price Commission, composed of representatives of the four associations, has a formal advisory function. The four associations decide on prices for the other milk products autonomously in the *Paritätische Kommission*. The standard wages for employees in the sector are settled on the side of the employers through the ÖRV and the respective sub-units of the BWK and on the side of the employees through the Union of Private White-Collar Workers and the Union of Manual Workers in the Food Industry. Both are affiliated to the ÖGB.

Although wages and prices are fixed by different institutions, they nevertheless are brought together into a corporate package during negotiations. The four associations deal with each through a well-coordinated procedure. They can fix the standard contractual wages and the prices for milk products autonomously. With respect to the price paid to the farmers and the retail price of milk, they reach an agreement in the Price Commission on a joint 'suggestion', which the minister then declares legally binding by decree. All prices and wages become simultaneously valid. On the basis of the agreement on prices and wages, the associations within the MWF then revise the standard costs used in the clearing system.

The comprehensiveness of the domains and of the representational functions mean that, not only the disposition of all parameters of the regulation of the dairy industry (procurement and sales markets, investments, prices, profits, wage-costs) are concentrated in the four associations, but that they can also be employed in a co-ordinated fashion. This accumulation of control capacity also increases the pressure to find compromises. Because the Austrian system of interest intermediation and policy implementation — the so-called *Wirtschafts-und Sozialpartnershaft* — relies upon the co-operation of the four large associations, failure to find a compromise in a major sector would jeopardize the entire system. For example, the regulation of the associations in the area of the MOG is the most important element of the *Wirtschafts-und Socialpartnershaft* for the PKLWK. Should the system of regulation that is grounded upon the MOG become blocked, then the co-operation of this association in other areas would become doubtful.

In all, these connections illustate a paradox of organized class power. In Austria, the associations have accumulated power to such an extent that they have become quasi-prisoners of their own corporate potential for disruption and are only able to make use of this capacity if they exercise it co-operatively. This accumulation of power has its basis not only in a comprehensive, secure domain, but also in the internal centralization of the decison-making processes within each respective association.

Decision-making process
Although the associations differ somewhat in their internal structure, they all have in common the centralization of important functions at their highest organizational level. The BWK, PKLWK, ÖAKT and ÖGB are all peak associations and possess a high degree of control over their affiliated sub-organizations. All problems which do not affect only the interests of a sub-unit are dealt with at the top. Since economic affairs are usually decided at the level of the entire economy, decisions about them fall almost exclusively within the competence of the peak associations. All sub-units, whether territorially or functionally differentiated, are subject to the control from above. These controls rest upon organizational factors which are both *internal* and *external*.

Internally, the leaders are not elected directly by the members in any of the peak associations. They are recruited by a stepwise process of delegation which is related to the total number of members and the heterogeneity of the domains covered. These choices of personnel have the purpose of unifying, by successive approximations, internal interest heterogeneity. The more complex and varied the organized interests are, the more differentiated tends also to be the process of delegation and leadership selection. In accordance with this principle, all peak associations are characterized by an especially large number of sequential elections. The autonomy of the top leaders with respect to the membership basis increases with these steps (Herder-Dorneich, 1973: 171). With the growth in autonomy of an association's leadership, its ability to arrange compromises through external negotiations partners also increase.

This process of rendering associational leadership autonomous is not without problems, especially over retaining the loyalty of members. The further removed from member calculations that decisions are made, the more unsure it becomes that the ensuing decisions will obtain the ultimate agreement and support of those affected. This problem of legitimacy is, however, defused by the fact that each of the four peak associations is firmly aligned with one of the two largest party-political camps in Austria. The integrative effect of these political traditions can be documented through elections. In all the associations, candidate lists are presented by the respective *Lager*. The electoral outcome inevitably reinforces the traditionally dominant camp. The great majority of members identify, therefore, with that political camp into which the association is integrated. Through this, a generalized loyalty is generated which contributes importantly to the securing of the legitimacy of the policies followed by the association's leadership.

With the formation and conservation of member loyalty resting upon other conditions and processes than those involving the making of decisions, the formulation of associational goals is thereby relieved to a considerable degree from the burden of sustaining motivation and compliance.[5] A central precondition for the assumption of public policy functions by private associations is thus fulfilled (Streeck, 1972; Weitbrecht, 1969).

An important *external* condition for the centralization of the associations is that only the peak organizations — and not even their sub-units — are regarded by state bodies as relevant partners for negotiation. The sub-units are only recognized as interlocutors if they have been commissioned by their peak associations to deal with a given problem. Futhermore, the peak organizations increase their capacity for control from above and for monopolization of access through their co-operation with one another.

Given these conditions it is possible for the peak associations to permit the articulation of group interests within their respective domains without being overwhelmed by them. Such 'sectoral', 'branch' or 'product' interests are introduced into the inter-association decision-making process in carefully measured doses. For example, three sub-units are responsible for the dairy sector within the BWK: one covers the industrial milk-processing plants, the second deals with trade milk-processing plants, and the third with matters of commerce. All three currently have representatives within the MWF. The final decision about delegates is made, however, by the leadership of the BWK because, in accordance with the MOG, only the BWK is formally represented in the MWF. The situation is similar in the ÖGB. In terms of internal differentiation and autonomy of its sub-units, it occupies the second place, behind the BWK. Both of the unions which are specifically responsible for the workers and employees in the sector are represented in the MWF, but they are delegated by the top leadership of the ÖGB. In addition to these representatives of the relevant sub-units, the representatives from the peak associations themselves also sit on board of the MWF. The respective unions and branches of the ÖGB and the BWK do have considerable autonomy in the area of wage policy. Collective agreements are negotiated and concluded by them. Nevertheless, they are also subject to the control of the peak organizations in this matter. The agreements made among bargaining sub-units require the approval of the *Paritätische Kommission*.

The centralization of the interest associations is illustrated very clearly by the composition of the personnel on the teams which negotiate wages and prices in the dairy industry. Although these take place in three different sites, most of the representatives take part in all three rounds of negotiations. The regulation and co-ordination capacities of the peak associations are also strengthened through this concentration of participation in the decision-making process.

Professionalization

All four interest associations have at their disposal an extensive staff of paid officials. For example, almost 4600 officials are employed in the BWK and its organizations; the ÖGB and its individual unions have about 1800 employees (Traxler, 1982a: 239). There is one staff member per fifty members in the BWK; the proportion in the ÖGB is one to 899. This high level of professionalization is of significance for the stability and the functional capacity of sectoral regulation because, when combined with a comprehensive domain of representation, the officials tend to develop an orientation which favours the assumption of public policy functions. In comparison with elected leaders, associational officials are oriented more towards macro-economic than sector-specific perspectives and adopt 'technocratic' rather than 'ideological' criteria. In Austria these officials of all associations have been a driving force behind the development of the 'Social Partnership' system during the 1960s (Marin, 1982). Their orientation stems from their specific interest position. Out of professional and career calculations, these officials are mostly oriented towards the higher levels of their own respective associational structures and, therefore, toward more comprehensive definitions of the interest situation. For the same reason, they orient themselves more towards organizational interests than the specific concerns of members. The continued existence of the association and the increase of its long-term influence are weighted very highly in their calculations. In Austria, the satisfaction of these organizational interests is closely connected with the assumption of official policy functions. If the associations maintain a 'responsible' policy-line, they increase their organizational power through co-operation with one another and with the state in a process of reciprocal transfer of resources. This political exchange (Lehmbruch, 1977; Pizzorno, 1978) is particularly attractive to the associations' officials because they then do not only prepare the policy decisions and negotiations, but they also participate actively in them. In this manner, they become directly responsible for the increase in organizational influence of their associations. All four associations send officials as delegates to the MWF with a view to ensuring their comprehensive interest orientation and the predominant role of the peak organization. For example, some years ago, the leadership of the BWK replaced an elected leader who withdrew from the MWF with an associational official in order to achieve greater autonomy for its representative in the MWF in relation to the lobbying by its member firms.

The role of the state revisited
In the dairy sector, interest associations have assumed regulatory duties of a nature and extent that the state alone would be incapable of accomplishing. Nevertheless, the associations require state assistance to fulfil these tasks. Their organizational bases alone are insufficient to ensure an effective functional capacity for regulation by associations. Two types of support from public authority can be distinguished: guarantees of regulatory capacity and guarantees of organizational security.

The legal basis for the regulation by associations rests on the MOG. By means of this law, the associations represented in the MWF are equipped with a series of formal competences to which the associations add their own resources. In order to implement regulatory measures, the MWF has at its disposal several legally-backed sanctions. Firms are obliged to present all information to the MWF that this organization requires for its clearing system. The MWF is empowered to set up and prescribe for the firms a unified system for the calculation of operating costs which corresponds to its needs.

Farmers whose milk does not meet the lowest quality standards can be excluded from the circle of milk suppliers. Furthermore, the MWF has the power to impose a fine upon or to withdraw subsidies from processing firms which do not conform to its norms.

Another organizational guarantee granted by the state is that only the PKLWK, ÖAKT, BWK and ÖGB have a right to send delegates to decision-making bodies within the MWF. The membership dues which the processing plants are obliged to pay to their association are recognized as a cost factor by the MWF for the clearing system. However, more important than these sector-specific matters are the overall guarantees of organizational security. As was mentioned above, the BWK, ÖAKT and the PKLWK rely upon the principles of compulsory membership and payment of dues.[6] In contrast, the ÖGB is a voluntary organization. Because no competing trade union movement exists in Austria and the legal framework of labour relations provides indirect help for recruiting union members (Traxler, 1981), the ÖGB is also well entrenched organizationally. In 1980 its density ratio stood at 59.5 per cent (Traxler, 1982a: 257). The PKLWK, ÖAKT and the BWK have a legally guaranteed right to consultation. The government is obliged to present all projected legislative and administrative acts to the Chambers for their opinion in the planning stage. The number of state consultative bodies in which the four associations are jointly represented has become enormous. In practice, the influence of the four associations is even greater than the formal guarantees would lead one to assume. A monopoly of representation for interests in their respective domains has been conceded de facto to the four associations by the Austrian state.

In so far as the assumption of official functions by the associations rests on state regulatory and organizational support, this system is not a case of quasi-political, completely private, self-administration.[7] From the juridical point of view, the MWF forms part of the national state administration and is, therefore, subordinate to other state agencies. The four associations have no formal authority to issue directives to their representatives within the MWF (Korinek, 1976). In practice, however, the weight of influence is quite differently distributed. As was shown above by the mode of controlling milk prices, decisions are de facto reached by the associations even in those areas which are not formally reserved to the MWF but supposed to be decided by the responsible ministry. Regulation of milk industry is licensed by the state, but associations jointly make their regulatory decisions with considerable autonomy.

By virtue of their organizational privileges, the four interest associations form a stable cartel of representation which excludes any secession of sub-group interests. Some years ago, an attempt on 'the part of the private milk-processing firms to set up their own association failed. It was simply not possible for the aspiring association to achieve any political relevance. It survives to this day, but only by providing certain economic services to its members.

This case demonstrates that an effective associational regulatory system relies not only upon certain structural preconditions of a specific organizational nature, but also upon conditions *external* to the associations themselves. The latter are necessary for the survival of the system because associations which fulfill public functions are especially subject to risks of destabilization and defection (Olson, 1965). These risks increase in direct proportion to the comprehensiveness of the domain they represent because the heterogeneity of the member interests tends to intensify problems of internal integration. This coincidence of internal and external preconditions cannot be generated by deliberate state planning, although the purposive mobilization of state assistance is necessary.[8] So far, the formation of such a system has not been a matter of conscious policy design.

On the problem-solving capacity of the system

If one views the efficiency of the system from the perspective of the stated aims of the MOG, its principle advantages are that it guarantees the protection of the domestic dairy industry, unified prices and the permanent provision of consumer products conforming to fixed quality standards. In addition, the system contributes to *Staatsentlastung* by generating a political consensus. Although a high conflict potential is present in the fixing of prices for milk and milk-products, they have remained outside day-to-day, publicly salient, controversies. Similarly, labour relations have functioned without manifest conflicts. Since 1974, there have been no strikes in the sector. In both areas, the precondition for this apparently frictionless regulation of conflicts is the all-embracing and co-ordinated wage and price-policy of the associations which is, in turn, grounded upon the neo-corporatist structure of the entire system. A more fragmented system in which, for example, associations engaged in labour relations were not simultaneously integrated into the MWF would have great difficulty in attaining such a level of co-ordination. The associations have such an impressive ability to solve problems about incomes policy that, since the setting up of the MWF, they have assumed additional functions in this area. Milk products, which were originally subject to state controls, were transferred to the responsibility of the autonomous pricing mechanism of the associations in the *Paritätische Kommission*. At the beginning of the 1980s, when state subsidies to domestic milk were cut down, the necessary measure of price-adjustment were carried out smoothly by the associations.

In opposition to these advantages of the system, some deficiencies can be seen. First, the system is somewhat ponderous. This can be illustrated by the fact that at the beginning of 1983, the final balance-sheet for 1981 had still not been completed. Second, some clandestine lobbying tends to be carried on by association members within the MWF in the furtherance of their private interests. This lobbying is aimed, for example, at making changes in the fixed procurement and sales markets or in the planning of investment. Participants in this are not only farmers and processing firms, but also employee representatives (*Betriebsräte*) from the firms concerned. On the question involving the approval of investments, the suppliers of the capital goods have also become active.

Both types of deficiency are, nevertheless, not specific to regulation by associations, but a *general* problem of political regulation that arises irrespective of whether the state or the other actors carry out the task. If the allocation of resources and the distribution of favours takes place, not through an anonymous market process, but through deliberate collective decision, then attempts at lobbying and colonizing of the agencies by the involved interests are to be expected.

Much more grave is the still unsolved problem of chronic overproduction in the sector. This perpetual expansion of supply stands in opposition to an extensive stagnation of demand. This problem is being tackled in two ways. First, attempts are being made to increase exports. In this area some success has been achieved. Milk products represent the highest proportion of exported Austrian foodstuffs. This strategy has, however, the disadvantage that these exports have to be financed by state subsidies. Second, according to section 3/1c of the MOG, attempts are being made to promote the concentration and rationalization of production so as to lighten the cost burden on the system by increasing productivity. The same factors which generally facilitate an associational assumption of public functions also tend to favour the adoption of this modernizing task. The comprehensiveness of associational interest domains means that alterations in the industrial structure only affect changes in members, but do not endanger the existence of a given, established association. Such associations are, therefore, relatively insensitive to changes in industrial structure. As has been mentioned above, a *Strukturplan* has been elaborated for the modernization of the sector by the MWF by investment planning. Each firm that wishes to make an investment and aspires to the recognition of this investment as a cost factor, has to make an application for MWF approval. In practice, however, the *Strukturplan* has only minimal significance. The reason for this is lobbying on the part of the individual firms applying, something which the members of the MWF can only evade with difficulty.

In spite of the ineffectiveness of the *Strukturplan*, the MWF has succeeded in generating structural improvements. This took place by bypassing lobbying. Instead of making a concrete decision on each application, a generalized mechanism was established which took over the function of modernization. This mechanism rests upon the fixing of standard costs. The standard costs are the decisive criteria for the allocation of subsidies and the imposition of contributions to individual firms. If in fixing the standard costs, no consideration is given to less efficient concerns, then they come under pressure from costs. In the long term, they have either to increase their productivity or cease production.

TABLE 1
Number of firms in the dairy industry and turnover/cost relationship per kilogram of milk supplied

Year	Firms in dairy industry		Turnover/costs ratio schillings	real % change weighted for inflation
	Number	as a % of 1950		
1950	526	100	—	—
1965	425	81	—	—
1969	346	66	3.9	100.0
1970	326	62	3.8	97.4
1971	306	58	3.7	94.9
1972	284	54	3.7	94.9
1973	256	49	3.7	94.9
1974	243	46	3.4	87.2
1975	237	45	3.3	84.6
1976	234	44	3.4	87.2
1977	231	44	3.4	87.2
1978	222	42	3.3	84.6
1979	217	41	3.3	84.6
1980	209	40	3.4	87.2

Source: Österr. Molkerei- und Käsereikalender 1981 (*Almanac of the Austrian Dairies*, 1981), p. 234.*Tätigkeitsbericht des Milchwirtschaftsfonds über das Jahr* 1980 (*Annual Report of the Milk Market Board*, 1980), Bd. B, p. 83.

The advantage of this mechanism for the interest associations resides in its quasi-market effect. The firm in question does not collapse *politically* as a result of the denial of specific investment, but *economically* as a result of a deficiency in its ability to compete. This allows the associations to exonerate themselves. They only have to reach one general decision instead of a multiplicity of specifically unfavourable ones. This decision about the standard costs can be legitimized by each association before its members by reference to the pressure to seek compromise. It has been above all, the worker and employee associations who have promoted modernization in this way.

Since the ÖGB and the ÖAKT also represent the consumer in the MWF, they have attempted to hold down prices by measures increasing productivity. They have been supported in their efforts by the staff of the MWF. The effects of this strategy of modernization can be seen in the development of the number of firms and the relation of turnover to cost per kilogram of milk supplied.

Table 1 shows that the process of concentration has slowed down significantly since 1975 and that improvement of productivity has come to a full stop. The reason for this is the changed economic situation. Since the recession of 1975 the maintenance of full employment and not rationalization has had priority within the ÖGB and the ÖAKT.

To sum up, the problem-solving capacity of private interest governance within the various policy areas of the dairy sector is considerable, but variable. While the associations have remained successful at regulating wages and prices without conflict, at present no initiatives for the improvement of the economic structure and performance of the sector can come from them. The period before 1975 shows that it is possible in practice as well as in principle for associational action to be successful in such reforms. The present passivity of the associations can be traced to their changed interest position. In phases of economic expansion, association with comprehensive domains can tolerate processes of modernization or even promote them actively. This is because structural change alters the composition of the membership domain, which expands through economic growth. Contrary to this, during protracted economic crises, the risk arises that associations will suffer significant losses in the number of members because of rationalization measures.

The variations in the ability of private interest governments to solve problems with respect to incomes' policy and industrial policy rest on the different interests that are involved in these areas and which are differently relevant to the associations. In incomes policy, associations are asked to defer the immediate interests of their members in favour of corporate interests. Centralized, comprehensive associations which are secured by organizational guarantees are able to meet that demand. On the contrary, modernization measures demand sacrifices not only by members but also by the associations themselves, at least under present circumstances. Although the economic significance of the dairy sector is small,[9] further rationalization measures are perceived as involving such a large risk of loss of members and employment, even by comprehensive peak associations with a strongly entrenched capacity for control, that they cannot disregard this in their political calculations. From this can be drawn the conclusion that it is not the violation of *member interests*, but the violation of *organizational interests* which sets the limits to the problem-solving capacity of associations involved in systems of private governance.

Notes

1. A review of the concept of and research on corporatism is given in Schmitter and Lehmbruch (1979) and Lehmbruch and Schmitter (1982).

2. On conceptualizing corporatism as a way of controlling the working class, see Panitch (1980).

3. On the 'political rationality' of *Staatsentlastung*, see Offe (1981: 125 ff.).

4. The *Paritätische Kommission* is the central institution of corporatist economic and social policy in Austria. Its chief function is incomes policy. All wages and about a quarter of all retail prices are subject to its control. In contrast to the MWF, the *Paritätische Kommission* is not a state licensed regulation system, but a system of autonomous co-operation of the four interest associations. For details of the *Paritätische Kommission*, see Marin (1982).

5. On the separation of the formulation of goals and sustaining of motivation by election procedures, see Luhmann (1969).

6. As far as ÖAKT and PKLWK are concerned, these principles are established with respect to their territorial subunits.

7. On the differentiation of systems of political regulation according to the degree of involvement of the state, see Ronge (1980) and Czada and Dittrich (1980).

8. The analysis of the development of co-operative industrial relations in Austria indicates that the evolution of the Austrian neo-corporatism has been rather an unanticipated side effect of the discrete policies followed by the collective actors involved than an intended result of their efforts at political design (Traxler, 1982b).

9. In 1980, only 0.22 per cent of the economically active population in Austria worked in the processing plants of the dairy industry.

9
Regulating milk markets: corporatist arrangements in the Swiss dairy industry

Peter Farago

As in other countries, the dairy industry in Switzerland is one of the most strictly regulated sectors of the economy. One reason for this is the economic importance of milk: it is the key source of income of Swiss farmers, and it has given rise to an industry of considerable size occupied with the transformation of the 'white gold' into a wide range of products. Moreover, the perishability of raw milk requires a vast organization for its speedy transport, processing and marketing. Both factors apply to other countries as well. Nevertheless, the actual regulatory systems differ considerably. The purpose of this chapter is to describe in detail the regulation of milk processing in Switzerland in two product groups, with particular emphasis on the corporatist arrangements existing in the system.

The structure of the Swiss dairy industry
The importance of milk as a raw material for the processing industry derives from its versatility. Milk can be converted into products such as cream, cheese, yoghurt, condensed milk or milk powder; the latter, in turn, is the base for chocolate, baby food or animal food. All these products are subject to different marketing conditions. Therefore, one cannot speak of one homogeneous milk market, but rather of several specialized product markets.

The different markets for milk products are of varying economic significance. Roughly half (46 per cent) of the raw milk in Switzerland is processed into cheese. Cheese manufacturing is by far the most important branch of the Swiss dairy industry. Liquid milk (18 per cent), butter (15 per cent) and cream (13 per cent) trail well behind. All other milk products together take up less than 10 per cent of the raw milk. Cheese is one of the few products of the Swiss food processing industry with a large export share, accounting for 32 per cent of Swiss food products exported. More than 50 per cent of Swiss cheese is exported. Export is based mainly on the traditional hard cheeses, among them the world-famous Emmental. These hard cheeses account for 70 per cent of Swiss production. During the 1970s, consumption of liquid milk and traditional hard cheese has stagnated while soft cheese and certain specialties such as yoghurt and curd have expanded on domestic markets.[1]

About 80 per cent of Swiss cheese, and almost 100 per cent of hard cheese, is manufactured in so-called 'village dairies' (*Dorfkäsereien*). Such dairies usually process the milk produced by the local farmers without any intermediary treatment. Village dairies are often family enterprises, employ only a few people and are spread all over the country. There are in Switzerland roughy 1500 such dairies. All other milk processing is done in industrialized, large-scale dairies. These are mostly situated near the main trading areas and in the big cities.

Organizations in the Swiss dairy industry

The milk processing industry in the strict sense of the word is organized into six associations. These can be divided into two groups:

1. One consists of the organizations of the cheese manufacturing village dairies. These organizations form a complex system of three interlocked associations. Two of them act as interest organizations of independent cheesemakers: the Association of Milk Buyers and the Association of Soft Cheese Manufacturers. The bulk of village dairies is organized in the former one.

2. The second group consists of three associations of the industrialized large dairies. One of them, the 'Milk Group' of the Association of the Swiss Food Processing Industry, covers the entire dairy sector. The other associations in this group have rather specialized domains such as the Association of Box Cheese Manufacturers and the Association of Ice Cream Manufacturers.

Both groups of associations organize almost all of their potential members. But whereas the associations of the cheese manufacturers have in general a large membership (more than 1000), those of the industrial dairies have only few (10–20). In the cheese manufacturers' associations, the high number of members and their territorial dispersion has given rise to a complex internal structure with many regional subgroups. The associations of the industrial dairies are structured in a much simpler way. The associations of cheese manufacturers have a full-time professional staff while those of the industrial dairies have delegated their affairs to a lawyer on a part-time basis.

The milk producers are organized into co-operatives. There are more than 4000 local co-operatives of milk producers forming thirteen regional associations of co-operatives. These, in turn, are united in the Central Association of Swiss Milk Producers (ZVSM), an association of associations representing all milk producers and, hence, a large share of the Swiss farmers. The local co-operatives as well as the regional associations of co-operatives are active in milk processing. The local co-operatives normally own the buildings and the machinery of the village dairies. Mostly, these dairies are leased to independent cheesemakers, but roughly 20 per cent of them are run by the milk producers themselves. The regional associations of co-operatives operate industrialized dairies which manufacture the whole range of milk products. Furthermore, they together own fifteen butter factories accounting for more than 80 per cent of domestic butter production. In recent years, the economic activities of the milk producers' organizations have grown remarkably: eight out of the thirty largest Swiss food processing companies are regional associations of milk producer co-operatives. As a consequence, the associations of milk producers act not only as interest associations but also as business firms.

Two big retailers, the consumer co-operatives MIGROS and COOP, also engage in milk processing. They are the leading food retailers, holding market shares of 24 and 15 per cent respectively. MIGROS manufactures practically all its milk products in its own dairies, and COOP runs a dairy with a regionally limited trading area.[2]

All associations mentioned in this section — together with associations of wholesalers and exporters — play a role in the milk processing regulation system. They represent different and, in part, contradictory interests. The milk producers are interested in high prices for raw milk, the processors in a high margin between the prices of raw milk and milk products, and the retailers in low retail prices. Since they are all taking part in a wide range of economic activities (production, processing, marketing), they have a common interest in the functioning of the regulation system as a whole. This is the basis for their collaboration in several regulatory agencies controlling milk processing at the national level. But this does not preclude differences on specific matters (for example, on producer prices).

The regulation of milk processing — the example of two product groups

An overview
Legally, the milk processing regulation system is based on a number of laws and decrees establishing, among other things, the rules of price fixing (especially for the price of raw milk), quality control, milk processing, and the marketing of milk and milk products (including foreign trade). Most important among them is a legal order of priority for the allocation of raw milk to the different kinds of processing:

 1. Liquid milk for consumption, 'fresh milk products', such as yoghurt, curd, etc.;

2. Milk powder, condensed milk;
3. Cream;
4. Skimmed milk powder;
5. Cheese;
6. Butter; and
7. Casein.

Highest priority is given to products that do not have to be subsidized by the state.[3] The order of priority is updated twice a year in a milk processing programme which allocates the expected amount of produced raw milk to the various milk processing channels. The manufacturers are supplied with raw milk according to the programme.

The milk processing regulation system is run by several semi-public bodies. The Special Commission on Milk (Fachausschuss Milch) is the advisory board to the respective office of the federal administration (Bundesamt für Landwirtschaft, Abteilung Milch). The commission supervises the functioning of the system as a whole and monitors the consequences of changes in the system (for example, price revisions). The implementation of the milk processing programme lies with Regional Programme Commissions (Regionale Programmkommissionen) which makes for a highly flexible handling of the programme. For the economically most important milk products, cheese and butter, there are special marketing agencies. The Käseunion (Cheese Union) is charged with quality control and the promotion on the domestic and the foreign markets. The BUTYRA has a monopoly on the import of butter. Both organizations are formally firms. The Käseunion is a joint stock company while BUTYRA is organized as a co-operative. They have an exclusive right to buy the products they are marketing from the manufacturers and, thus, are able to control the respective markets comprehensively. Another semi-public board, with mainly technical functions, is the Swiss Milk Commission (Schweizerische Milchkommission) which, among other things, issues binding quality regulations for milk and milk products.

Each of these semi-public bodies includes the full range of interest organizations concerned with the production, processing or marketing of milk and milk products (Table 1). The federal administration — mostly represented by the Office of Agriculture — participates in an advisory function.

The only association present in all four bodies is the Central Association of Milk Producers. This association has a unique position in the regulation of milk processing since it has a legal responsibility for the administration of the system as a whole. Partly in collaboration with

TABLE 1

The representation of interest organizations in the most important semi-public boards of the milk processing regulation system

	Fachausschuss Milch	Käseunion (Verwaltungsrat)	BUTYRA (Vorstand)	Schweizerische Milchkommission
Producers' organizations				
Central Association of Milk Producers	X	X	X	X
Regional associations of milk producer co-operatives	X			
Processors' organizations				
Association of Milk Buyers	X	X	X	
Association of Soft Cheese Manufacturers				
'Milk Group' of the Association of the Swiss Food Processing Industry	X			
Association of Box Cheese Manufacturers	X			X
Association of Ice Cream Manufacturers				X
Retailers' organizations				
MIGROS		X	X	X
COOP		X	X	X

the Käseunion and BUTYRA, it regulates milk production and milk processing, quality control and marketing. For this purpose, the association disposes of considerable resources. Its staff exceeds that of the respective division of the federal administration. The decisions of the association and its agencies are legally binding. If firms do not agree with a decision, they can appeal to the Federal Office of Agriculture. On the regional level, the regional associations of milk producers' co-operatives play a role similar to that of their Central Association on the national level; in particular, they control the allocation of a possible surplus of raw milk to the processing plants.

The assumption by the milk producers' associations of a prominent role in the regulation of milk processing is, from their point of view, a way of representing the interests of their members. A central objective of the regulation system is to stabilize the income of farmers by guaranteeing a base price for raw milk and by marketing the processed milk. At the same time, however, the milk producers' associations are themselves economically active in the industry they regulate. This has become a subject of public debate in Switzerland. The suspicion is that the associations might, for example in the allocation of raw milk, favour their own processing plants. Association officials deny this, pointing to the right to appeal against their decisions and to the control functions of the Federal Office of Agriculture. Up to now, milk producers' associations have not been proven to favour their own economic interests in regulating milk processing. Nevertheless, the combination of economic activity and para-state functions in the same industry remains a critical issue.

The following sections explain the regulation process for two product groups, cheese and fresh milk products. A description of the entire system of milk processing regulation would be beyond the scope of this chapter. The two product groups represent the range of comprehensiveness of regulatory measures. The cheese market is an example of a 'closed', tightly regulated market whereas the market for fresh milk products is comparably 'open'. Furthermore, since cheese is by far the most important milk product, its regulation constitutes a key element in the regulation system as a whole.

The cheese market as an example of a 'closed' regulation system

The supply of raw milk. Since the milk producers' associations collect virtually all the milk that is not consumed by the farmers themselves, cheese manufacturers have to buy their raw material from the milk producers' co-operatives. Quantities, prices and terms of delivery are set by a system of contracts. This system operates on three levels:

1. *National level:* a long-term skeleton agreement between the Central Association of Milk Producers and the Association of Milk

Buyers regulates the general business conditions between the sellers and buyers of raw milk.

2. *Regional level:* annually renewed collective contracts between the regional associations of milk producers' co-operatives and the regional sections of the Association of Milk Buyers regulate prices and various levies to be paid by milk buyers.

3. *Local level:* annually renewed milk buying contracts between the local milk producer co-operatives and the milk buyers they supply, regulating subjects such as the schedule of milk delivery, the rent for cheesing facilities, etc.

The most important contracts for the processors are those at the regional level. In addition to general rules obliging the contracting parties to observe the legal prescriptions, these contracts are concerned with economic parameters — such as the price of raw milk — that are contested between sellers and buyers. Local level contracts have to be approved by the regional associations of milk producers' co-operatives to become legally binding on both sides. The associations determine whether local contracts are in line with the regulations of the milk processing programme. They thus have complete information and control over the amount of raw milk used for cheese manufacturing. A new entrant into cheese production would first have to ask the milk producers' associations to assign him the amount of raw milk needed. However, priority is given to existing contracts. As a result, practically the only way to enter into cheese manufacturing is to lease an existing outlet. Normally, this is possible only if a contract holder retires.

The situation on the supply side is difficult to influence by the processors or their associations. It is controlled by the associations of milk producers, especially with respect to the approval of buying contracts. Processors can intervene only in bilateral regional negotiations by which prices and conditions are fixed collectively.

The regulation of manufacturing. Even after the contracts have been approved, individual cheese manufacturers remain subject to the control of the milk producers' associations. The collective contracts oblige all milk buyers to furnish the milk producers' associations, on a monthly basis, with comprehensive production statistics. The data enable the regulating agencies to fine-tune production regulation measures. For example, the Central Association of Milk Producers can require processors to reduce their output — either in response to excess production (for example, if the Käseunion reports that a particular kind of cheese can no longer be marketed at justifiable prices) or if a dairy continues to turn out cheese of minor quality. Dairies are not allowed to change their products without notifying the Central Association; all changes of production need its approval.

The far-reaching authority of the milk producers' associations in the implementation of the milk processing programme strictly curtails the dairies' economic freedom of action. It also constrains their associations. As members of the Regional Programme Commissions and of several semi-public boards, they can take part in the administration of milk processing regulations, and they have a word to say if, for example, one of their members is ordered to reduce his production. But in practice, there is no way they can compete with the legal authority and the information advantage of the milk producers' associations.

The marketing of the final product. On the marketing side, there are different regulations for different kinds of cheese. All of the traditional hard cheese is marketed exclusively through the Käseunion, and producers are legally required to sell their output only to this organization. Other brands (like, for example, the widely known Appenzeller) have separate marketing organizations which also collect the entire production but operate without legal authorization. Still other brands have their own marketing agencies, but there is no obligation, legal or otherwise, for the dairies to sell their production to them. Finally, there are brands with completely unregulated markets. In the last two categories mentioned, we mainly find soft cheese and cheese specialties.

Cheese markets vary from complete regulation to complete openness. The less economically important a type of cheese, the less regulated its market. On the other hand, soft cheese had the highest growth rates in the 1970s of all kinds of cheese. This is a result of the growing surplus of raw milk being used to produce a range of new cheese brands to face the competition of imported soft cheese. Since this coincided with growing demand, regulation was deemed unnecessary. In contrast, the market of the traditional hard cheese is stagnating. This is in line with the principle that stagnating markets are more likely to be exposed to regulatory measures than expanding ones. The Käseunion would have the legal possibility to extend its regulatory function to other product markets if the economic situation were to change.

The role of the processors' associations in the various cheese markets depends on the way in which markets are regulated. Their main activity is the regulation of soft cheese. The Association of Soft Cheese Manufacturers operates several marketing agencies which have, however, no public status. By contrast, in the Käseunion the associations of processors are a small minority, with merely two out of the twenty-four seats on the board of directors. The Central Association of Milk Producers, by comparison, has ten seats.

Summing up, the cheese market is thoroughly regulated.

Regulation measures cover the distribution of raw milk as well as the processing and marketing of the most important product groups. Processors' associations, except for those parts of the market where there (still) is no legally-based regulation scheme, are limited to representing the economic interests of their members.

The associations of milk producers play the dominating part in the regulation of the cheese market. They are further strengthened by the fact that they are themselves direct market participants. Not only do they run their own dairies, but they also engage in wholesale trade (in traditional hard cheese, they hold a wholesale market share of approximately 30 per cent). As a result, independent cheese manufacturers find themselves surrounded by the producers of milk; they have to buy their raw material and lease their equipment from them, and often their product is marketed — after the intermediary station of the Käseunion — by firms owned by the milk producers.

The market for fresh milk products as an example of an 'open' regulation system
There is a wide range of fresh milk products in Switzerland, the most popular of them being yoghurt. The different kinds of yoghurt account for more than 80 per cent of the total turnover of fresh milk products. Other products in this category are curd, cottage cheese, and various dessert specialties. The range of products has expanded in the 1970s, and this trend is continuing. Although in comparison with cheese or butter, fresh milk products are of minor economic importance, they have outstanding growth rates. This makes them interesting for processors. In contrast to cheese, fresh milk products are manufactured exclusively in large-scale industrialized dairies. These are represented by the 'Milk Group' of the Association of the Food Processing Industry.

The supply of raw milk. Like in the cheese industry, the producers of fresh milk products have to buy their raw milk from the milk producers' co-operatives, and contracts require the approval of the associations of milk producers. However, the situation is simplified by the fact that there is not such a complex system of contracts on different levels as in cheese manufacturing. The reason for this is that there are only a small number of dairies that produce fresh milk products. Contracts are made between these dairies and the regional associations of milk producers' co-operatives. In practice, the dairies collect the raw milk at the farm gate and transport it to their plants themselves. Contractual relations between farmers and processors are as stable as in the cheese industry, and opening a new dairy would meet with the same difficulties. Since negotiation and approval of buying contracts have become highly routinized, the interest association of the fresh milk products manufacturers does not need to get involved.

The regulation of manufacturing. Fresh milk products are given high priority by the milk processing programme. Apart from this, they are not subject to specific regulations. This makes them attractive to dairies since it allows them virtually unlimited possibilities for product innovation. It is possible that this has contributed to the expansion of this product group in recent years.

The marketing of the final product. There are only few regulations here, one of them being the fixing of maximum prices. This, however, has no practical significance because the market is highly competitive. Rather than trying to keep prices high, processors try to win market shares by offering discounts or even selling below costs.

Except for the regulation of the raw milk supply, the market for fresh milk products is relatively open. The reason for this is the limited quantitative importance of these products for milk processing as a whole and their relatively recent appearance on the market. Fresh milk products form a niche in the milk processing regulation system which allows for almost unlimited initiative on the part of processors. As a result, this market is characterized by economic competitiveness rather than by associational action. While the associations of milk producers continue to play a role in the management of the supply of raw milk, the interest association of the dairies does not perform regulating functions.

The protective function of the milk processing regulation system

Undoubtedly, the milk processing regulation system is an element of planning in the capitalist market economy of Switzerland. It is undisputed that the system secures a continuous supply of milk and milk products irrespective of seasonal variations in milk production and consumption. But there is a price to be paid for this. The annual loss of the milk processing regulation scheme amounts to about 800 million SFr which are covered largely by state subsidies. The official legitimation for this is the preservation of a *Bauernstand* as stipulated by the federal law on agriculture. A less obvious function of the regulation system is to protect the small cheese manufacturing dairies by fixing the retail prices of cheese in consideration of their higher costs in comparison with the large dairies. Nevertheless, there has been growing criticism in recent years of the high costs of the system. However, although several improvements have been suggested, up to now nobody has proposed a complete change. Its organization and the collaborative ties between public and private actors, then, are unlikely to undergo major revisions in the near future.

Corporatist arrangements in the regulation of milk processing

The main characteristic of the Swiss milk processing regulation system is the central role of private interest organizations in the execution of regulatory measures. Such an inclusion of private actors in the implementation of public policy is called a corporatist arrangement. In the case of the milk processing regulation system, two types of corporatist arrangements can be observed: first, the authorization of a single interest association, in this case the Central Association of Milk Producers (which can be referred to as delegation). Secondly, the collaboration of public and private actors in joint organizations such as the Special Commission on Milk, the Käseunion or the BUTYRA (co-operation). The milk processing regulation system in Switzerland is a combination of these two types of corporatist arrangements. The question then arises as to what the reasons for such a combination might be. To answer this question, it is helpful to look at the specific conditions for the different types of arrangements.

Cost effectiveness

The participation of the milk processors' associations in the regulation of milk processing is based on two factors. One is that the milk processing regulation scheme serves to protect the farmers; since farmers' incomes are concerned, the milk producers' associations have a vital interest in these regulations. Secondly, there can be no doubt that the technical performance of the milk producers' associations as regulatory agencies could be matched by the state only at substantively higher costs. In part, this is due to the fact that producers — for reasons one can readily understand — prefer to be controlled by their own organizations. It also has to do with the traditionally weak resources of the Swiss federal state rendering it incapable of dealing with such a formidable task as the regulation of milk processing.

The efficient execution of the milk processing regulation is made possible by the high degree of organizational development of the milk producers' associations. The Central Association of Milk Producers as well as most of the regional associations of milk producers' co-operatives are characterized by a comprehensive domain, high density ratios, differentiated organizational structures and considerable financial and personal resources. This enables them to manage highly complex regulative tasks such as the limitation of milk production at the farm level without external help.

The case of the milk producers' associations demonstrates two basic conditions for the emergence of delegation as a corporatist arrangement. The first relates to problems of legitimacy, the second to problems of organized interest representation. In principle, the execution of public policy programmes is one of the core fields of state action. If such a function is to be passed over to private actors, there is a need for additional legitimacy in two respects: the private actor in question should have a recognized right to be involved, and the issue in question should be 'non-political', at least in so far as it does not directly raise problems of political power. These two conditions are typically met where so-called 'technical issues' are at stake. The most common examples of delegation are the elaboration of standard specifications (for example, for mechanical engineering) or of quality regulations for certain products. Since associations of the affected firms are closer to the technical and economic developments in the industry and since they enjoy their members' confidence, they usually solve such problems more efficiently and at lower costs than state agencies. However, if issues formerly perceived as 'technical' become politicized, even already existing delegation arrangements can lose legitimacy. In the last decades, this has happened to the 'technical' problems of environmental protection. The legitimacy of delegation as a corporatist arrangement, then, is by no means historically stable and is affected by changes in the social or political environment.

This does not necessarily mean that delegation is unstable in itself. This is because it rests on a second basic precondition which is the organizational structure of the private actor involved in it. Delegation presupposes a high degree of organizational development. Organizational structures are persistent; they do not change at the same pace as their environment. If the delegation of public authority to a private interest association goes together with developed organizational structures, these by themselves help to stabilize the corporatist arrangement. Delegation arrangements that are based on strong organizational structures have a relative autonomy from their political surroundings which resembles that of the developed association vis-à-vis its members. Corporatist arrangements based on delegation may thus survive the political circumstances in which they have been created.

Authority to enforce
Using the example of the limitation of milk production at the farm level, it has been shown that the milk producers' associations are able to implement public policy programmes with binding authority. The question then arises why the same does not apply to the regulation of milk processing. Milk processing involves not only the producers of raw milk but also the processors, the wholesalers and the retailers. For each of these groups, there are interest organizations with a legitimate claim to particpate in the regulation process. The Swiss tradition of

granting representation to all organized interests concerned precludes the allocation of overall responsibility to only one of these organizations. On the other hand, none of the associations of processors, wholesalers and retailers is similarly developed organizationally as the milk processors' associations. They are more heterogeneous, less elaborately structured and less comprehensive in their domains. This prevents them from assuming overall responsibility for the regulation of milk processing. As a consequence, co-operation seems to be the best solution to the problem of including all interest organizations concerned.

Co-operation does not raise the questions of legitimacy and organizational capacity with the same severity as delegation. Since the state participates in the various co-operative boards, and since their decision-making processes are — at least formally — open to public scrutiny, the state does not have to pass its full authority to a single private actor. Thus, it remains unchallenged in its role as the promoter of the public interest. Furthermore, since co-operation requires the presence of a large number of interest organizations, the structural properties of each one of these are of less importance. They only have to represent reasonably well their respective constituencies, and they must be able to participate regularly in the co-operative bodies. Co-operation, then, is the appropriate type of corporatist arrangement if many associations with divergent organizational structures are affected by a particular issue.

Heterogeneous structure
The combination of the two types of corporatist arrangements in the Swiss milk processing sector reflects its heterogeneous structure. The milk producers form a coherent group with a highly developed associational system whereas processing and marketing are differentiated by product groups with divergent representational structures and associational systems. In such a case the emergence of a uniform corporatist regulation system is unlikely. The implementation of public policy programmes by private actors has to be accomplished by a complex interplay of different types of corporatist arrangements. The prominent role of the milk producers' associations in the milk processing regulation system is partly based on the fact that they are involved in production as well as in processing and marketing. This legitimates them both to participate in all the co-operative bodies and to perform the encompassing control functions that have been delegated to them by law. The strong position of the milk producers' associations vis-à-vis the other interest associations shows that delegation bestows on an association a power which is hard to match by other associations without delegated functions. Delegation

may thus confer on private interest associations attributes of a government not only vis-à-vis their members but also vis-à-vis their market partners.

Notes

This paper makes use of the results of an investigation on associational structures and activities in the Swiss food processing industry which was conducted under the auspices of the Swiss country study in the comparative project on business interest associations co-ordinated by Schmitter and Streeck (for more details on this project, see Schmitter and Streeck, 1981). The research report on the Swiss food processing industry (Farago et al., 1984) is based on the legal and statistical sources and association publications which are unlikely to be available outside Switzerland. I shall therefore not reference this literature explicitly. Neither shall I, to improve readability, reference citations from the research report mentioned; basically, all of this chapter relies on it. The report (which is writen in German) can be obtained from the author.

1. Moreover, there is — in spite of restrictive measures such as tariff barriers — a considerable amount of imported cheese competing directly the Swiss products on the domestic market.

2. In other regions, COOP buys from the dairies of the regional associations of milk producer co-operatives.

3. Cheese is the milk product which needs the highest amount of subsidies: the marketing of the three most important brands of hard cheese causes an annual loss of approximately 250 million SFr.

10
Private organizations as agents of public policy: the case of milk marketing in Britain

Wyn Grant

In 1983 the Milk Marketing Board for England and Wales celebrated fifty years of successful operation. Similar boards were created for the three milk-producing areas in Scotland in 1933 and 1934, while the Milk Marketing Board for Northern Ireland came into being in 1955. Despite many vicissitudes and a number of difficult problems, the basic shape of the milk marketing scheme has remained unchanged since its formation. It is the theme of this chapter that the Milk Marketing Board (and its Joint Committee with the Dairy Trade Federation) can be taken as a successful example of private government, and that by examining the factors that have contributed to its success, it is possible to arrive at a better understanding of the conditions which permit private organizations to act as agents of public policy.

It is necessary to add a number of caveats to this statement. First, the Milk Marketing Board (MMB) is not simply a private organization in so far as it operates within a framework laid down by statute, although it is not part of a central government department. Moreover, the Dairy Trade Federation (DTF) — a private organization — is closely involved in the operation of the milk marketing scheme. Second, although the MMB may have successfully regulated a particular agricultural market, this process has not been without its costs. Some agricultural economists would argue that the prices of dairy products would be lower in Britain without the board and that it has inhibited product innovation. On the other hand, there is a case for arguing that, without the Board, many farmers would go out of business and that, in the long run, prices of dairy products would rise. These arguments have been reviewed elsewhere (Grant, 1983a) and are not the main focus of this chapter. However, at the very least, it has to be conceded that the pursuit of governability in this particular product market has some opportunity costs. Third, even if the Milk Marketing Board can be regarded as a successful private government, it may not be possible to replicate its success elsewhere, even in other agricultural markets (see Grant, 1983a) because the necessary favourable conditions are absent.

The milk marketing system in Britain

The origins of the scheme
The scheme was introduced against a background of serious depression in British agriculture. The position of the dairy farmer was not eased by the early development of concentration on the processing side of the industry, so that by the 1920s half a dozen dairy companies controlled a large part of the total milk market in England and Wales. For a variety of reasons (for example, larger farms than in mainland Europe) the farmer co-operative movement made little progress in Britain and the government had to intervene to create what was, in effect, a state sponsored producers' co-operative. In particular, government intervention solved the 'free riding' problem that arose in voluntary attempts at co-operation (see Giddings, 1974: 10). Nevertheless, 'the fundamental concept throughout remained that of producer self-government. It had been recognised from the beginning that anything looking like "farming from Whitehall" would antagonise the agricultural community and hence be unworkable — even if it was acceptable to Parliament ' (Giddings, 1974: 11).

In 1931 the Government passed an 'enabling' Agricultural Marketing Act. The 1931 Act did not require anyone to set up marketing organizations, but created the legal basis on which such organizations could be built if the producers of any farm commodities so wished. In 1933 the National Farmers' Union drew up a Milk Marketing Scheme using the provisions of the 1931 Act and incorporating many of the ideas suggested by an official committee set up to investigate the re-organization of the milk industry. The scheme was approved by Parliament in July 1933 and subsequently endorsed by a poll of milk producers, 96 per cent of whom voted in favour of the scheme. What is interesting about the foundation of the scheme is the way in which it arose from a mixture of state initiative, interest group involvement and consent by the individual producer, a formula which could be said to be designed to maximize the legitimacy of the new institution.

How the scheme works
  The constitution of the board. The Board has fifteen members elected by the farmers (each farmer has one vote plus an additional vote for each ten milch cows in his possession) and three members appointed by the Minister of Agriculture. These three outside members are not representatives of the minister; rather they should be seen as 'non-executive directors' who bring special skills (for example, in marketing) to the work of the Board. The powers of the Board are strictly defined and limited in the Milk Marketing Scheme (as laid

down by the Minister with Parliamentary approval) which has the objective of ensuring that the interests of the dairy trade and of consumers are recognized and respected as well as those of the farmer. For example, the Board is prohibited from producing margarine. The Minister has the power to override any Board decision if he thinks it is harmful to other interests, but that power has never been used. He appoints a Consumer Committee which reports to him periodically on the working of the Scheme.

Market structure
In 1980, 47 per cent of the milk utilized by dairies in the UK was processed for liquid sale to the consumer (compared with 17 per cent in the other nine EEC countries taken as a whole) and the remainder was used for manufacturing, principally for butter (25 per cent) and cheese (15 per cent). Liquid milk sales have shown a long-run tendency to fall, and the use of milk for manufacturing has become far more important than was once the case.

The dairy industry in England and Wales (less so in Scotland) is relatively highly concentrated. By 1980 the Milk Marketing Board's commercial arm, Dairy Crest, which it has developed by building its own plants and also by purchases from other dairy companies, was the largest buyer of milk in Britain (around 27 per cent). The MMB is relatively unimportant in the liquid milk trade, but is the largest manufacturer of butter and skimmed milk powder and the major producer of hard cheeses. The three largest dairy companies — Unigate, Express (part of Grand Metropolitan) and Northern — accounted for around 30 – 35 per cent of milk purchases. The retail co-operatives took another quarter, leaving the remaining 15 per cent or so for smaller companies.

How the scheme works. A farmer who wishes to produce milk for sale has to market his milk through the Board or be licensed as a producer retailer or producer processor, selling off his own round or direct to local shops. However, the overwhelming bulk of milk produced by farmers is sold to the Board. They pay the farmer an average price for his milk based on the total income for all markets (with small regional adjustments and, in some cases, quality penalties or incentives). Milk sold for manufacturing purposes fetches a lower price than milk processed for the domestic consumer.

Liquid milk prices have been subject to substantial state control, although this is to be relaxed in 1985. In 1984, the system worked as follows. The Minister of Agriculture fixed the maximum wholesale price; this was normally the price at which the Board sold to the liquid milk processor and distributor, although on one occasion the dairy trade refused to accept a price increase. The Minister also fixed a maximum retail price for liquid milk. The difference between these two prices was known as the distributive margin and was made up of handling and processing costs and the dairy's profit margin. The Minister monitored these costs in a sample of dairies and also prescribed a target rate of profit.

There are a number of prices for manufacturing milk depending on the use to which the milk is to be put. These prices are negotiated between the Board and the DTF, representing the dairy industry, in a Joint Committee. After 1985, liquid milk prices will also be negotiated between the Board and the DTF. The composition and powers of the Joint Committee are laid down in a statutory instrument approved by Parliament and cover matters apart from prices for manufacturing milk such as allocation of supplies and quality control. It should also be noted that the income of the DTF is collected by the MMB through a levy written into the contract issued to first hand buyers of milk. The levy is obligatory rather than compulsory, as it can be struck out of the contract, and it is believed that one small processor refuses to pay it.

How much have you understood?
Readers of earlier versions of this chapter, which went into much more detail about the operations of the scheme, have said that they have not fully understood how it works. It is doubtful whether anyone except a handful of staff at the MMB understand all its ramifications, but as a learning device, a self-assessment test has been included at this stage. This should be attempted before reading further; the answers are at the end of the chapter.

1. A farmer decides to sell milk on his own account without registering with the MMB. Can he or she do this?

2. Under the arrangements operating in 1984, the maximum wholesale price at which milk may be sold for processing for consumption is laid down by the Minister of Agriculture. Is this the price accepted by the Board and buyers as the actual selling price?

3. 'The Milk Marketing Board's involvement in the marketing of milk stops short of the delivery of milk to the individual consumer.' True or false?

4. Does the individual farmer need to worry about the negotiations between the DTF and MMB which fix the various prices for milk for manufacture?

5. An aunt has left you some shares in an English dairy company which confines its operations to processing liquid milk and selling it through a system of rounds to the final consumer. Is the company a good long-term investment? Answer yes or no.

Conditions that favour a corporatist mode of policy-making

It should be remembered that corporatist arrangements, even at the meso level, are the exception rather than the rule in Britain. There is a strong tradition of consultation with sectional interests, but it is unusual for the state to designate a particular organization (in this case, the DTF) as the representative of a particular category of interest and to delegate powers to develop and implement public policy to a private government (in this case, the Joint Committee of the DTF and MMB).

It is not hard to explain why corporatist arrangements have not flourished in Britain; prevalent liberal values do not encourage such devices. What is more difficult to account for is their occurrence in particular environments. In general, one can say that just as plants which are not common to the British Isles flourish in particular sheltered locations (for example, sub-tropical plants in the far South-west), so there are specific environments which are conducive to the development of corporatist arrangements. Agriculture is such a case, and the corporatist arrangements that develop there may to some extent be seen to 'spill over' to those parts of the food processing industry 'close to the farm gate'. For sturdy individualists, farmers have been willing to accept a quite remarkable degree of state intervention in their affairs. However, although the state extends beyond the farm gate, it does so through acceptable forms of intervention such as financial assistance and technical advice. The provision of these forms of aid to the farmer facilitates a good working relationship between individual farmers and the 'field' representatives of the state (see Grant, 1983b).

However, it is not sufficient to say that agriculture is special; one has to say *why* it is special. Even liberal economists accept that agricultural markets are prone to inherent instabilities (which arise from the very nature of the production process itself) and there has therefore been a broader consensus than in other areas that some measure of government intervention is necessary. One solution has been for government to structure the market by setting certain key prices. However, the setting of key prices does not, of itself, reconcile conflicts of interest; indeed, it may exacerbate them as parties with different interests seek to influence the price setting authority. Hence, the need arises for mediating institutions on the borderline between the public and private domains which can promote co-operative relationships without eliminating competition.

Such a general explanation of the tendency for corporatist arrangements to develop in agricultural markets does not tell us why the Milk Marketing Board has flourished while other agricultural marketing arrangements in Britain have failed to get off the ground or been dissolved by their members. For example, it was never possible to form boards for fatstock or cereals and the boards for eggs and tomatoes and cucumbers were brought down by a campaign waged by some of their own producers. Of the two other remaining boards, the Potato Board has faced considerable opposition from disgruntled producers and the Wool Board is of minor importance.

In looking at any of these cases, there are often specific factors which would need to be highlighted in a more detailed account (for example, the problem of producer retailers in the case of eggs or the opposition of the millers to the proposed cereals board). However, it is suggested that there are some general factors that account for the greater success of the Milk Board (for a more detailed comparison with the other boards, see Grant 1983a). The first of these factors is the perishability of the product. It is not possible for an individual producer to 'play the market' by withholding the product until prices change (an important skill for large scale cereal farmers). If milk is not transported quickly to the dairy, it becomes worthless. Second, milk does not need a complex grading system, the administation of which can lead to endless disputes with producers. Such a scheme would be necessary, for example, for a livestock marketing board. Third, some of the boards operate or have operated in markets with a large number of marginal producers (such as smallholders) who may resent any form of outside intrusion into their businesses in a way which more established farmers do not. These marginal producers are often in the forefront of campaigns to dissolve the boards (as has been the case with potatoes in the early 1980s).

What all this seems to suggest is that corporatist arrangements in Britain are likely to have a low birth-rate and an even lower suvival rate and such an assessment would not be far from the truth. One set of circumstances in which they are successful is where there is agreement that indirect state intervention would in some way benefit the operation of a particular market. However, as will be pointed out later, the current ideological climate in Britain is not favourable even to indirect state intervention; there is a new virus going around which threatens even formerly healthy corporatist species.

Reconciling representation with regulation
All private organizations which act as agents of public policy are likely to face a tension between their tasks of representation on behalf of their members, and regulation on behalf of the state. Fully developed democratic procedures within the private interest government can go a long way towards reassuring members that their concerns will not be neglected. As Cawson points out, 'In the final analysis democracy means voluntary co-operation, in the sense of active rather than

passive consent, in collective social arrangements ' (Cawson, 1982: 112).

The MMB places considerable emphasis on its democratic procedures. The farmer votes for the majority of members of the board itself, a regional committee and certain specialist committees, and can also attend the annual general meeting (where there is usually some vigorous questioning of the board by farmers). Candidates for board membership wishing to represent a paraticular region (there are slightly different arrangements for the three members elected on a national basis) must be nominated by twenty registered milk producers in the region or by a county branch of the National Farmers' Union. The election is advertised in the Board's own journal and *The Times*. A deposit of £20 is payable which is returnable if the candidate polls at least one-eighth of the total votes cast or one-quarter of the number obtained by the most successful candidate. For £500, the Board will reproduce a 1000-word election manifesto written by the candidate and distribute it to all voters.

The scrupulous care which the Board takes with its election arrangements is demonstrated by the steps it takes to avoid the bovine equivalent of impersonation; remember that the franchise in England and Wales is based on the milch cows rather than just the farmers — in the 1978 referendum on the board's future a separate result was recorded for producers and cows. For a sample of producers, the number of milch cows eligible to be counted in the voting procedure is checked against their recorded production; if there is a discrepancy, a board official will literally go 'into the field' and count the cows.

Democratic procedures do not, of course, ensure that everyone's interests are protected all of the time (nor are they meant to), and not all farmers have benefited from the MMB's activities, even if there have been more gainers than losers. As Winter points out, the replacement of churn by bulk collection disadvantages many older, smaller producers who were effectively forced out of production because of the capital costs involved in the new system of collection (Winter, 1983). Moreover, the equalization of prices brought about by the marketing system benefited farmers in the pastoral west, but disadvantaged larger producers near the conurbations, many of whom were producer-retailers. As Winter points out, 'Such farmers remain a small but highly vocal minority opposed to or critical of the Board's activities ' (Winter, 1983: 17).

However, the Board is not there just to represent producers' interests without consideration of the broader consequences. It operates within a market considerably influenced by the exercise of various governmental powers, including in more recent times the setting of intervention prices by the European Community. It is required by statutory instrument to negotiate with the DTF in the Joint Committee on a wide range of matters. The Board and the DTF each have one vote in the Joint Committee, and the Committee is deemed not to have reached a decision until both votes have been cast in the same direction. Although there is an arbitration procedure in the event of a failure to agree, the way in which the Joint Committee is constituted reinforces a willingness to compromise which already exists between the two parties.

The chairman of the MMB has pointed out that the 1933 scheme gave producers power they never had before, but not infinite power. The Board has had at times to accept compromises with other powers such as the Government, the EEC and trade and consumer interests (see *Milk Producer*, April 1981). The success of the MMB is due to a considerable extent to the nature of the scheme itself which represents a set of checks and balances, offsetting the Board's statutory monopsony by devices to protect all other affected interests from the abuse of such enormous power, for example, the Joint Committee and the Consumers' Committee. The particular success of the milk marketing scheme rests on the fact that it combines in one arrangement: considerable democratic rights for the producers (including ultimately the right to dissolve the Board); enormous marketing powers for the Board itself; statutory negotiating rights for the processing industry; and considerable opportunities for the government to exert influence on the operation of the scheme (reflected in a practical working relationship between Milk Division at the Ministry of Agriculture and the MMB).

The contribution of the state

Both the Board itself and the Joint Committee are established on the basis of statutorily based schemes which confer certain powers on them. For example, the Board has a Disciplinary Committee which has powers to fine producers for breaches of the scheme's regulations. It is clear that without state intervention it would not have been possible to develop a satisfactory marketing scheme for the industry as a whole. Voluntary attempts to bring farmers together in the 1920s failed because the dairy companies could always find farmers desperate to sell at almost any price.

It has been argued that the milk marketing scheme really represents a mechanism for covert state control of the industry. John Cherrington, a farmer and agricultural correspondent of the *Financial Times*, has argued:

> Milk was a special case and the Milk Marketing Board was used as a means of securing Government control of the milk market, a task which would have been impossible without it. Again I doubt if farmers really suffered

from this policy, but I do not think they realised how what they thought was their Board was being used. (Cherrington, 1979: 139)

In stressing the 'dual personality' of the marketing boards, Giddings has remarked that 'The boards are responsible to their registered producers, not to the Minister and Parliament. But the Minister's control over the context in which the boards operate means that, while independent, they are subject to his powerful influence.' (Giddings, 1974: 227). As Winter points out, within the limits set by the minister, Parliament and the producers, 'the Board has considerable autonomy and is able to develop policy in a number of ways through internal and external negotiation.' (Winter, 1983: 11). Some of the most important negotiations are, of course, with the dairy trade through the Joint Committee.

Part of the success of the MMB derives from the fact that it has a relationship with the state from which it obtains significant organizational resources and stability, yet it is not seen by its members and others as part of the state. If it were generally perceived as part of the state, its purchase of sixteen creameries from the privately owned Unigate group in 1979 would have been politically controversial and it might have become a target for 'quango hunters'. It is able to project itself simultaneously as one of the largest agricultural co-operatives in the world, and as a huge manufacturing organization operating successfully in a highly competitive market.

From the point of view of government, the milk marketing scheme regulates what would otherwise be a highly unstable market without the necessity for direct state ownership or intervention. A potential problem area is thus taken away from central government, at least to some extent. If producers complain about the operations of the Board, the minister can always point out that they can change its composition at the next board elections if they so wish.

How incorporation affects private governments

In a country in which business interest associations are often poorly resourced, the DTF stands out as a well-endowed organization. Although it represents only one sub-sector within the food processing industry, its income (£716,000 in 1980) was almost as large as that of the Food Manufacturers' Federation (£746,000 in 1980) and substantially higher than the 'umbrella' organization for the industry, the Food and Drink Industries Council (£316,000 in 1980). Reference has already been made to the unique way in which the DTF's income is collected through a levy imposed by the MMB, and it would appear that this method of raising funds, which is a reflection of the partnership between the MMB and DTF, has provided the DTF with greater organizational resources than would otherwise be the case.

Systems of business interest representation in Britain are often characterized by their lack of cohesion in the sense that one can find a large number of associations with overlapping functions, with no hierarchically ordered relationship between them, and sometimes competition for members and influence over government. The dairy sub-sector is an exception to this general pattern, and this may reflect the special status accorded to the DTF by the state. The DTF is an association of associations which brings together the private manufacturers, the co-operatives and the retail dairymen; the dairy trade federations in Scotland and Northern Ireland, and the Federation of Milk Marketing Boards, are DTF affiliates. The only organizations outside this network (apart from the producers of ice cream which is not seen as a dairy product in the UK) are some small organizations representing farmhouse cheese makers and the producers of milk and milk products from dairy goats and sheep (these animals are not covered by the marketing scheme). The importance of the decisions made in the Joint Committee to dairy processors creates a special need for an effective organization to represent them. The smoothness of the DTF's internal decision-making procedures is illustrated by the fact that the constitution requires that decisions should normally be made without voting.

Coping with instability
There are five potential threats to the stability of the existing milk marketing arrangements in Britain: dissatisfied producers; dissatisfied processors; dissatisfied retailers; government worries about the ideological correctness of market regulation; and fundamental changes in the milk regime introduced by the EEC in 1984.

Each of these problems will be considered in turn. As far as farmers are concerned, there is nothing new about generalized grumbling by some of them about the Board. However, there are some new difficulties which, if they are not solved, could produce a more serious level of dissatisfaction with the scheme. Above all, there are the cuts in milk production brought about by EEC policy changes which are discussed in more detail below. Other problems are the increasing use of milk for manufacture which realizes a lower price which processors are naturally not keen to increase; the threat to the doorstep delivery system; and the prospects of imports of cheap UHT milk from the EEC. Against this background, it is not surprising that some farmers (particularly those with large herds near urban centres) have been tempted to purchase their own pasteurization plants and sell to the consumer as producer retailers, or to shops or retail dairymen as producer processors. The Board is not opposed to farmers opting to become producer processors if they so wish, but the chairman has warned that 'if this trend extended into a general belief that every producer would be better off doing his own thing, we would be endangering the very thing that has sustained the industry for the past forty-eight years — the corporate, co-operative strength provided by the producer marketing board system' (*Milk Producer*, April 1981).

There are some signs of disquiet among manufacturers. In 1984, the DTF and the MMB had to resort to a government appointed arbitrator to resolve what was regarded as a particularly intractable dispute over the price that manufacturers should pay for the milk they bought to make Cheddar cheese. The MMB insisted that the price paid should provide a reasonable return to farmers, reckoned as the intervention price plus a premium supposed to guarantee continuity of supply. The manufacturers argued that the price should reflect the returns to be obtained from Cheddar, depressed in 1984 by a glut on the market.

It is also possible that some companies may come to the view that the cost of having a stable and co-operative framework for the conduct of relationships with their raw material suppliers is too high in the sense that it prevents them from maximizing their profits. Low returns in dairying may not disturb companies whose main base is in the industry and which have become accustomed to its state of affairs. But it may be less acceptable to conglomerates which can compare the profits obtained from dairying with the returns from their other activities. Grand Metropolitan has interests which range from hotels through holidays to health care, but its food divisions — effectively Express Dairies — was the only major area of activity to report lower trading profits in 1982, and again in 1983. Grand Metropolitan complained in its 1983 annual report that 'the panoply of controls and constraints on commercial freedom in the UK, stemming from our own Government's control of the liquid milk margin coupled with the monopoly powers and commercial activities of the Milk Marketing Board, continues to distort competition in the domestic market' (Grand Metropolitan, 1983: 14).

These underlying tensions between dairy companies and farmers have come to the surface more in Scotland than in England, in part because the Scottish MMB was for a time dominated by 'radical' farmers, in part because the first-hand selling price of milk has been as much as 10 per cent higher in Scotland, a situation resented by Scottish dairymen. There was a lengthy dispute over the price of wholesale milk in 1981, which was only settled by arbitration and in June 1983 a new 'war of words' broke out between the Scottish DTF and the Scottish MMB. The President of the Scottish DTF claimed that the Scottish MMB was more concerned with increasing producers' income than with the protection of their premium market; continued to seek more and more money from principal customers in spite of the market's signals of declining consumption; was a 'cosseted organization' protected by its statutory monopoly position; and followed a 'blinkered' policy which could price it out of the market. (*Farmers' Weekly*, 10 June 1983).

In order to understand the potential problems in the retail area, it is necessary to know that the retail sector in Britain is highly concentrated and becoming increasingly so, particularly in the more prosperous parts of the country. For example, in London, the two leading store chains were taking 55 per cent of packaged grocery sales in the summer of 1982; in the South the figure was 45 per cent and in Anglia 41 per cent. The retailers have used their oligopolistic powers to obtain highly favourable terms of sale from the food manufacturers.

However, although they have exerted some pressure on dairy products, supermarkets have been less successful in breaking into liquid milk sales. Supermarket chains allege that supplies are denied them if they sell below the doorstep delivery price or that dairies collude to charge shops higher prices. The admission of imports of UHT milk into Britain from EEC countries following a European Court of Justice decision in February 1983 opened up new possibilities for the retailers and was seen as constituting a new threat to the milk marketing scheme. However, despite some alarmist predictions from the trade, including one advert from a milk packaging firm which asked 'Is Britain's fresh milk industry about to be engulfed by a tidal wave of cheap imported UHT?', the European Court decision had little immediate impact, although it might have in the longer run.

These threats to the scheme posed by changes in market conditions are paralleled by political problems. The ideological climate in Britain in the early 1980s has not been favourable to market regulation, even by private governments. In its first term of office, the Thatcher Government phased out milk price control in Scotland and, although there were special reasons for taking this step in Scotland, it was also seen as an experiment which could be followed up by similar action in England and Wales. One consequence of the 'drying out' of the Thatcher government after the 1983 election was that a 'wet' Minister of Agriculture (Peter Walker) was replaced by the government's former Chief Whip, a post which is usually held by government loyalists. In February 1984, the government announced that it intended to decontrol liquid milk prices in England by the end of 1985. However, this decision enhances the importance of the Joint Committee as a private government, as it will probably be the forum in which liquid milk prices are negotiated between the MMB and DTF.

An even bigger change in the circumstances of the industry seemed likely to result from the introduction in April 1984 of a package of measures designed to cut back EEC milk production by about ten million tonnes. These unprecedented and substantial cuts in milk production led to widespread protests by farmers. However, what is interesting about the protests that took place is that to a large extent they were directed at the government (particularly the Minister of Agriculture) and the EEC, rather than the MMB. There were some criticisms of the MMB for being too concerned about the processing end of its operations, for lacking adequate contingency plans for a substantial cutback in production, and for supposedly believing that it could market its way out of any difficulty. Small-scale farmers who had recently expanded production, and who had few alternative ways of making a living, were understandably particularly aggrieved and formed themselves into action groups (most notably in west Wales). These action groups were more critical of the MMB, but even they did not call for its abolition, concentrating their fire on the cow vote system, and calling for the introduction of a 'one producer, one vote' arrangement in place of the cow-based franchise. Despite their dislike of the EEC's reforms, most farmers know that they would be worse off without a private government in the form of the marketing boards.

Conclusions

The milk marketing system in Britain offers an interesting example of the way in which intermediary organizations can assume public policy functions. In this case, the intermediary organization has also taken over some of the functions of the market, as is symbolized by the MMB's acquisition of a large portion of the Unigate business. The scheme has thus substituted for market failure and state failure a more satisfactory way of dealing with the problems of the product sector. Indeed, the MMB has tried to apply its entrepreneurial skills to other parts of the food processing industry, having unsuccessfully led a consortium of co-operatives in a bid for the ailing meat processing firm, FMC, formerly owned by the National Farmers' Union Development Trust. The MMB seems to be a classic case of an organization which is more flexible than state agencies, closer to the problems it attempts to resolve, and better able to win the co-operation and support of those directly affected.

An examination of the milk marketing system in Britain can thus contribute to the debate about whether there really is a 'third way' between the market and the state. However, one must be cautious about the extent to which generalizations can be based on this particular case. In many ways, the milk sector is untypical of agriculture as a whole, particularly in the sense that it has a higher political profile; one indication of this is the strong feelings that consumers have about the retention of the doorstep delivery system. As Winter points out, 'Milk ... assumed considerable importance, which it still retains today, as a "political" commodity with symbolic importance ... For the voting public, and the farming lobby too, milk was a commodity which came to symbolise the success or failures of agricultural policy.' (Winter, 1983: 10).

Despite the political salience of milk in Britain (at least in comparison with many other aspects of agricultural policy), it is by no means clear what the public interest in relation to milk is, and therefore it is difficult to determine whether the organization of group interests in the sector is compatible with the pursuit of the public interest. This fact, of itself, gives the MMB considerable freedom of manoeuvre in reconciling the various interests it has to deal with. Nevertheless, there are growing doubts about whether the present set of arrangements are the most satisfactory that could be devised, in part because of growing political concern about the ideological acceptability of such forms of regulation in a country committed to the pursuit of free market solutions; and in part because of changes in economic conditions in the sector. It is difficult to be confident that the milk marketing system will still be in existence to celebrate its hundredth birthday. However, nothing lasts for ever, and perhaps one of the characteristics one should look for in intermediary organizations is a willingness to undergo periodic metamorphoses as economic and political conditions change.

Answers to self-assessment questions

1. This is a trick question. Strictly speaking he can, as there is no requirement for a producer of milk from goats or sheep to register with the board; the board is not concerned with these highly specialized markets. However, farmers producing milk from cows (other than for their own use) have to sell their milk through the board, or be licensed by the Board as a producer processor or producer retailer (under the 1978 regulations, producer-retailers with fewer than twenty cows have the right, if they wish, to opt out of the scheme altogether).

2. Usually, but on one occasion, the DTF at first refused to accept the higher price determined by the minister. Scottish DTF members refused to pay a price increase for milk from the Board in 1981, but had to accept almost all the increase after an arbitration decision.

3. False. The writer gets his milk from Dairy Crest, the commercial arm of the MMB. But only 5 per cent of milk is delivered by the MMB, so there is only limited vertical integration from the farmer to the final consumer of liquid milk.

4. Yes. The farmer may have better things to think about, but at

least his union should be worrying for him. It is true that the amount the farmer receives in his monthly milk cheque is determined by the average price received by the MMB (and, of course, his own level of output), but around half of that price will be determined by the prices negotiated for milk for manufacture.

5. No. You should probably get rid of them, although it is a matter of judgment when to sell (it is possible that someone may make a takeover bid). Remember that the general profit margin available to such companies has been determined by the minister, using a formula which takes the low end of the range of profits of a group of food manufacturing companies (because of supposedly low risks in dairying). Of course, your company could do better than other companies, but that seems unlikely — doorstep delivery is a labour-intensive operation and profit margins are vulnerable to any small falling away of custom. In some areas, collecting the round money can be dangerous, and theft of milk is a problem. Of course, if your company was making a new yoghurt or expensive dairy-based desserts for the catering industry, that would be a different matter....

11
Varieties of collective self-regulation of business: the example of the Dutch dairy industry

Frans van Waarden

Introduction

Entrepreneurial action in capitalism — i.e. under conditions of competition and class conflict — is guided, if not determined, first of all by the imperatives of the different markets for final products, raw materials, capital and labour. During the course of development of capitalism new limitations to free enterprise have been set by state regulation. In between the constraints of the market and the rules imposed by the state, a third source of control can be distinguished: collective self-regulation by capitalists themselves. In order to compensate for shortcomings and the self-destructive logic of the market while at the same time pre-empting state intervention, capitalists have banded together and agreed on mutual rules of conduct which limit their individual autonomy in their own collective long-term interest. Whenever such forms of self-regulation involve the state to a greater or lesser extent, one can speak of corporatist arrangements where the private and the public sphere are interwoven. This may be the result either of private assistance in formulating and implementing public policy, or of state assistance in the formulation and implementation of private regulation.

Depending on the degree of state involvement in such arrangements and in their genesis, Schmitter (1974) has distinguished two sub-types of corporatism, 'state' and 'societal' corporatism. Schmitter uses these concepts to characterize whole societies, but they can also be used to characterize different arrangements within one society, or even within one branch of industry. Thus, even 'state corporatism', which Schmitter reserves for totalitarian states, could conceivably be found within the kind of society that he associates with 'societal corporatism': the liberal capitalist welfare state. As will be shown in this chapter, such is indeed the case.

'State' and 'societal' corporatism are highly general types which can be interpreted as positions on a continuum ranging from very little to very heavy state involvement in capitalist self-regulation. A first aim of this chapter will be to describe the variety on this continuum and develop an instrument for distinguishing between different forms of collective self-regulation. To this end, a number of variables have to be introduced. Schmitter (1974) paid attention primarily to the structural aspects of corporatism. Here the functional side will be stressed first. The following sub-functions, which may either be performed by the state or by the industry, can be distinguished.

1. The formulation of, or giving advice on, general rules;
2. The confirmation of rules, either de facto or formally;
3. The formulation of operationalizations and norms necessary for the implementation of the general rules;
4. The actual implementation and administration;
5. The control of the observation of the rules;
6. The supervision of implementation and/or control;
7. The sanctioning of transgressors; and
8. The handling of appeals.

Attention next will be directed to the structural side: what type of organizations do perform these functions and what influence do the state and the industry have on these organizations? The following organizational characteristics will be distinguished:

1. Initiators of the organization;
2. Legal recognition. Is the organizational structure regulated in formal law? Or less extreme: is state permission required for changes in the organizational structure?
3. Influence of the state on the governing board;
4. Finance by the state;
5. Statutory or de facto monopoly within the domain of the organization;
6. Statutory or de facto compulsory membership;
7. Statutory or de facto 'tax authority', and
8. Statutory or private sanctions (on the basis of public law, disciplinary law or the civil code).

Two characteristics are of primary importance: rule-making and instrumentation with statutory powers. They will be used to distinguish three main types of regulation:

1. *Pure private regulation.* Regulation and implementation is done by the industry without state support.
2. *State-assisted private regulation.* Rules are made autonomously by private organizations or private representatives on semi-public bodies with the (indirect) backing of statutory powers.
3. *Private-assisted state regulation.* State rules laid down in law are to a significant extent implemented by private or semi-public bodies.

On the basis of this distinction several types of regulation will be grouped.

In addition to a description of varieties of self-regulation, an attempt will be made to analyse some conditions for their emergence and to evaluate their success and their stability.

Sector selection

For practical reasons, the study has to be restricted to one industry. The choice has been the dairy industry because it probably has the largest variety of forms of self-regulation in the Dutch economy. In addition, these often have had a long history and have shown considerable stability, even though the organizational characteristics may have changed over time. Inside the sector there exist examples of all the different forms of corporatism that can be found elsewhere in the Dutch economy. Investigation of the dairy industry hence presents us a cross-section of corporatist arrangements. In addition, the dairy industry has some corporatist arrangements which are peculiar to the industry. In fact, the variety is such that for reasons of space this paper had to be limited to seven types of corporatist regulation selected from the many more that are present in the sector.

The Dutch dairy industry

The dairy industry is an important part of the Dutch economy. This is due less to its contribution to the GNP than to its connection with the agricultural sector. The Dutch economy has, until well after the Second World War, been an agrarian economy supplying the surrounding industrialized nations such as Germany and Britain with food. Even now, the food processing industry as a whole is one of the largest economic sectors. Within the food processing industry, the dairy industry is the largest branch — which is not surprising given the fact that two-thirds of all farming land is used for dairy cattle farming.

International trade is very important. Not counting consumption milk (which is primarily sold on the domestic market), 84 per cent of all products are sold abroad. With a share of 30 per cent in the world dairy trade, the Netherlands is the world's largest exporter of condensed milk, milk powder and cheese, and second to New Zealand in butter.

The sector has gone through a strong merger movement. Around 1900 — when industrial dairy production originated owing to a number of technical innovations — there were over 900 firms. By 1980 this number was reduced to 62. Among them are four very large firms, each located in a different part of the country, which account together for two-thirds of national production.

An important distinction in the industry is that between co-operatives owned by farmers and proprietary firms. While the respective market shares of the two categories in 1910 were about equal, the strength of the co-operatives has since then grown steadily. By now, co-operatives account for 90 per cent of all production.

Pure private regulation: the Frisian dairy union

The Dutch dairy industry is organized in twelve voluntary interest associations. The co-operatives have four regional dairy unions which, together with a few individual cooperatives in areas where there is no regional union, form a national association, FNZ. The small private industry has one national organization. Furthermore, there are six product-specific associations which organize both private and co-operative firms.

The purest form of collective private regulation is found within these associations. Their rules are formally binding only on their members, but as they organize almost all firms in their respective domains, they in fact regulate the entire industry. The strongest case is that of the Frisian dairy union, one of the four remaining regional co-operative unions. It has the largest number of binding rules of all dairy unions and actively controls and sanctions them.

For example, there are rules that regulate competition for raw materials. These concern both price and supply. Co-operatives pay a weekly advance on the milk price to their farmers. At the end of the year, the final price is determined. This is done in order to calculate the profits of the co-operatives away in the costs of raw materials. The members of the co-operatives get their 'dividends' in this way for tax purposes. In the past, factories used to compete continually, luring farmers away from one another with a high advance on the milk price. Most regional dairy associations have tried to reduce this competition by introducing binding rules on the methods of calculation of the advance on the milk price. The Frisian union even went so far as to determine the advance centrally every two weeks. In addition, this organization succeeded in getting the power to determine which farmer should supply which factory. Furthermore, the Frisian union and other regional associations prescribe bookkeeping techniques, require that the accounts of the firms are monitored by the association, and regulate investment of member firms.

All sub-functions around these regulations are performed privately. At no stage is there government interference, except of course in so far as the state registers the constitutions of private associations, requires them to satisfy the civil code, and backs internal associational rules by private contract law.

The existence of these forms of self-regulation can only be explained by the past. Both the need for them and their possibility stem from the structure of the industry in former days. The *need* for such regulation developed out of two factors: the fierce competition between factories for milk suppliers; and the lack of trust between the members of the co-operatives on the one hand and the directors of their factories on the other.

Competition resulted from the existence of many small factories. Market entry was easy because of the still low degree of capital investment needed. To maximize the price co-operatives could pay to their members, they had to increase efficiency, among other things by using economies of scale. This required more milk which, in turn, required more suppliers.

The distrust of farmers vis-à-vis the management of their factories was a result of their lack of expertise. Farmers had to rely on management as they lacked the knowledge of the trade. But they did not like this dependence because they were fully liable for all debts and because the director was not 'one of them'. Having received academic training he also usually came from another region. Thus the farmers turned to the regional dairy associations to control the books (and the directors) of the co-operatives for them.

An important condition making self-regulation *possible* was the emergence of a rather autonomous regional association with a secretariat wielding a high degree of authority. This was the result again of the opposition between the farmers and the director of the co-operative, the lack of knowledge among farmers, and the need for central services such as collective buying of machines and materials. In addition, a strong sense of social identity among the members further enhanced the possibility of self-regulation. This was based on the common property structure and the ties of the co-operatives to the agricultural world and its organizations. The exceptionally strong organization in Friesland has to be explained by the deep-seated sense of regional identity in that part of the country, owing to the separate culture and language of the Frisians and conflicts of economic interests with other regions.

The self-regulatory arrangements developed by the Frisian Dairy Union have been quite successful. Competition was reduced, and the broad consensus on self-regulation further enhanced the legitimacy of interest associations involved and reinforced social cohesion. State intervention was not necessary to deal with the problems dealt with by private regulation. Regulatory arrangements were stable over the years and would likely be continued were it not for the fact that they might in the future become redundant as a result of the unabated merger movement. In this case self-regulation between firms will be replaced by intra-firm rules. Horizontal consensus will then cease to be the basis for regulation; it will be replaced by hierarchical authority.

State-assisted private regulation

Case one: quality control of raw materials
Milk, as an organic matter, is a sensitive raw material. It deteriorates quickly and is easily polluted. This is not only a danger to public health but also to the efficiency of the production process. In order to stimulate farmers to produce good quality milk, factories voluntarily introduced already at an early date the principle of payment according to quality (cleanliness, presence of bacteria, antibiotics residues, etc.) In 1958 the state made this compulsory for the whole country. It delegated the necessary rule-making however to the representatives of the private industry in the statutory trade association (STA, see next section).

This payment system led to a need for an objective assessment of milk quality. Factories could of course perform quality controls in their own laboratories. But the farmers did not trust their factories enough to allow them to do this without external control. Furthermore, given their need for a large number of suppliers, factories were often tempted to apply less rigorous standards.

At an early date, the provincial co-operative dairy associations accepted responsibility for quality control. This fitted in well with their other self-regulatory activities, control of the books and reduction of competition for farmers. However, when nationwide compulsory payment by quality was introduced, the state wanted to have more control over quality assessment. Since at that time the statutory trade associations were established, it was held this was an appropriate task for them. But the industry opposed such a transfer of authority from its existing private associations to a semi-public institution. In a pre-emptive move the voluntary dairy associations jointly established a new private control system which was somewhat independent from the voluntary associations. The state consented with this arrangement.

Almost all sub-functions in the present milk control system then are in private hands. Only the basic regulation, the obligation to pay milk according to its quality, is a semi-public responsibility. Furthermore, the STA passively supervises implementation in so far as the private supervisory agencies have to be registered with and recognized by the STA. All other sub-functions are carried out by private foundations created by the industry. They provide binding operational rules, carry out the analysis, control and supervise, sanction transgressors and even handle appeals.

Most of these tasks are in the hands of eight Regional Organs for Milk Control (ROM) which are co-ordinated by a Central Organ for Milk Control (COM). The chemical analysis is performed by six Milk

Control Stations spread out over the country. Milk is graded by them. For third-class milk, farmers have to pay a fine; for first-class milk they receive a bonus which is paid out of the fines. For the presence of pesticides and antibiotics an especially high fine has to be paid. The amount of the fines is so calculated that a farmer will not benefit from intended adulterations.

ROMs are foundations, not associations. This was a conscious choice in order to give them greater autonomy from firms. Since foundations have no members, the firms to be controlled have no direct influence on their board. They have however an indirect influence since board members are appointed by their voluntary associations.

ROMs have a monopoly in their territory because the COM recognizes only one ROM for each region. Affiliation is compulsory by regulation of the STA, in an indirect way. The STA has issued a by-law stipulating that only factories that are affiliated to a recognized milk control organization are allowed to process and sell milk and dairy products. This indirect method has been chosen because compulsory membership in private organizations is formally unconstitutional. Even this 'detour' may be illegal but, contrary to the situation in quality control for final products, no one has yet challenged the arrangement in the courts. The whole dairy industry consents to this element of compulsion which was created voluntarily by itself.

Given the ROM's monopoly status and the practice of compulsory affiliation, all their further authority can be based on the same simple civil law which regulates the internal affairs of any other private organization. Appeals are also handled privately. The COM has instituted and regulated a private Council of Appeals where firms can appeal decisions of the ROMs.

Quite separate from this private arrangement, there are also state agencies that could perform the same activities. They have no supervisory authority over the private control system but they exist next to it. In principle, they would be able to supervise the functioning of the private control system but this they hardly do any more. The Food and Drugs Inspection Boards which in the past used to carry out thousands of controls among milk suppliers now analyse no more than one or two samples a year. This is a clear example of private offloading of state activity.

The arrangement has been a rather stable one up till now. It has been successful in 'offloading the state' and has legitimacy, not only towards the state, but also towards the industry. Some minor changes are however pending. State influence will probably increase somewhat as the fresh milk control system will be brought under a new, general 'Quality of Agricultural Produce Act'. The General Inspection Board of the Ministry of Agriculture will then get supervisory authority over the private control system.

Case two: the statutory trade association: autonomous activities

The most important organization in the dairy industry is probably its statutory association (STA, in Dutch *Produktschap Zuivel*), created under the 1950 Act on Statutory Trade Associations. This act has been a pure expression of explicit corporatist ideology as developed in catholic thinking. The Act created a national tripartite formal advisory council of industry, the Social Economic Council. Furthermore, it made it possible to establish tripartite statutory trade associations regulating specific economic sectors. This can be done on request by voluntary organizations of the industry. Under certain conditions however, the state can also take the initiative. Two types of associations are provided for: so-called *bedrijfsschappen* which organize a sector horizontally, i.e. all producers at a certain production stage; and so-called *produktschappen* which organize a complete product column from raw materials producers to retailers.

Fifteen vertical *produktschappen* and forty-two horizontal *bedrijfsschappen* have been created since 1950. They are mostly located in agriculture, food processing, trade, mining, and leather and shoes. For the dairy industry, a vertical *Produktschap Zuivel* was set up. This was however not a new phenomenon for this industry. Ever since the Second World War semi-public bodies had existed here, with varying degrees of state influence, to administer distribution policies (in wartime) and agricultural crisis policies (in the 1930s).

In a sense, the STA is a part of the state run by the industry. Its legal status is perhaps best compared with that of a municipality. Whereas the domain of a municipal government is a territory, that of the STA is an industry. Both function under public law, have the authority to tax their 'inhabitants', and may enact, within the limits set by the central state, autonomous legislation with the power of law. In both, the central government is represented through its appointment of the 'chairman' (Dutch city mayors are appointed by the central state), but apart from this they are governed by their 'inhabitants'. These are, technically speaking, not 'members', but 'subjects' to their authority. A difference however is that the city council is elected directly by the subjects (with candidates being nominated by political parties) whereas the executive board of the STA is made up of representatives not only nominated, but appointed, by the various voluntary associations of dairy farmers, the dairy industry and the dairy trade, to the extent that these are recognized by the state. The affiliated firms are hence only indirectly represented on the board.

As far as organizational structure is concerned, the statutory status of the STA implies heavy state influence. The STA has a statutory monopoly in its domain, statutory affiliation of all dairy firms, statutory tax authority, statutory authority to enact binding legislation within its domain, and its decisions are public law. In return for this, its status and organizational structure are regulated in law. For example, the organization cannot autonomously change its structure; rules and decisions are subject for formal state approval; and the state is represented on the governing board by a state-appointed full-time chairman and a number of civil servants who have the status of observers without voting rights.

Originally, the STAs were given three types of binding authority vis-à-vis the industry in their domain: they had the power to issue so-called 'autonomous rules' (which however required formal state approval); they were authorized to participate in the implementation of state regulations (so-called 'co-government'); and they were entitled to issue 'general administrative rules' necessary for their own functioning, such as the requirement for firms to register with the STA, to pay levies, to provide information, etc.

In the years before the formation of the Common Agricultural Policy of the European Community, the autonomous rule-making activity of the STA was extensive. Generally speaking, the STA formulated and implemented market-ordering regulations more or less of the same kind as those later included in the dairy policy of the EC. In fact, European dairy policy was heavily influenced by the STA regulations in the Netherlands. The architect of the EC dairy policy, the European Commissioner Sicco Mansholt, came from Dutch agricultural circles and knew the Dutch system of regulations well. He had been Dutch minister of agriculture before. Many of his civil servants in Brussels came in fact from the Dutch STA.

All this changed when regulatory powers were raised to the supranational level in 1964. The autonomous rule-making authority of the STA was drastically reduced. Only a few autonomous rules remained, such as:

1. The rule on payment to farmers by quality and fat and protein content of the milk;

2. The rule establishing a minimum retail price for milk, intended to protect the small retail business against supermarket competition; and

3. Rules on compulsory levies for special activities, such as collective advertising and collective research.

These rules are formulated and confirmed by the industry through its representatives on the STA executive board. The STA also formulates the necessary operationalizations, supervises implementation and control, and in a number of cases administers and controls the observation of the rules themselves. The STA does not levy sanctions. It has no right to impose disciplinary measures. The STA can however declare transgression of certain rules a criminal act. Prosecution and trial are a matter of the judiciary. Appeals are also handled by the state. They go to a special Court of Appeals for Trade and Industry.

The STA as an organization has been rather stable. Its staff has grown continuously, and in 1980 it employed 241 people. Its autonomous activity has however decreased. The large staff is primarily employed for activities that are performed in co-government (see below).

Private-assisted state regulation

Case one: quality control of final products
Quality control regulations exist not only for raw materials, but also for final products. Both are however completely distinct control arrangements. The organization structure is different and state influence is greater in the control of final products.

Adulteration of quality, understood as composition (fat and water content) became a serious problem for the dairy industry by 1890. Merchants and factories tried to enrich themselves by mixing cheaper margarine or water in the butter and selling it for the price of regular butter. Competition forced honest producers and traders to follow in the adulteration practices with the result that the quality of Dutch butter and cheese and their reputation abroad deteriorated ever more. In 1903 for example a much publicized lawsuit was held in England against a Gouda cheese with only 1.6 per cent fat and 57 per cent water.

The voluntary associations tried from their start to curb these practices. Some were even formed especially for this purpose. They instituted a voluntary system of quality control within their associations. Member factories could have their produce controlled and then stamped with a trademark, guaranteeing a minimum fat content. This trademark was supported by advertising abroad. The voluntary arrangement however could not solve the problems. Many producers were afraid to join. Their customers, the dairy wholesalers, prohibited them to do so. And if it was not for this reason, competition with the non-participants prevented others from joining.

State support was needed for an effective system of quality control. The Butter Act of 1889 and the later elaborations thereof were among the first new forms of state intervention in the economy after the short Dutch experience with the liberal 'nightwatch' state. These state rules were not yet binding rules. That went too far for the liberal tradition of those times. Instead they offered the industry the use of state guaranteed trade marks as alternative to private trade-marks. The industry responded by establishing formally independent Butter and Cheese Control Stations in different parts of the country. These private institutions became authorized to issue the state butter and cheese marks to firms which voluntarily submitted themselves to quality control by these stations.

The control system remained voluntary until the First World War. During that war, permission came to be required for export of dairy products. Such a licence was only given for controlled products. After the war this export prohibition of uncontrolled products was continued. Only then did the system become really effective.

This system has existed until 1982. Altogether there were five Butter Control Stations, four Cheese Control Stations, one Control Station for Milkpowder and one special control station for evaluating smell, taste and look of the different products. The first two categories coordinated their activities each in Central Committee. The organization network was completed by two Central Councils for Appeal.

Basic legislation was provided by the state in the Act on the Export of Agricultural produce (*Landbouwuitvoerwet*) of 1928 and the different product decrees based on this Act. The Act also formulated conditions for formal recognition of private implementation agencies and for authorizing them to issue state certificates. Operationalization of these state rules was done by the different control stations. They issued binding inspection rules and created a disciplinary by-law. The organizations carried out the chemical analyses, administered them, and sanctioned transgressors. Appeals to disciplinary action were handled by the special Councils for Appeal. These had a semi-public character. The council members were all appointed by the state, but a minority of its members was nominated by the private control institutions.

Formal state supervision implied that state assent was required for the constitution, for the disciplinary by-law, for rules on rates of control, and more generally for the financial report. Furthermore, state representatives had to be admitted to the board meetings. The appointment and dismissal of the chief of staff required state approval.

The organizations had a monopoly in their regional domain. The state recognized only one control station for each territory. Affiliation was, as indicated, de facto compulsory. Until 1979 all organizations were privately funded. Since then the state subsidizes 50 per cent of the costs.

Some organizations were legally associations, others were foundations. Associations had however not firms as members but voluntary interest associations of the dairy industry, the same which in the foundations formed the executive board. Hence the firms to be controlled nowhere had direct influence on the policy of the control stations.

The stations gave very high fines and did this frequently. This was because they used a system of 'calculated offences'. Fines were so high that they compensated benefits which might be earned by adulteration. This was used as an argument in favour of private control and sanctioning on the basis of disciplinary law. In a criminal court judges would be unlikely to impose the high fines, necessary to play this game, for such 'insignificant' offences as a little more water in the cheese.

The arrangement outlined so far has, however, been changed recently (1982). This change was caused by the EEC. Under EEC policy it is not permitted to have different quality legislation for exports and for the domestic market. The old Act of 1928 was therefore replaced by a new one in 1974, a general Act on Quality of Agricultural Produce (*Landbouwkwaliteitswet*). It took another eight years before decrees for different dairy products under this Act were announced.

The state used this opportunity to simplify the organization structure of implementation. Integration between the different control organizations is increased. The new structure is modeled on the one created in 1957 for quality control of fresh milk discussed above. The old control stations are gradually brought into one single organization, the COZ or Central Organ for Dairy Hygiene. Except for this formal integration nothing very much has changed.

An interesting recent development is that compulsory membership has been challenged by some new affiliates, the cheese traders. Under the new act cheese wholesalers are also considered producers, since cheese is sold to them and taken to their warehouses when it is fourteen days old. It can however only be sold to consumers after another fourteen days of ripening. This is now also considered production and hence wholesalers have been forced to join the control organization. Unlike the dairy industry they have not consented to this and have challenged compulsory membership of private institutions for the European court in Luxemburg. The first verdicts have been in their favour. This resulted in great anxiety both in the industry and the relevant state agencies. New compromises are sought to fit the law. No solution has been found yet while one is waiting for the result of appeals procedures.

Case two: the statutory trade association in co-government
After the establishment of the Collective Agricultural Policy of the EEC in 1964 the STA has become involved in the implementation of this policy in the Netherlands. The national government has delegated its responsibility for this policy to the STA, but of course supervises the STA activities in this field.

Involvement of the STA in policy formation and confirmation is here of course minimal. The STA has the legal right to be heard by the national government whenever it considers new measures relating to the dairy industry. Furthermore, the STA represents the Dutch government in the Advisory Committee on Management of Milk and Dairy Products in Brussels and in this way it can influence European dairy policy. When it comes to operationalization the STA however has more authority. It can decide under what conditions to give advances on export restitutions or how to use the fund filled by the co-responsibility levy. Such operationalizations, so called 'measures in co-government', require state approval.

The basic activity of the STA under this regime is implementation and administration. It is a kind of semi-public tax and customs office. It collects the levies and provides the subsidies and restitutions, instituted by the EEC. Since quite large amounts of money are involved — in 1980 about one billion dollars — the financial supervision of the implementation is tight. At least five state and suprastate agencies are involved in it.

Supervision, control, sanctioning and appeals are all handled by state agencies. In implementation too state influence is great since the structure involved is almost the same as that for the autonomous activity of the STA. The only difference is that the STA receives state subsidies for this takeover of state responsibilities. Thus in this case state influence is even greater.

Case three: social security
In contrast to the five policy areas just mentioned the two remaining ones to be discussed are not specific to the dairy industry. All economic sectors have privately manned 'Sector Associations' (*Bedrijfsverenigingen*), which are involved in the implementation of social security legislation. They carry out the workmen's compensation plans, that is those social security schemes for wage labourers which insure against loss of income due to unemployment, illness or disablement. Altogether there are twenty-six bipartite sector associations, among them one specifically for the dairy industry. They are supervised by a tripartite Social Insurance Council. Appeals are handled by ten regional tripartite Councils of Appeal, supervised by a

Central Council of Appeal. The latter is the only body involved, which is not made up of interest representatives. It consists for 100 per cent of professional lawyers.

Rule-making in this policy area is the responsibility of the state. All plans have a public law status. There is however room for private operationalization of these rules. The sector associations have the authority to issue rules, norms, conditions and prescriptions, necessary for implementation and binding for everyone in their domain. Employers are obliged to register with the association, to supply certain information and to follow guidelines regarding the wage administration. The associations can set the premiums for some insurance plans. They also have the right to exempt employers from participation in the general sickness fund, if they care to take the financial risk themselves.

Responsibility for administration rests with the sector insurance associations as does control on the observation of the rules. Sector associations have the right to track down illegal benefit recipients and premium dodgers. To this end they have their own criminal investigating department. The controllers employed by them have the right to enter premises of employers and workers. In so far as sanctioning means the withholding of benefits, the sector associations are also responsible for this task. Appeals by prospective benefit recipients to decisions of sector associations are handled by the tripartite Councils of Appeal, which have priority over the civil courts.

The organizations are of course legally recognized. But more than that, their structure is exactly prescribed by law. They are endowed with statutory powers. All firms are compulsorily affiliated, the sector associations have a monopoly in their domain, and they have 'tax authority' in so far as they levy premiums, to be paid by all subjects in their 'territory'. The state has no direct influence on the sector associations but it appoints one-third of the members of the peak Social Insurance Council, including the chairman. The executive of the sector associations is made up of representatives of those employers' associations and trade unions, which are recognized by the state. Firms are here also only indirectly represented.

The sector associations as such were a private initiative, although not in the dairy industry. Around 1900 some employers established the first sector insurance associations to implement privately initiated insurance schemes, which were intended as an alternative to plans for compulsory state accident insurance then discussed in parliament. The enactment of other insurance plans, such as for invalidity and sickness, was retarded for years because of political conflicts over the question whether the schemes should be administered by public or private organizations. In the meantime the number of private insurance plans in collective agreements increased. Voices were heard to sanction these forms of self-regulation publicly (i.e. declare them generally binding, just as with collective wage agreements) and to delegate formal authority of implementation to the existing bipartite sector insurance associations. A problem was however that not all employers were a member of a sector insurance association and compulsory membership of private associations was not considered acceptable yet.

In 1930 therefore the implementation of the new sickness insurance act was delegated to the sector associations, but these did not get a monopoly, nor was compulsory membership required. Unorganized employers had to affiliate themselves with state controlled regional Councils of Labour for the insurance of their workers. In addition, there could be more than one private association in each sector, i.e. even as sector associations they did not have a monopoly.

This compromise lead to fierce competition among sector insurance associations and between these and the state-controlled organizations. The different associations tried to recruit employers as members, among other things by competing with lower premiums. As this turned out to be to the detriment of the benefits which workers received, the trade unions asked for monopoly recognition of sector insurance associations and for compulsory membership. Only after prolonged discussions was this introduced by the 1952 Social Security Organization Act which regulates the status of the present insurance associations.

The stability of this form of corporatist self-regulation is presently threatened. State influence is increasing, not only in rulemaking, but also in implementation because too lenient benefit distribution is seen as one cause of the skyrocketing expenditures. In addition concern has grown over the complexity of the implementation structure and the unclear division of responsibilities. Apart from sector associations, social security plans are implemented by regional tripartite councils of labour, private health insurance associations, municipalities and their horizontal and hierarchic co-ordination structures. In a recent study by state civil servants both rising costs and overcomplexity have led to a questioning of the whole corporatist implementation structure.

Factually, the system is hardly corporatist any more. The implementation agencies have grown so large and their tasks have become so complicated — with the development of jurisprudence — that implementation is controlled more and more by the many bureaucrats and professionals employed by the sector associations. They, rather than the representatives of the interest associations, take the decisions, as one of these representatives recently complained

(Van Brussel, 1979). What is happening is a well-known phenomenon, only it is not usually associated with corporatism: the rise of bureaucracy, but within corporatism. A paradox indeed: corporatist structures, in earlier days defended as an alternative to (state) bureaucracy, have turned by their growth into the very alternatives they were to prevent.

Case four: supervision of works councils
The Netherlands has since 1950 an Act on Works Councils which has been twice renewed and extended, in 1971 and 1979. The 1950 Act also provided for so called 'Sector Committees' (*Bedrijfscommissies*), made up of representatives of employers' associations and trade unions, with the task to supervise the implementation of the works council act in their domain. Since then seventy-one sector committees for works councils have been formed, including one specifically for the dairy industry.

The formulation and confirmation of rules is here a complete state responsibility. The government act prescribes the structure and authority of works councils in such great detail that little room is left for sector committees to decide on interpretations and operationalizations of the law.

Their most important task is to mediate in conflicts between employers and their works councils and to provide binding arbitration in a number of cases. In addition, an employer may appeal to a sector committee for approval of his personnel policy when the works council declines to provide this, as is required by law. Sector committees should further mediate in cases where the employer declines to help initiate a works council before the state court can force him to do so. The basic idea is that of self regulatory conflict resolution under the expectation that where this does not succeed at the firm level, it might perhaps succeed at the higher sector level. Finally, sector committees have some tasks in the appeals procedure. Employers and/or employees can not so much appeal the law as well as request exemption. Sector committees have the power to grant such exemptions or allow firms to deviate from some legal requirements, such as the number of council members.

The sector committees have been a state initiative. They are legally recognized and their structure is closely prescribed in law. The establishment of individual sector committees is however a task of the semi-public Social Economic Council upon request by the relevant employers' associations and trade unions. Their legal recognition is a monopoly recognition. There is only one committee for each economic sector.

The state is not represented on the committee. Decisions are taken autonomously but financial affairs are controlled by the Social Economic Council. The activities of the committees are to be paid both by the employers' association and the trade unions.

The basic motive for the establishment of the sector committees was not so much a need felt by the industry but the corporatist ideology which was very influential in government around 1950. It was thought that a task such as the supervision of works councils could best be delegated to the organizations of the industry as they would be able to take account of specific sector conditions in implementation. Furthermore, it was seen as just another institutional linkage between the organizations of the different classes, conducive to harmonious class relations. This function remained however undeveloped due to the unimportance of the sector committees. Their activities have been very limited. Many sector committees met only once a year, confining themselves mainly to written communication.

This scant activity has led to a discussion which threatens the future of the present arrangement. The Social Economic Council noted in a study that as a result of the lack of activity many sector committees got insufficient experience with mediation and hence have not been able to build up expertise. Also, the government has become more inclined in general to solve the contradiction between decentralization and equality-before-the-law in favour of the latter. Plans are being discussed to abolish the sector committees and replace them with a general industry-wide council assisted by a staff of professional lawyers. Interest may give way to expertise, corporatism to technocracy.

Some comparative observations

The different cases presented in the preceding paragraphs show a wide variety of corporatist arrangements. All represent a mix of state and private responsibilities in the creation and implementation of binding rules and the related administration of justice for a circumscribed category in the population. In all cases, private industry and their interest associations partake in the state monopoly over the legitimate exercise of force, the state monopoly of taxation and, derived from these, the monopoly over the creation of rules that are binding on all subjects within a certain territory.

Collective private self-regulation by an industry with more or less state assistance is the principal distinguishing element of corporatism. Corporatism is therefore not primarily a 'system of representation' as in the famous definition of Schmitter (1974: 13). It is not the articulation, aggregation and representation of interests vis-à-vis the state which is characteristic of corporatism but rather the opaque mix of public and private responsibility in government which not only includes the formulation of rules (to which interest representation is directed) but also the implementation, control, sanctioning and handling of appeals.

At the same time, many of the examples of corporatism presented here also fit the structural elements of Schmitter's definition. The respective organizations have a monopoly within their domain and have formal or de facto compulsory membership or affiliation. They perform different regulatory activities in different policy areas and are hence functionally differentiated. They are singular and hierarchically ordered, as for example the Regional Organs for Milk Control which are co-ordinated by the Central Organ. Except for the first case, all are recognized by the state, either directly or indirectly, through the semi-public statutory trade associations or the Social Economic Council. Some of them have even been created by the state. They have been granted their statutory powers in return for state influence on the selection of chairmen and members of the executive boards or on the selection of the associations that can appoint their leaders.

Apart from these common elements — which define them as forms of corporatism — there are significant differences. The most important one relates to the degree of state influence on regulation and on the instrumentation of the arrangements. A rough distinction has been made between state-assisted private regulation and private-assisted state regulation. Table 1 provides a summary of the seven cases of regulation discussed. It indicates which sub-tasks are performed by the industry, the state and/or semi-public organizations and what influence the state has on the structure of the organizations that were specially created to perform regulation. On the basis of a five-point scale of state influence on each variable, an additive indicator has been constructed of state influence in corporatist arrangements. The cases have been ordered by increasing state influence.

Is there a systematic relationship between degree of state influence and policy area? It turns out that in all cases of strong state involvement other organized interests are also involved. The regulation of social security and the supervision of works councils are matters in which trade unions (and certain political parties) have an interest. Quality control of final products is a concern of consumer groups and is an area where the general public interest is at stake. Market ordering through co-government by the STA is a case where there is external influence on the national government by the European authorities. The strong state involvement in these areas

TABLE 1
Functional and structural characteristics of seven cases of regulation

	The Frisian Dairy Union	Quality control of raw materials	STA: autonomous activities	Quality control of final products	Social Security	Supervision of works councils	STA: co-government
Subfunctions							
Formulating rules (3x)[a]	0	¾	¾	1½	1½	3	2¼
Confirming rules (3x)[a]	0	¾	1½	3	3	3	3
Formulating operationalizations	0	0	½	½	½	½	½
Implementation	0	0	½	0	½	½	½
Control	0	¼	½	0	½	¾	1
Supervision of implementation	0	0	½	1	½	½	1
Sanctioning	0	0	1	0	¾	1	1
Handling appeals	0	0	¾	½	½	½	¾
Structure							
Initiators	0	0	0	0	0	1	1
Legal recognition	0	½	1	1	1	1	1
State influence on board	0	0	½	½	0	0	½
State financing	0	½	0	½	0	0	1
Monopoly in domain[b]	½	1	1	1	1	1	1
Compulsory affiliation[b]	½	1	1	1	1	1	1
Tax authority[b]	½	0	1	1	1	0	1
Sanctions[c]	0	½	1	½	1	1	1
Additive indicator of state involvement	1½	5¼	11½	12	12¾	14¾	17½

Coding: 0: private business responsibility. No state interference, no statutory powers. 1: state responsibility, state influence, statutory powers. ¼, ½ or ¾: mixed responsibility, or responsibility of semi-public organizations such as Statutory Trade Association or Social Economic Council.

[a] Given the special importance of rule-making, the variable was given a weight of 3.

[b] ½: de facto; 1: formal

[c] 0: sanctions on the basis of the civil code; ½: sanctions on the basis of disciplinary law; 1: sanctions on the basis of criminal law.

could hence be explained from a pluralist perspective: the presence of other competing interests does not allow for too much self-regulation by the industry but presses for more neutral state intervention.

Another difference between state-dominated and industry-dominated types of regulation is that the former concerns subjects that are not specific to the dairy industry. Regulations on works councils and social security apply to industry as a whole. Quality control of final products and the agricultural policy of the EEC impose rules that affect the whole food processing industry. Most of the more private regulations, on the other hand — such as those on the relations between factories and farmers and on the quality of raw materials — are specific to the dairy industry. While general regulation concerning all industries alike seems to have been difficult to delegate, this was less the case for sector-specific regulation. Whenever possible to discriminate between general and specific, the state has done so. In the dairy industry even more than in other sectors, regulation has been devolved to the industry, or the state has allowed the industry to regulate itself. The industry, on its part, has always preferred self-regulation over state intervention and has been prepared to regulate, control and even police itself.

All regulations, except for some concerning the whole economy (works councils), were originally private initiatives. They originated from a felt need to reduce competition. Whereas in other sectors firms pursue such interests individually — 'the capitalist way' — through the competitive struggle, the dairy industry has already at an early stage of its development agreed to act on these interests collectively, trying to reduce competition through regulation rather than through forcing competitors out of the market. Competition, however, is not only a motive for regulation but also a barrier to it. Competition often creates prisoners' dilemma problems which undermine collective regulation. Such has been the fate of many a cartel. In the dairy industry this problem has been overcome due to the particular *structure of the industry*.

First of all, the sector has known a high degree of social cohesion. Several factors contributed to this: its co-operative ownership structure, its ties with the world of agriculture and farmers' organizations, and its extreme territorial dispersion (owing to the need to locate factories near the raw material supply as milk was difficult to transport without loss of quality). Territorial dispersion led to the creation of regional associations of factories which represented regional collective identities, and this further enhanced social cohesion.

A second factor explaining the early development of well-resourced and relatively autonomous (regional) associations was very small firm size which created a need for central staff resources. Lack of knowledge and expertise in business affairs on the part of the farmers also played a role, as well as the opposition which developed between the co-operators and the directors of their factories.

A third factor was the presence of 'enemies' such as the private dairy industry and the established dairy merchants. This too enhanced associability. The bulk character of the product contributed also as it produced a high degree of homogeneity of interests.

Originally self-regulatory measures were taken by voluntary interest associations. Some of them were later on delegated to special organizations differentiated out of these general voluntary interest associations. As a result, the latter could remain relatively small and flexible whereas the functionally specialized organizations assumed a more neutral image.

Self-regulation emerged out of a need for reduction of competition and was made possible by the particular structure of the sector. It was made possible too by the absence of state intervention as well as state opposition to self-regulation. There was in fact state support for private regulation. This tolerant, if not positive, attitude was due to the fact that the state always had a strong interest in the industry. The dairy industry is important both for public health and for economic policy objectives such as a prosperous agricultural sector, regional industrial balance and foreign currency earnings. These interests were articulated and defended within the state by a powerful Ministry of Agriculture, with strong ties to the agricultural and food processing community. As a consequence the state has allowed, if not supported, measures to be taken in the interest of the industry even if they were contrary to other interests such as those of domestic consumers. Given the strong ties between the Ministry and the industry's associations, the state easily consented for a long time to regulation being treated as a private affair. Self-regulation was also supported by the state because of the explicit corporatist ideology which was influential between 1920 and 1960.

Nevertheless, the influence of the state on sector regulation has increased and is still increasing. Only a few of the many pure cases of private self-regulation of the past have remained, such as the internal rules of the Frisian dairy union that regulate competition for raw materials. Others have sooner or later been publicly sanctioned (quality control of milk) or have been replaced by state regulation (quality control of final products, social security, European dairy policy). Not only the rules have become more public. So have the involved orgnizations. The first step was the differentiation of functionally specialized organizations out of general interest associations. After that, these new, originally voluntary and non-monopolistic organizations gradually became de facto compulsory or were vested with a statutory monopoly, statutory membership or affiliation, and sometimes statutory tax authority. Often this happened in the early 1950s when corporatist ideology was most influential in government. In those years the statutory trade associations, the fresh milk control organizations, the social security associations and the sector committees on works councils were created — all, except for the last category, out of pre-existing voluntary or already compulsory organizations. In this sense, the difference between ideological corporatism and neo or incremental corporatism is less great than is often supposed. The introduction of ideological corporatism in the Netherlands was basically a formalization and continuation of incremental forms of corporatism which have prevailed from 1900 to 1950.

There were several factors contributing to this development. First of all, it turned out that many regulations were only effective under conditions of compulsion and monopoly. Social security was not very well attended to as long as there was competition for members between different associations. Quality control became really effective only when it was made a precondition for receiving an export licence. The obvious need for tighter regulation could be satisfied in part because there was enough consensus in the dairy industry over this necessity. Again, close cohesion and strong voluntary associations were important conditions for this. In addition, there was the initiative of the state to increase regulation. The popularity of the corporatist ideology has already been mentioned. Furthermore, the policy of crisis management which the state developed during the 1930s consisted basically of 'compulsory market ordering'. This was both the result of economic experience — self-destructive competition — and of popular economic theories based on catholic corporatist thinking and social democratic ideas on economic planning.

Corporatist self-regulation in the dairy industry has generally been successful. Quality control, market regulation and reduction of competition for raw materials all seem to have improved the industry's economic position. At least they have certainly not hurt it. Rationalization and modernization have not been retarded by reduced competition between domestic producers as some would have expected. The Dutch dairy industry has improved its position continuously in relation to its competitors in other countries, due to its efficiency, large scale of production, high quality, tight organization and effective private market agreements. It submits relatively little to the European intervention bureaus. It usually succeeds in selling its products at higher than intervention prices. The present (1984) shortage of domestic milk supply (due to the co-responsibility levy of the EEC) has led Dutch factories to start buying milk surplusses in other European countries such as Belgium, France, Scotland and Ireland.

Corporatist self-regulation has been successful not least in the sense that it has preserved its legitimacy, in particular vis-à-vis the industry itself. It also has unburdened the state. Without the private and semi-public agencies, the state bureauucracy for the dairy industry would have to be much larger. In fact, in neighbouring countries it is larger.

Instead of a state bureacracy, however, a highly complex private/public type of bureaucracy has evolved around the state. It employs over 1200 people, serving an industry with only about 22,000 workers. The number and status of its different organizations and the relations between them and with the industry and the state have become so complicated that this bureaucracy is probably less accessible and transparent than a state bureaucracy should be.

This has led to pressure for change and it is one reason for the present relative instability of corporatist self-regulation in the Dutch dairy industry. Pressure from the state for simplification of the organizational structure has recently led to a reorganization of the quality control arrangement accompanied by an increase in state influence. Similar reorganizations could follow in the arrangements for social security and for supervision of works councils, as was indicated. Changes in the organization of social security are in addition motivated by budget problems of the state. Similar problems in the European dairy policy could also lead to still greater state influence on market ordering and on the statutory trade association implementing it. Opaqueness of organizational structures and rising costs of government programmes could hence result in a continued trend towards more and more state influence inside corporatist arrangements.

Finally there are also changes in the economic structure of the sector, which threaten the stability of existing arrangements. Concentration of property has become very high. Four firms now dominate the industry. There are almost as many regulatory organizations as there are firms in the industry. Some quality control stations work already basically for only one large firm. If this trend continues — and there is no reason why it should not — the present interorganizational system will become untenable. It either could develop altogether into a central staff bureau of a future 'Dutch Dairy Inc.' — then its independence from the subject to be regulated and controlled would disappear — or the different organizations could be reorganized, simplified and integrated within the state apparatus.

That would be the end of corporatist self-regulation in the Dutch dairy industry.

Acknowledgement
This paper is based on research funded by the Dutch Organization for Pure Scientific Research ZWO (Grant no. 50-174). A longer version comparing twelve different types of regulation has appeared as Working Paper no. 108/84 of the European University Institute, Florence.

12
The governance of the American economy: the role of markets, clans, hierarchies, and associative behaviour

J. Rogers Hollingsworth and Leon N. Lindberg

This chapter addresses some issues of the governance of the American economy in the 1980s. Our concept of governance refers broadly to the full range of institutional possibilities for deriving collective decisions in an economy. The objectives of economic governance are efficiently and adaptively to co-ordinate the activities of firms and their 'relevant environments', that is, customers, suppliers, competitors, labour, technology generators, government agencies, etc. (Lawrence and Dyer, 1983). We argue that one can identify in any modern capitalist economy four distinctive forms of governance and that their characteristics must be taken into account if we are either to understand economic performance or to derive proposals for public policies. Because the American economy is so large and complex, consisting of hundreds of different sectors, one can, however, only gain a modest perspective on the subject of governance in the space allotted here.

Instead of focusing on the entire economy in the aggregate, as is often the strategy of economists, the concern here is with the sectoral level — for example, such things as the dairy, meat, textile, construction, steel, semiconductor, pharmaceutical, aircraft, computer, etc. industries. Just as Streeck and Schmitter in their introductory chapter to this volume confronted the problem of how the community, markets, the state and associations interact to promote societal order, this chapter employs many of these same concepts in order to understand how various sectors of the American economy are governed.

Economic governance

Governance refers to the several institutional mechanisms through which firms as complex organizations have come to deal with other organizations or actors in response to problems of *resource scarcity* (uncertainty with respect to the availability of capital, raw materials, human resources), and *information complexity* (uncertainty with respect to competition, products, markets, technology and government regulation). Specifically, governance in regard to various sectors addresses the following type of questions: what are the mechanisms by which prices are set and demand stabilized, production levels determined, the activities of production and distributing units co-ordinated, relations with labour managed, product innovation and development occur, capital is allocated, information about product quality is disseminated, and norms of fair competition and product standards are generated. In order to understand the governance of specific economic sectors, the strategy employed herein is to integrate the general political and sociological theoretical insights of Streeck and Schmitter (1984) with those of other scholars who have studied the structure of American industry in recent years: Chandler (1962, 1977), Ouchi (1977, 1980, 1984), Williamson (1975, 1981), Hage and Clignet (1982), Lawrence and Dyer, (1983). From this literature, one learns that the governance of economy occurs *via* a variety of mechanisms: markets, hierarchies, the clan or community and associations. Of course, each of these mechanisms despite common elements, operates according to a different logic.

Markets provide the arena for buying and selling, with prices supposed to convey the information for the efficient allocation of goods and services (Ouchi, 1977: 540; Zysman, 1983: 17). Under some conditions, however, there are market failures, and when this occurs, prices fail to convey the necessary information.

However, there are alternative mechanisms for allocating resources and co-ordinating activities, one of which is *hierarchy*. There are two forms of hierarchy which may replace market mechanisms as devices for the co-ordination and allocation of resources. These are the state and the modern corporation. Of course, the modern corporation and the state are by no means functional equivalents, but with both, economic actors are dependent upon hierarchical coordination for economic activity. Of course, the state has much more legitimate authority and coercive capacity than the corporate structure. And while oligopolistic and monopolistic types of corporate structure often take the place of markets in co-ordinating economic activities, it is rare that a corporate firm becomes totally independent of markets. Within both the state and the corporate structure, however, bureaucratic structures operate according to systems of hierarchical surveillance, evaluation and direction.

Drawing on a long sociological tradition, Streeck and Schmitter (1984) employ the concept *community* as a mechanism which is involved in the governance of total societies. Focusing at the sectoral level Ouchi (1977, 1984) employs the concept *clan*; he sees the clan as a loose form of organization in which the members are bound together over a very long time, and in which there is mutual understanding, and the expectation of mutually rewarding long-term involvement. Clans often substitute not only for markets but for hierarchies as well. For example, market prices are a relatively sophisticated form of decision-making, but 'correct' prices are often difficult to establish because of technological interdependence, novelty, and other forms of ambiguity. Hierarchies perform well in so far as there are established rules to cover contingencies. But decision makers within hierarchies must be familiar with the structure of rules in order to apply the correct one in any specific situation. Exceptions to rules are either denied or referred up the chain of command in the hierarchy. But in situations of considerable uncertainty and complexity, the number of excecptions can overload the hierarchy. Shared norms among different actors, however, are alternative mechanisms to markets and hierarchies for governing behaviour (Ouchi, 1980). Clans are mechanisms for reducing differences among individuals and organizations. In a society with high levels of technological complexity with technology changing frequently, close communication is necessary in closely integrated industries. But if markets and bureaucracies cannot provide effective communication among individuals and organizations with different goals, clans do have the potential to mediate differences and to promote goal congruence. In a society as heterogeneous and as mobile as the United States, however, the effectiveness of clan activity to cope with economic problems is lower than in societies with greater ideological, ethnic and racial homogeneity.

Associational behaviour is still another mechanism involved in co-ordinating economic activity in a modern economy. This form of governance is distinctive in that it involves structural negotiations among a limited set of business firms which mutually recognize each other's status and entitlements and seek to reach and implement relatively formal and stable compromises in pursuit of their interests (Schmitter and Streeck, 1981, 1984). Such associations and systems of interrelated associations may become highly developed vertically and horizontally across a range of the activities of firms in any given sector. Association staffs may over time develop a certain autonomy from member firms which facilitates the pursuit of long-term strategies for the management of the problems of a sector and stabilizes relationships with the state and other forces in the environment of a sector. In these ways business associations may provide an institutional basis permitting firms to define a set of common interests and to develop a sufficient consensus to resolve disputes. It is through such arrangements that business frequently attempts to regulate or govern itself, and it is here that business often develops its most active and continuing interface with other organized groups and the state.

Business associations are less important in governing the American economy than they are in several European economies, and the importance of associations as a governing instrument varies from sector to sector in the United States, as it does in most societies. Similarly, the role of markets, hierarchies, clans, and associations varies from sector to sector. Each of these mechanisms is in varying degree involved in the governance of each sector of the economy. The primary concern of this paper is to offer a preliminary description of the variation in the role which these mechanisms play in the governance of a representative array of sectors of the American economy. In this sense, the purpose of the paper is quite modest. It is only a beginning of an effort to study the governance of the American economy.

It is not enough to know that the governance of the economy occurs as a result of these four different mechanisms. We must try to understand what sectors of the economy tend to be co-ordinated or governed by what specific mechanisms. In order to advance our understanding of how these mechanisms operate in specific sectors of the American economy, it is expedient to do two things:

(1) to develop a typology of the American economy (see Figure 1); and

(2) to specify the relative importance of the four types of governing mechanisms in various sectors of the American economy.

The typology will help us to understand some key differences among various sectors of the economy. Our strategy is to lay the groundwork for a more complex research agenda which will confront the following type of problems: why do markets, hierarchies, clans and associations vary in their capacity to co-ordinate economic activity across sectors of the American economy? Why do different forms of governance develop in different sectors? How does the mix of governing mechanisms influence performance? Is there in some sense an optimal mix of governing mechanisms in view of the resource scarcity and information complexity characteristics of different sectors? What does this imply as far as government efforts to improve economic performance?

A typology of the sectors in the American economy

There are, of course, many dimensions along which one may compare various sectors of the American economy. However, the typology portrayed in Figure 1 captures some of the broad contours that seem to be most important in conditioning firm's behaviour across the different sectors. These dimensions permit the development of a four cell table into which one may fit the various sectors of the contemporary American economy. The dimensions along the horizontal axis are the size of the firm, the size of demand at the firm level, and the level of investment required by a firm for entry into the sector. The dimensions along the vertical axis are the level of technological sophistication and the rate of technological change. Note that the horizontal axis captures variation across firms and their environments in particular sectors, while the vertical axis captures variation across products. The various sectors of the economy are arrayed within each of the cells.

FIGURE 1
A typology of the American economy[1]

		Size of firm Size of demand at the firm level Level of investment	
		Low	High
Technological sophistication and rate of technological change	Low	*Cell One:* Relatively small firms with low technological complexity	*Cell Two:* Large firms with low technological complexity
		A | B	*Examples*
		Firms producing undifferentiated products | Firms producing differentiated products	Autos Steels Canned foods Soft drinks Producers of fabricated metal products
		Examples Agriculture | *Examples* Residential construction Printing Publishing Apparel Textiles Furniture Banking Savings institutions	
	High	*Cell Three:* Relatively small firms with high technological complexity	*Cell Four:* Large firms with high technological complexity
		Examples Pharmaceuticals High performance plastics Ceramics Specialty steel Radioisotopes Various electronics industries	*Examples* Mainframe computers Nuclear energy Aircraft firms Telecommunications

At this point, it is important to point out that this typology deliberately does not attempt to address the issue of why firms within the same sector vary in their performance. That question would require a fundamentally different set of variables, ones which would capture structural as well as social psychological variables at the firm level.[2] Rather, the typology here attempts to capture variation across sectors of the economy, acknowledging that there will be considerable variation in the behaviour and performance of individual firms.

Cell One is called simply 'Relatively small firms with low technological complexity'. Sectors within this cell are made up of firms which are relatively small, which require relatively little capital in order to enter the industry, and which tend to be quite competitive. Sectors in Cell One should be distinguished as to whether they produce undifferentiated products or differentiated products. The agricultural sector would be the former, while the latter would consist of publishing, printing, textiles, apparel, housing, furniture, banking, savings and loan associations, as well as others. Industries in these sectors require little energy and relatively small amounts of complex machinery, as they are quite labour intensive. The volume of output is relatively low at the firm level, and mass advertising is relatively unimportant for these industries. In the American economy, workers in these sectors have a relatively low level of unionization. And when they are organized, they tend to be organized into craft instead of large industrial unions. In general, wages, job benefits and job security among workers in these sectors tend to be low, while job turnover rates are relatively high.

Of course, the technological complexity of industries is not static, and for this reason, industries may historically move from one cell to another. The four cell table tends to capture the variation in the American economy around 1980.

Cell Two is called 'Large firms with low technological complexity'. Sectors within this cell are made up of firms which are relatively large and which require considerable capital in order to enter the industry. The sectors tend to be oligopolistic in nature. Whereas some of the sectors in Cell One attempt to produce customized products (for example, housing, banking, etc.), sectors in Cell Two tend to specialize in the production of standardized products. In the production of consumer durables, large sums of money are spent on advertising, and firms have sizeable sales forces. Of course, there are many types of industries in Cell Two. There are:

(1) mass producers of low priced, semi-perishable packaged products which adopt large-batch and continuous-process technology (for example, manufacturers of canned foods, soft drinks, beer and liquor, breakfast cereals);

(2) processors of perishable products for national markets (for example, large meat packing and processing firms);

(3) manufacturers of mass produced consumer durables which use continuous process technology and which require specialized marketing services in order to be sold in volume (for example, manufacturers of automobiles, heavy farm equipment, sewing machines, etc.);

(4) makers of somewhat complex producer goods which are standardized (for example, manufacturers of elevators, heavy electric motors, etc.);

(5) producers of primary metals (for example, steel, copper, aluminum, etc.); and

(6) producers of fabricated metal products (for example, manufacturers of cans).

Industries in Cells One B and Two were well developed prior to 1945 and, by contemporary standards, these are industries in which the level of technological complexity and rate of technological change has not been very high. A high proportion of the manufacturing sectors in these two cells consist of industries which are either in decline or are in a stage of transition. Many of the newly industrializing countries have enormous labour cost advantages over firms in Cell One B and Two, meaning that a number of firms in these cells must reduce their output, exit from the industry, or seek governmental protection. However, there are few sectors in which decline is inevitable. Instead, most manufacturing sectors in Cells One B and Two are in a stage of transition. Firms in these sectors are faced with the same choices as those which are declining, but with the additional choice of altering their products and/or production processes. In part, the mix of markets, hierarchies, clans and the associational structure determines the strategy which manufacturing sectors in transition will employ (Zysman, 1983; Ouchi, 1984; Lawrence and Dyer, 1983).

Cells Three and Four contain industries which are based on scientific knowledge, especially on the application of scientific theory to product development. Cell Three would include firms producing pharmaceuticals, specialty chemicals, specialty steels, high performance plastics and ceramics, radioisotopes, and high technology electronics. As in Cell One, firms in Cell Three tend to be highly competitive and relatively small. Entry into this sector tends to be based more on knowledge than on capital. The life of most products is relatively short, and the survival of firms in Cells Three and Four is very dependent on considerable investments in research and development. And as Hage and Clignet (1982: 82) point out, the high technological sophistication of these sectors has tended to enlarge the range of products. Hence, firms in Cell Three have the potential to develop many more product lines than those in Cell Two.

Also in contrast to Cell Two, firms in Cell Three have a much smaller proportion of the labour force organized into trade unions. On the other hand, many of the employees in this sector are highly educated, enjoy considerable work autonomy, and receive attractive wages and work benefits.

Firms in Cell Four are involved with technologies having relatively short lives as far as markets are concerned. Similarly, the level of technological complexity is quite high and firms spend considerable sums of money on research and development. Barriers to entry are based on both knowledge and large sums of capital. Examples of industries are those involved in the production of mainframe computers, aircraft, telecommunications equipment and services, and nuclear power plants. Because of the vast capital required to operate in this sector, entry is difficult and market price competition is not very important. Indeed, sectors in this cell tend to be either oligopolistic or monopolistic.

For firms to perform well in Cell Four sectors, harmonious work conditions are essential. In general, a high proportion of employees are unionized and are well compensated.

The role of governance mechanisms
Obviously, firms vary greatly in their capital requirements and their need for governmental intervention, a high quality labour force, extensive research and development funds, and countless other resources. Most everyone seems to know this. Even so, the bulk of the scholarly literature fails to recognize that if there is great variation in the structure and in the resource needs across sectors of the American economy, there is probably great variation in the way in which sectors of the economy are governed. True, there is a strong ideological predisposition among Americans to prefer market solutions. American legal norms and constitutional doctrines further elevate a liberal conception of the state and a separation of the public and private spheres. Partly as a result, there is insufficient recognition that the governing mechanisms that actually shape economic activity are quite complex. For example, the political economy literature places great emphasis on the weak American state, stressing the way in which its executive authority is dispersed and is vulnerable to interest group pressure (Krasner, 1978; Lowi, 1969; Katzenstein, 1973). While it is true that the weak state/strong state formulation is helpful in comparing the political capabilities of states in cross national research, this perspective is somewhat overly simplistic and fails to recognize that the American state's ability to act in one policy area is very different from its ability to act in another (Zysman, 1983: 297). Similarly, the political economy literature on the nature of markets in

the United States misses important variations. For example, John Zysman (1983) in his very informative comparative study of financial systems argues that there are basically three models of finance in advanced industrial societies and that the American model is a capital market-based system in which security issues (for example, stocks and bonds) are the predominant source of funds for American firms. However, contrary to what Zysman argues, all three of his models are present in the American system. As we will try to show below, financing in some sectors is credit-based with government administered prices, while in others, the flow of long-term credits is bargained or determined by other organizations. Only a more in-depth analysis across a number of sectors of the American economy will reveal the more diverse nature of financial institutions in the United States.

In short, the nature of markets, the state, clans and associative behaviour is far more complex in the governance of the American economy than most political economy scholarship has recognized. By focusing on several economic sectors in each of the four cells in Figure 1, the remainder of this chapter is designed to provide examples of this complexity and to make a modest first step in the specification of what mix of markets, hierarchies, clans, and associative behaviour occurs in each of the four cells.

Cell One A (relatively small firms with low levels of technological complexity, producing undifferentiated products)

Agricultural sectors seem broadly representative of this category. Even so there is diversity in the way they are governed. Many agricultural sectors have the characteristics of a market economy. For example, in most meat and vegetable sectors, there are large numbers of sellers, no one of which can affect market prices. Entry into the industry is relatively easy. Within modest limits, prices are determined by markets in which offers from sellers and bids from buyers are made. Prices are determined in a highly competitive way, and on a given day, prices change frequently. It is not unusual for the total value of output of some agricultural sectors to vary as much as 20 per cent from year to year. In these sectors, the state plays a very modest role in intervening in markets, and clan type activity and associative behaviour are not well developed.

On the other hand, there are agricultural sectors which are governed very differently, sectors in which prices are very stable, government intervention is extensive, and clan type activity and associative behaviour are pervasive. A good example, is the dairy industry. The key to understanding the dairy industry is to be found in the vast system of dairy co-operatives. Co-operatives function extensively in certain sectors of agriculture because of the Capper-Volstead Act of 1922 whereby Congress granted agricultural marketing co-operatives partial immunity from federal anti-trust laws.

Co-operatives have tended to develop in those sectors of agriculture in which the size of firms is relatively homogeneous, as in dairying and wheat farming. Moreover, in those geographical areas where co-operatives have been extensively developed, there has been a common culture among the producers — a culture which has often been ethnically based. On the other hand, farms in the meat and vegetable sectors have been much more heterogeneous in size and there has been little common culture among producers. As a result, co-operatives have been much less common and very competitive markets have been the dominant method of shaping prices.

Co-operatives play a very important role in shaping economic activity in the dairy industry, handling approximately 80 per cent of milk produced in the United States. Co-operatives bargain with milk processors for the price to be paid to producers, represent dairymen at hearings for federal milk marketing orders, and provide for the transfer of milk from the farm to the factory. Some co-operatives are even processors, producing cheese, butter, and other dairy products. The functions of dairy co-operatives extend far beyond the marketing of milk. Indeed, dairy co-operatives have become the functional equivalents of business trade associations. In this respect, co-operatives lobby for dairy legislation, provide insurance for their members, provide advertisements to increase the demand for dairy products, and disseminate to members information designed to create greater efficiencies on dairy farms.

The state and the dairy industry have combined to influence the price of milk by creating federal marketing orders and dairy price support programmes. Under federal marketing orders, milk processors are required to pay dairy farmers *via* their co-operatives a specified price for the milk which is used in the fluid milk industry and a lower price for the milk which is left over and which is processed into such manufactured items as ice cream, cottage cheese, skim milk, dry milk, etc. Under a marketwide pooling agreement, each producer receives the same blend-price for his milk, whether the milk goes into the Class I fluid milk classification or a manufactured milk classification.[3]

The federal government also intervenes in the dairy industry with a price support programme. In order to support milk prices, the federal government, through the Community Credit Corporation, agrees to buy cheese, non-fat dry milk, and butter at designated prices. Because the prices of these commodities are tied to the price of all milk through the milk marketing orders, the net effect is to support the price of all milk.

The dairy industry in the United States, like that in Canada and most West European countries, can be described as 'neo-corporatist' in nature, because of the importance of associations and clans and because of the extent to which public and private sectors are intricately intertwined. As a result of extensive governmental involvement, prices in the dairy industry are highly stable and producers and processors have relatively high returns on investment. In comparison with the prices of steers, hogs, broilers, corn, potatoes and oranges — i.e., those sectors in which co-operatives are not well developed — there is very little variation in milk prices. And the key variable in explaining variation in behaviour between the dairy industry and the meat and vegetable industries is organizational structure. Where there are extensive co-operatives, trade associations, and clan type activities involved in governing an industry — as in dairying — there is much greater price stability and much closer government-industry collaboration than in those sectors in which co-operatives are poorly developed and trade associations have little autonomy to represent the interests of the industry. Sectors with the latter characteristics have prices determined much more directly by the market.

We have seen that there is considerable variation across agricultural sectors in the role that state plays in the pricing of agricultural commodities. The state is a major player as well in other economic activities in the agricultural arena. For example, the state is very much involved in providing capital for agriculture and in promoting agricultural research. Largely as a result of the role of the state, the United States is one of the world's most efficient producers of agricultural commodities and is the world's leading exporter of agricultural commodities, and there are a number of indicators that suggest that its comparative advantage is growing (Evenson, 1982). In providing direct expenditures and credit, the state is heavily involved in the entire agricultural economy. The federal government, through the Commodity Credit Corporation, provides extensive support to agricultural producers when the national average market price for a commodity is below the target price set for it. The state, also through the Commodity Credit Corporation, provides credit in the form of loans to agricultural producers to finance their crops. Credit programmes are distinct from price supports and other direct expenditure programmes in that non-governmental financial institutions are often involved in implementing the federal programme. Basically there are two forms of agricultural credit programmes: direct government lending and government loan guarantees (for example, promises by the government that it will repay principal and interest in the event of default by borrowers: Bickers, 1984). It is the powerful role of major farm organizations (for example, American Farm Bureau Federation, National Farmers Union), as well as co-operatives and trade associations in individual sectors interacting in a close symbiotic manner with the US Department of Agriculture, which has led to heavy involvement of the state in the providing of capital to the various agricultural sectors.

Research conducted in the agricultural sector is of special interest. It is the interaction of the state, associative organizations, and clans that has contributed to making American agriculture so remarkably innovative. More specifically, the federally supported experimentation stations in affiliation with land-grant state universities and farmer interest organizations constitute the world's most complex system of agricultural research. While much of the research is funded at the federal level, very little research takes place in federal institutions. Throughout the country, there are 52 State Agricultural Experiment Stations which are integrated with state universities, state extension programmes, and local farm groups. The research, extension, and teaching programmes are generally state specific in nature. Thus, farmers are able to see to it that particular technologies are advanced as quickly as possible (Nelson, 1982: 466 – 7). The close clanlike relationship which exists among farmer organizations, state and federal government officials, and university researchers to promote and to disseminate agricultural innovations has been highly successful. Indeed, in no other sector of the American economy do agents of the state, industry representatives, and members of the research community work so closely in order to keep their sectors at the forefront of technological change.

Cell One B (relatively small firms with low levels of technological complexity producing differentiated projects)
Manufacturing sectors in this cell are made up of firms which are highly competitive and market-oriented, although hierarchies play some role in shaping prices and production quotas, in allocating capital, and/or in providing funds for research and development. Under certain conditions, hierarchies have become more extensively involved with sectors in this cell, via the corporate conglomerate-type firm. When large conglomerate firms have acquired ownership of firms operating in Cell One B, one finds a tendency for the corporate office to allocate capital to firms with a high yield and to monitor the efficiency performance of each firm. Because the central office can monitor the internal operations of a firm more effectively than external financial markets, there is some evidence that conglomerates

have more efficient resource allocation properties than banks or financial institutions external to the firm (Williamson, 1975).

The overwhelming majority of firms in this cell are not part of conglomerate operations, however. Because sectors in this cell are involved in labour-intensive production processes with low skill requirements, it has been relatively easy for less developed countries with only modest amounts of capital, technology, and skilled labour to enter the American market, meaning that firms compete vigorously not only with other American but with foreign firms as well.

The textile industry is fairly typical of manufacturing sectors in this cell. In order to promote stabilization and co-operation in the industry, firms have developed business trade associations. However, the trade associations have never been able to match the effectiveness of the bureaucracy of oligopolistically oriented sectors (for example, those in Cell Two) in achieving stability. Because of anti-trust legislation, business associations in this cell have also been unable to regulate prices and production levels. Nevertheless, manufacturing firms have engaged in associative behaviour in the standardization of products, the testing of materials, the promoting of markets, the development of industry codes of ethics, and the influencing of governmental policy.

Governmental policies are much more at arm's length in these sectors than in agriculture. In general, these are policies not designed to prevent problems, but policies designed in response to difficulties. The American government's use of Orderly Marketing Agreements (OMA) as a form of protectionist policy is an ideal-typical example of the role which the American state has played in the governance of several manufacturing sectors in Cell One B. An OMA is an agreement between two countries about the nature of their trade in regard to specific goods (for example, shoes, textiles, apparel, etc.). OMAs are generally used as protection against foreign competition in order to help well-organized, highly visible and vocal interest groups at the expense of consumers who are very diffuse. Because alternative policies, such as direct subsidies and credit policies are much more visible and more easily resisted, protectionism is preferred as a low cost, workable political strategy where direct state involvement and associative capacities are minimal. In the short term, plant closings are avoided and jobs are saved, though the long-term effects in terms of efficiency are another matter.

Whereas the associative structure of industry and state-industry relations is quite well developed in sectors in Cell One A, this is somewhat less true with sectors in Cell One B. As a result, firms, associations, and the state in Cell One B appear to have limited capacity to develop policies designed to promote sectoral innovation and readjustment. Partly because of the way in which American agriculture is governed, it is as efficient as any in the world. However, the weak associative structure, the lack of well-developed state policies, and a poorly developed set of networks (e.g., clans) tying together the key actors in the manufacturing sectors of Cell One B have meant that the market has been left with the major responsibility for governing these sectors. And it is problematic whether market forces have the potential to provide the readjustment required by mature industries in a stage of decline or transition.

The residential construction industry is another major sector in Cell One B, and its governance machinery is somewhat different from that in the manufacturing sectors. In both manufacturing and construction, the sectors are co-ordinated very much by market forces. Because of variation in consumer tastes, the construction industry is highly decentralized and fragmented into many different firms. For example, in the 1977 census of construction, there were approximately 100,000 firms in construction. Most firms were quite small, as more than 90 per cent of the firms employed fewer than 10 persons full-time.

However, mechanisms other than market forces are also important in governing this sector. Indeed, it is a mixture of market, hierarchical activity, and clan type networks, exemplified by the relationships that exist between general contractors and sub-contractors. Because general contractors and sub-contractors usually tend to work together over a long period of time, the relationship is somewhat clan-like in nature. In keeping track of materials and equipment, there are a variety of bureaucratic practices between contractors and sub-contractors and because contractors and sub-contractors work autonomously, their relationship is also governed by market forces.

While the state plays some role in this sector, its activities are less prominant than the market as a co-ordinating mechanism. Because of decentralized political jurisdictions and the diversity in the climate, there is great variety in building and zoning codes, meaning that construction regulations tend to be local rather than national in nature. Given the fragmentation of the industry and the large number of firms, the federal government has had little capacity to regulate the industry. The central government's main influence in the housing industry has been more indirect, resulting from its macroeconomic policy. As a result, the construction of residential housing has been subject to short-term cycles of three to five years, eight such cycles occurring between 1950 and 1980. The leading cause of this volatility has been a result of fluctuating interest rates. Of course, the federal government has also influenced the housing market, through massive mortgage loan guarantees and by subsidizing interest rates through VA and FHA housing loans.

While national level business associations have been generally weak, there are in the construction industry several of real importance: notably the Associated General Contractors Association and the National Association of Home Builders (Lawrence and Dyer, 1983). But the most important form of economic co-ordination of an associational nature in this industry is at the local level, in the form of employers' associations.[4]

Not only do local employer associations negotiate labour contracts, but they provide the following services for their members: public relations, lobbying, legal services, insurance. Of course, it is not only in the construction industry that employer associations play an important role in co-ordinating economic activity. They are also important in the following industries in Cell One B: hotel and restaurant, apparel and shoe, metal fabrication and scrap metal, printing, beer and liquor, food processing, retail trade. This is very much in contrast to the model of collective bargaining in the mass production industries with very large, nationally organized firms (see Cell Two). Those firms (for example, automobile, steel, rubber, oil refinery, among others) tend to conduct their own labour relations rather than rely on associational representation. But in the highly competitive sectors of Cell One B, dominated by small and medium sized firms, multi-employer bargaining at the local level through employer associations has been a common practice (Derber, 1984; Lawrence and Dyer, 1983).

Cell Two (large firms with low technological complexity)
While market forces are of some importance in the governance of sectors in this cell, most governance takes place through the hierarchical structure of the oligopolistic type firm or by what Chandler (1977) has called 'the visible hand'. Firms in many of these sectors are vertically or horizontally integrated so as to monitor and to evaluate complex economic activity, to allocate capital, technology, and personnel not only within the firm but also across industries and functional activities. Whereas historically transactions took place between firms at different stages in the production-distribution process or in different geographical areas, salaried managers within a single giant firm have taken over basic economic functions that had previously been carried out through market mechanisms. Refiners of products merge backward into exploration and production of raw materials, while manufacturers move forward into marketing and distribution.

The hierarchical structure of the firm (and managerial elites) enjoys substantial autonomy in the governance of these sectors. External controls from boards of directors, owners, banks, institutional investors and government regulators are all relatively weak. Where firms cannot finance investment out of retained earnings they tend to rely on capital markets in which stocks and bonds are the dominant source of industrial finance. Instead of exercising direct influence on the management of firms, investors and financial institutions tend to exit (e.g., sell their securities) if they are dissatisfied (Herman, 1981). In this way, financial markets somewhat paradoxically reinforce both the autonomy of managers and hierarchically organized firms and make them highly sensitive to short-term rate-of-return considerations as management seeks to prevent investors from exiting (Zysman, 1983).

Where there are oligopolistic sectors, there are also trade associations, but their functions are not as important in the co-ordination of economic activity as is the case with associations in Cells One A and One B. In the oligopolistic sectors, giant firms can carry out their own technical and market research, advertising, lobbying, and cost benefit analysis, whereas the small and middle sized firms in Cell One rely more heavily on business trade associations to carry out these functions. Most large firms in Cell Two have their own public affairs office, with many even having offices in Washington, while the smaller firms in Cell One B are much more dependent on trade associations in order to conduct public affairs.

Even if business trade associations are less important in the governance of oligopolistic sectors, the business elites of firms in these sectors are quite active in various types of informal networks (e.g., interlocking boards of directors) and in organizations which cut across many sectors of the economy, such as the Conference Board, the Business Council, the Committee on Economic Development, the Council on Foreign Relations. Somewhat clan-like in nature, these organizations attempt to transcend company, regional and sectoral considerations, and play an important role in influencing economic policies of an aggregate nature — policies affecting the entire economy instead of policies that are sector specific (Useem, 1984).

In Japan, steel, auto, and other firms in Cell Two industries have strong clan-type relationships with banks, suppliers and politicians. In the United States, however, relationships are more arm's length among firms in these sectors. For example, in Japan, there are very close clan-like ties between auto companies and their suppliers. This relationship promotes close communication out of which there is a steady stream of new ideas from which innovative products emerge. In the United States, however, auto firms and suppliers lack this clan type of relationship. Instead, the ties between auto companies and suppliers are primarily contractual, formal and rigid in nature. And this more formal relationship at the sectoral level seems to lead to less innovativeness and greater standardization on the part of American producers (Zysman, 1983).

Because clan-like organizations (such as the Business Council and the Conference Board) which transcend specific sectors are far more influential than sectorally specific business associations in the shaping of state policies, it is not surprising that state policies tend to reflect the interests of the former more than the latter.

In so far as there are sectorally-specific policies designed for sectors located in Cell Two, they tend to be regulatory in nature (for example, auto safety, fuel emission control, pollution standards for the metal industries, pure food in the food industries). In so far as non-regulatory policies are concerned, business firms in this sector and the state have tended to prefer policies with aggregate objectives, believing that economic co-ordination should be handled primarily by the firm or by market forces. There is a distinctive 'industrial culture' (Dyson and Wilks, 1983) shared by the business elites of this cell (just as there is a different type of industrial culture operating in some of the agricultural sectors). As Kurth (1979) demonstrates, the expectations of government are shaped very much by the stage in the product life cycle at which the industry first developed. In the US, these sectors were well established before they were mature industries vis-à-vis the world economy. Hence, they developed without strong state assistance, and there has grown up among government and the business elites involved the expectation that the state's role should be kept to a minimum. As these sectors have matured on a worldwide level and American firms have become threatened by exports from foreign countries, business, and government elites involved have found it difficult to re-define a role for the state to play in the restructuring of these sectors.

Aggregated oriented policies, especially the manipulation of interest rates, influence the sales of steel, autos, farm equipment, etc. In addition, investment tax credits have some benefits for capital goods industries. Aggregate policies are designed to enhance market mechanisms, not to replace them. They are consistent with a widely shared belief that government intervention should not overtly discriminate among sectors and/or firms. On the other hand, there are protectionist policies which are sectorally oriented, but they are perceived as exceptions to policies which are legitimate to this sector and are generally ineffective in restructuring particular industries. Distressed industries or firms seek help from government in an ad hoc manner, while successful firms or industries prefer to remain quite autonomous from government.

Because of the type of industrial culture which is typical among sectors in Cell Two, the Department of Commerce does not have the close ties to these sectors which the Department of Agriculture has to various agricultural industries. Hence, the state does not systematically support research and development, nor does it play an active role in reporting to firms the type of innovations which are taking place in other countries.

Of course, there are limits to the power of corporate hierarchies to co-ordinate economic activity. For example, anti-trust laws present an obstacle to sector wide collaboration on production, commercial and trade matters. Firms cannot by joint agreement fix or stabilize prices, allocate territories, limit market entry, or regulate production. Moreover, anti-trust activity regulates the pooling of research and development, as well as the pooling of technical and marketing information. While the Capper-Volstead Act has exempted many functions of agricultural co-operatives from anti-trust legislation, trade associations in these sectors, as well as in sectors in Cells One B, Three, and Four are also very much constrained by anti-trust legislation.

In sum, Cell Two sectors are very much co-ordinated by the visible hand of large corporate firms, though limited by anti-trust legislation. Markets, particularly financial markets, are of some importance in economic co-ordination. Most state policy is regulatory in nature and is interventionist in specific sectors only on an ad hoc basis at times of distress or crisis. In general, state policy is sectorally neutral with aggregate rather than sectorally specific goals.

Cell Three (relatively small firms with high technological complexity)
As suggested above, the technology of sectors in this cell is quite complex and changes very rapidly. On a world-wide scale, American firms in these sectors have performed very well. However, the governing mechanisms have been quite different from those in Cells One and Two.

Because most firms in these sectors are in the early stages of the product life cycle, business trade associations are not very well developed, and their functions are somewhat less important in the overall co-ordination of these sectors than is the case with associative behaviour in Cells One A and One B. Rather, a great deal of economic governance in this cell occurs primarily as a result of market activity. And in contrast to Cell Two, most companies in Cell Three are too small for the visible hand of the corporate firm to play an important role in governing an entire industry.

On the other hand, the state through its research, development, and procurement policies, as well as through its patent policies has played an important role in governance. However, the American state has no systematic set of policies for intervening in fast-growing high tech sectors. Indeed, there is a policy for the state not to be actively interventionist except when national security interests are defined as being involved. However, a number of such sectors have fallen within this category, particularly those involving military and space programme activities.

The semiconductor industry is an excellent example of how a sector in this cell is governed when it is alleged to involve national security considerations. In comparison with sectors involving aviation and agriculture, the role of the state in the development of the semiconductor industry has been modest. Nevertheless, the procurement of electronic components and systems by the American military, and public support for research, development, and production engineering by the military, NASA, the National Science Foundation, and the National Bureau of Standards (Levin, 1982: 9; Borrus, Millstein, and Zysman, 1983) have been very important in advancing the industry. However, the bulk of innovative work in the development of semiconductor technology has taken place in private firms, with government labs playing an insignificant role.

In contrast to the structure of industry in Cells One B and Two, there are numerous clan-like networks in most of the industrial sectors in this cell. For example, in the semiconductor industry, there have historically been close networks among people in government, industries, and universities. Indeed, it is not an exaggeration to suggest that clan-like activity has been pervasive in this industry. Networks have been so close that Levin argues that one can easily trace a genealogy of the industry. For example, Bell Labs begat the Shockley Transistor, Shockley begat Fairchild, Fairchild begat Signetics, General Microelectronics, and Intel, among others, and each of these fourth-generation firms has numerous progeny of its own (Levin, 1982: 28). And throughout the semiconductor industry, there is a strong professional culture which has facilitated the free exchange of technical information and the mobility of personnel. A clan of university researchers has been very much involved in these networks from the beginning. In fact, it was the electrical engineering faculties of Stanford University and nearby University of California, Berkeley which were responsible for the location of numerous semiconductor firms in the Santa Clara Valley of California. But despite these extensive networks, the commercial potential of the industry was not understood well in the early years of the semiconductor industry. However, the military and NASA were willing to provide substantial money for research and development as incentives for companies to enter the field. Moreover, the large procurement orders by the government provided a cumulative production experience for contractors, facilitating the learning necessary to reduce costs. While few major innovations emerged directly from government-funded research and development, the government did move flexibly in response to each new technology early in the life cycle with substantial research development funds. Because the government was not a disinterested player but was the major consumer of the new technology, it was in a strategic position to evaluate alternative forms of technology and to provide valuable feedback to contractors. Of course, the government's willingness to purchase high volumes of the industry's output at very attractive prices did much to accelerate the pace at which the industry developed. However, the government was willing to lead the industry by specifying clear technological objectives without rigidly specifying the means to achieve them (Levin, 1982: 89).

By 1980, the industry had reached a more mature stage, and the state was no longer in a position to direct the industry's technological changes in accord with its needs as a consumer. Indeed, commercial users have become more important than the military and NASA. Meanwhile, the technological advances have become incremental and rather predictable. In sum, the history of this sector is one involving the state in high and complex technology before the commercial potential of the sector was well understood. Significantly, an alternative set of government policies was not likely to have had a major effect in developing the industry in such a short period of time. For example, the government's patent policies were relatively unimportant in the development of the semiconductor, and they had little potential to develop the industry. Large-scale integrated circuits could not be patented because they could not be described in the form of a valid patent claim. Also, the technology was changing too rapidly for firms to benefit significantly by the monopoly conferred by patents. Moreover, there is no reason to think that tax credits for research and development or some other form of undirected state subsidy would have been highly productive in a relatively short period of time.

In the pharmaceutical industry, however, patents are an important part of the innovative process, very much in contrast to the semiconductor and several other technologically complex industries. In theory, patents provide firms a stimulus to engage in innovative activity by granting them monopoly rights to exploit their inventions. In addition to providing patents, the state is involved in the pharmaceutical industry in several other respects. First, the state provides funding for basic research in the medical sciences, some of which is channelled toward pharmaceutical research. This has been the case in such diverse fields as immunology, molecular biology, and enzyme chemistry. Even so, the state's *direct* role in the development of new pharmaceuticals has been limited, in contrast to the semiconductor industry. An area in which the state has been directly involved in the development of new drugs has been in cancer research under the authority of the National Cancer Institute Drug Development Program with an annual budget in excess of $200 million. Another has been in the development of so-called 'orphan drugs'. These are drugs for rare diseases, but because there is such a limited market for them, it is unlikely that commercial firms will attempt to develop them.

Markets and the state are the two most important mechanisms involved in the governance of this industry. Aside from its patents policies, the state is heavily involved in regulating the pharmaceutical industry. By law, the Food and Drug Administration is required to certify that each new drug is not only safe but is efficacious as well. As a result of extensive governmental regulations, numerous studies have postulated that the costs of discovering and developing new drugs have increased so much that there has been a decline in the number of new drug innovations in the United States. While the overall consequences of the regulatory process is open to dispute, there appears to be little doubt that the regulatory process has more than doubled the costs of developing new chemical entities in the pharmaceutical industry since 1962. Moreover, government has delayed the introduction of new drugs into the American market in comparison with countries with a different regulatory process. Of course, the length of time required to test for the safety and the efficacy of new drugs reduces the effective time that a company may enjoy the monopoly privileges conferred by a government patent. Partly as a result, the average effective patent life for new chemical entities declined in the United States from 13.6 years in 1966 to 9.5 years in 1979 (Grabowski and Vernon, 1982; Wardell, 1979; Wardell and Lasagna, 1975).

Business trade associations are relatively unimportant in the governance of most industries in Cell Three. In the United States, associative behaviour tends to be more important in declining industries — or those in a stage of transition — rather than in those which are in the early stages of the product life cycle. On the other hand, clan-type activity is important throughout industries in Cell Three. Where the state is involved in a regulatory or adversarial role, however, the state is generally not part of the clan-like network — as was the case in the semiconductor industry, or in the agricultural sector. However, there are close networks involving the personnel of major pharmaceutical firms and university researchers. Many of the clinical studies required for FDA approval of new drugs are conducted at university medical centers, and major pharmaceutical firms provide substantial research grants to universities. Moreover, business and university personnel attend many conferences together and are active in many professional and scientific associations. It is as a result of this close interaction that scientists in many pharmaceutical companies frequently collaborate with university scientists on joint research projects.

In sum, associative behaviour is not very important in the governance of sectors in this cell. The state is important in product development, either through patent policies, research and development funding, or procurement policies. Finally, clans, or networks are important in most every sector in this cell. It is through informal networks that scientific and technical information flows horizontally among firms and various elements in their environments. Moreover, these informal networks provide the kind of links among sectors which permit the rapid diffusion of information about new markets and technologies.

Cell Four (large firms and high technological complexity)
Like the sectors in Cell Two, governance among the sectors in Cell Four is done very much by hierarchy, both by firms and by the state. However, clan activities are also very pronounced in some sectors. Trade associations, however, are relatively unimportant as co-ordinating mechanisms because, as suggested earlier, American trade associations generally provide fewer governance functions where oligopolistic firms dominate. The following discussion of the aircraft and computer industry are suggestions of how some sectors in this cell are governed.

In both sectors, federal research and development funding as well as procurement have been important in product development, as in the semiconductor industry. For example, a large proportion of the innovations in commercial aircraft design were originally developed by manufacturers for military application. Such a list would include the DC-3, as well as the DC-8, DC-10, the L-1011, and the Boeing 747 jumbo jet.

Because of the high degree of complexity of the products used in the aircraft industry, there is considerable borrowing from other industries. And this has meant the development of close, clan-type relationships among firms in complementary industries. The aircraft industry has developed such relationships not only with firms in the metallurgical and electronics industries but also with firms in the manufacture of equipment involving communications, navigation, radar, and instrumentation. While the aircraft industry is not vertically integrated, it is through clan-like networks that very close relationships have developed between manufacturing firms and their major sub-contractors. Most major airframe producers lack all the in-house expertise to develop and produce aircraft. Hence, clan-type relationships through sub-contracting have become increasingly important in the industry. For example, in the 1930s, sub-contracting constituted less than 10 per cent of the industry's operations. By the 1950s, Lockheed was subcontracting for almost 40 per cent of its major products, while at the present, Boeing in the production of the 747 jumbo jet sub-contracts for almost 70 per cent of the assembly costs. And increasingly, the sub-contractor and the prime contractor share substantially in the development costs. But it has been the state through its research and development funding which has been responsible for each new major innovation in the American aircraft industry. In general, it was the assurance of a market for military aircraft which provided manufacturers with the incentive to develop highly complex and costly new technologies (Mowery and Rosenberg, 1982; Rae, 1968).

A comparable process was also quite evident in the history of the mainframe computer industry. In the face of imperfect market information and technological uncertainty, the state through research and development funding, was directly and intimately involved in the development of the first and second generation mainframe computers. However, in the early stages of the industry, there were well-developed, clan-like networks. For example, in the late 1940s there were frequent conferences involving key players, the participants coming from the Departments of the Navy, Army and the National Bureau of Standards, the nation's leading universities, and from about a dozen major corporations. Many of the participants knew virtually everyone in every major organization interested in research on computers.

But the key to the early development of computers was the influence of the Department of Defense, for until the mid 1950s there was no commercial market for mainframe computers. Moreover, the first attempts to develop computers for a commercial market were basically by-products which were developed in response to government funding. It was only after 1960 that there was a decrease in the state's influence on the development of the computer industry. Throughout the 1960s and 1970s, however, the state, as a major consumer of computers, continued to have a substantial effect on the industry's future. Eventually, however, a few firms were able to survive whether or not they had government funding. But in the early stages of this industry, public and private hierarchies, operating through clan-like networks, were far more important than markets and associative behaviour as mechanisms driving the industry (Katz and Phillips, 1982; Goldstine, 1972; Hurd, 1980).

State and corporate hierarchies have also predominated in the governance of industries in the telecommunications and nuclear power sectors, although the efficiency and adaptability record differs sharply between the two. Both are what we might call infrastructure sectors in that their development is closely tied to the dynamic evolution of other economic sectors or they provide essential services to all consumers. Both sectors involve closely co-ordinating the activities of numerous industries, each based on highly complex and volatile technologies of great public salience. For these reasons both sectors have been subject to extensive state regulation and general participation in financing research.

The coming of electric and electronic communications transformed the structure of American business, making possible the growth of large-scale hierarchical enterprise (Lawrence and Dyer, 1983: 197 – 8). Furthermore, the industry was itself a pioneer in the evolution from family-owned small firms to the large bureaucratic organization dominated by professional managers. After early stages marked by chaotic competition and instability (i.e. price wars, duplication of equipment, shoddy construction, bankruptcies and predatory competition), monopoly firms began to emerge as early as the 1860s and 1870s: first Western Union, then Western Electric, Bell Laboratories and the AT & T system. Between 1913 and the 1930s the telephone business came to be considered a public utility and natural monopoly, and these large firms were granted virtual national monopoly status, combined with public regulation of rates of return and competitive practices.

Until the 1970s this combination of state regulated national monopoly and the hierarchical structure of AT & T effectively supplanted markets, as well as associations and clans as governance mechanisms in this sector. During this period of market dominance, AT & T (and Bell Labs) chalked up an impressive 'sustained record of innovation and efficiency' and were 'responsible for most of the significant inventions and new technologies in the communications industry during this century' (Lawrence and Dyer, 1983: 222).

In the 1970s, however, new transmission technologies and the development of increasingly sophisticated terminal equipment spelled the virtual disappearance of the distinction between data processing and data transmission. New competitive products and services emerged outside of the AT & T system to meet rapidly expanding demand. These forces have provoked major changes in the governance of the sector. Pressures from competition, combined with government initiated and court ordered regulation, to produce the partial break-up of the AT & T system. Whether hitherto relatively weak associational activity and clan structures (Ouchi, 1980: 162-163) will evolve to take up the slack in co-ordinating activities in the increasingly interactive network linking government regulators and procurement agencies, to transmission, terminal and switching equipment and service industries, remains an open question. Some expect such giant firms as IBM and the revamped AT&T gradually to restore a pattern of hierarchical governance to the sector.

In the nuclear power industry the state's role as regulator, political sponsor, and research and development funder has been closely bound up with the military origins and public safety implications of the technology. The whole development of the nuclear reactor industry, which has been dominated by General Electric and Westinghouse, is closely linked to federal government political and policy initiatives and to research carried out in a network of government laboratories (often managed by private contractors). But co-ordination mechanisms *across the sector* have not been able to stabilize relationships among relevant actors, as is exemplified by the declining fortunes of several of the component firms since the mid 1970s. The technology has proven to be singularly 'unforgiving' in terms of admissable error and public reaction. Intra-industry competition prevented agreement on a standardized reactor design, and free rider behaviour by the industry left open the back end of the fuel cycle (nuclear wastes). Successful development of the industry seems to require a degree of vertical and horizontal integration among capital markets, architect engineers, reactor vendors, providers of nuclear fuel and waste disposal services, reactor operators (investor-owned public utilities), and regulators at the state and federal levels, that corporate and state hierarchies in the United States have to date been unable to provide (Campbell, 1984). Clan structures and associations like the Electrical Power Research Institute, the Nuclear Power Forum, and the Edison Electrical Institute have been unable to fill the gap.

Conclusion
The previous discussion has focused primarily on the various mechanisms by which different sectors are governed in the American economy. Because of its complexity and diversity, it was not possible to cover more than a few sectors representative of four different categories of resource and information constraints. Nevertheless, by focusing on a few key sectors within each of the four cells, it is possible to gain an initial appreciation of the variety of governance arrangements that mediate the relationships of firms and their environments in the American economy.

Figure 2 presents a brief summary of the mix of governance mechanisms in the various cells of our typology of the American economy. The particular mix that prevails in the United States is of course conditioned and constrained by general political and institutional factors: the pattern of inter and intra-industry competitiveness; the relatively low capacity for collective action; the distribution of power and ideological persuasion; institutional fragmentation; the character of the financial system; the selective strength of the American state; and established constitutional and legal norms.

FIGURE 2
Strength of governing mechanisms in various sectors of American economy

Cell One A	Cell One B	Cell Two
Small firms with low levels of technological complexity producing undifferentiated products	Small firms with low levels of technological complexity producing differentiated products	Large firms with low levels of technological complexity

Markets
Hierarchy
  State[1]
  Corporate structure*
Clans[1]
Associations[1]
[1] In this cell, either a) markets are **** and the following relationships exist: state*** clans*, associations*, or b) markets are, * and the following relationships exist: state****, associations****, clans***.
	Markets***
	Hierarchy
	  State*
	  Corporate structure*
	Clans*
	Associations***
		Markets*
		Hierarchy
		  State*
		  Corporate structure***
		Clans*
		Associations*

Cell Three	Cell Four	
Small firms with high technological complexity	Large firms with high levels of technological complexity	

Markets***
Hierarchy
  State***
  Corporate stucture*
Clans***
Associations*
	Markets*
	Hierarchy
	  State***
	  Corporate structure***
	Clans***
	Associations*	

The strength of various governance mechanisms:
very strong****, moderately strong***, of some importance**, quite weak*

In Figure 2, one observes that each form of governance is found in each cell, though their importance varies from cell to cell. While the previous discussion has focused primarily on the various cells, the following is a brief summary statement regarding the different governance mechanisms.

The State. While the state is somewhat less involved in the American economy than is the case in most highly industrialized societies, its role in governance varies across sectors and with the level at which regulation occurs (national, regional, local). The state has been a very active player in the development of technology in industries involving agriculture (Cell One A), semiconductors, and pharmaceuticals (Cell Three), aircraft, computers and nuclear power (Cell Four). In agriculture, much of the state's involvement has been very decentralized, with the consequence that farmer organizations have played in important role in shaping the state's research and development programmes through active university and extension research programmes. In the aircraft, semiconductor, nuclear, and computer industries, the state — at the central level — has supported complex technologies early in their product life cycle. Because the state was a major consumer of the technology, it was intimately and directly involved in evaluating and developing alternative types of technology in each industry. Once viable commercial markets existed in these sectors, however, the government's role declined in the shaping of technological change.

The state's patent policies have been quite important in shaping technological change when there are specific products which have somewhat stable lines. However, an industry such as the semiconductor is so unstable that patents have provided firms with little incentive for technological development. Moreover, patents are of little consequence in the computer, the automotive, or the aircraft industry, for in these industries it has been the engineering of an entire product which has been important. However, the government's patent policies have been of great importance in promoting new products in the pharmaceutical industry.

Of course, the state is very much involved in regulating economic activity. Local governments regulate the construction, restaurant, and numerous other industries in which local officials can efficiently obtain information. In some industries in which the firms are national in scope, however, the federal government is the major regulatory agency. Thus, the federal government is very much involved in regulating air and water pollutant emissions from factories, workplace practices which impinge on the health and safety of workers, product safety, and so on. While there has been considerable discussion about the negative consequences of state regulatory practices on performance, there is very little evidence that state regulations, measured in the aggregate, have had much of a negative impact on the economy (Christiansen and Haveman, 1982).

Corporate hierarchies. These seem to develop where market co-ordination is allowed to prevail in monopoly or oligopoly sectors. They have to a substantial degree internalized many of the functions of markets, clans, and associations in sectors in Cell Two. In Cell Four interdependent corporate and state hierarchies predominate over markets and associations as governing mechanisms. Cell Two sectors and industries seem to have developed managerial hierarchies where demand has been sensitive to marketing instruments, where capital and energy-intensive technologies allowed economies of scale in processing and assembling large volumes of raw materials and semi-finished goods into equally large volumes of standardized producer or consumer goods, where a relatively high share of fixed costs makes profits volatile, or where products are perishable and processing and distribution time are central to profits (Chandler and Daems, 1980).

In Cell Four, the infrastructural character of the goods and services provided, the complexity of products, the pace of technological change, and the dependence on research and development have encouraged the development of stable hierarchically organized firms enjoying monopoly or oligopoly positions. Here too, we have seen the development of the large industrial research laboratories (or state-owned, industry managed public labs) where research activities need to be closely linked to marketing and production operations.

The allocative and dynamic efficiency effects of such corporate hierarchies have been generally neglected by economists. Some scholars (Piore and Sabel, 1984) now suggest that the mass production industries represented in Cell Two may be irretrievably in decline unless they change their structures, due to changes in technological and competitive conditions that render their internal and external governance arrangements dysfunctional. Similarly, several Cell Four sectors that have been government-regulated monopolies are being transformed by competitive pressures and by government deregulation or reregulation. Whether these changes will improve their efficiency and adaptability remains to be seen.

Associative behaviour
If co-ordination by corporate hierarchy developed later and somewhat less extensively in Western Europe than in the United States (see Chandler and Daems, 1980), associative behaviour in the form of horizontally and vertically integrated systems of associations (or government-sanctioned cartels) has been much more important in most sectors of European economies. Government policies and

constitutional constraints, and the prevailing preferences of managers, are important factors explaining such differences. In the United States associational behaviour is most developed in Cells One A and One B. Business associations are least important in the governing of sectors which are very early in their product life cycles (e.g., Cell Three). Moreover, the oligopolistic type firms in Cell Two and Cell Four fulfil many of the functions of business associations; that is, they conduct much of their own advertising, research, lobbying, public relations, etc.

In general, peak associations are very weak — almost non-existent in the United States. Of course, there are ad hoc alliances, joint task forces, and the sharing of facilities among associations in all cells. American associations tend to enjoy very little autonomy from their members, with the exception of a few sectors in the agriculture area — notably the dairy industry.

Even though there is a low level of organizational development among business associations in the United States, the role which business associations play in the governance of the economy varies over time and across sectors of the economy, depending on a host of characteristics. Schmitter and Brand (1979) have argued that capitalists organize in response to:

(1) the prior organization of workers;

(2) conflicts with and the prior organizational efforts of other capitalists in competing sectors;

(3) changes in the division of labour, market complexity, the structure of product competition, and the stage of the product life cycle;

(4) changing conditions of international competition;

(5) changing imperative of public policy; and

(6) unforeseen events such as war, production failures, and product substitution.

Clan type co-ordination. Although co-ordination through clans is not as well developed overall in the United States as in some other countries, notably Japan (see Ouchi, 1984), there are important sectoral variations. Clan-type co-ordination is far more involved in the economic activity of Cells One A, Three, and Four than in Cells One B and Two. In industries with high levels of technological complexity, there are serious efforts to develop effective communication among suppliers, researchers, financiers, management and workers. Individuals in complementary firms have a fairly high capability to converse and to think in highly specialized languages and dialects. In more mature industries (Cells One B and Two), however, clan type activity is less common. Partly as a result, American firms producing more standardized products find it far more difficult to adjust rapidly to product changes than their Japanese competitors who are firmly embedded in clan-like networks.

Thus, while the corporate hierarchy plays an important role in governing the American economy in sectors located in Cell Two, firms in this cell are not integrated into effective clan like networks. As a result, information about innovations is often slow to percolate up the chain of command in the hierarchical structure of the American corporation. Observers who have studied the failure of American steel firms to invest in the latest technology in the 1960s place considerable emphasis on the lack of a clan like structure which could have facilitated the communication of information about the latest technology (Adams, 1971).

Markets. Although widely held to be the most important mechanisms co-ordinating the activities of firms and their relevant environments in the American economy, markets in fact operate very unevenly. Indeed, they appear to predominate only in Cell One B. Firms in that cell, in contrast to those in Cell Two, have historically had a high ratio of variable to fixed costs, have been more labour intensive, and have had relatively low potential for scale economies in either production or marketing. As a result, small firms with price and production flexibility have historically been able to enter industries in this cell. In all other cells market co-ordination is supplemented or mediated — in some cases supplanted — by other collective decision arrangements. The analysis presented in this chapter suggests that these 'non-market' governance mechanisms emerge as part of an ongoing process of adaptation by complex organizations to technological change and to changes in business structure and competitive conditions.

Most economists tend to see these either as unimportant or as deformations or pathological growths impeding economic efficiency. The material presented here suggests it is doubtful that either view takes us very far in understanding how and why these other mechanisms emerge and what role they play in furthering allocative efficiency, economic stabilization, or adaptation to political and economic uncertainty.

Of course, market *ideology* is much more dominant in the United States than in most other countries. So too, is the autonomous corporation and its managerial elite less bounded by or integrated into a web of relationships involving the state bureaucracy, labour, banks, and other organizations. Together these may indeed permit public and private initiatives which are *market regarding*, at least in early stages of the product cycle, and to limit or roll back the intrusions of labour or the access of non-business interests to the state bureaucracy and state budget. Whether this encourages long-term economic and political stability and adaptation is somewhat less clear.

This chapter has demonstrated that the governance of the American economy is far more complex than most of the scholarly literature would have us believe. To understand the governance of the *entire* American economy however, a very large research agenda is necessary. This chapter has been limited to a descriptive sketch of the role of markets, hierarchy, clans, and associative behaviour in the governance of a few sectors. This analysis needs to be refined and extended to a wider range of sectors and industries, and we need to probe more deeply into the reasons why a particular mix of governance mechanics has emerged in particular kinds of sectors. Furthermore, three topics important to future study have been entirely neglected.

Firstly, we now need to move to a more complex level of analysis. Specifically, we should attempt to specify how the various mixes of governing mechanisms influence the *static and dynamic performance* of each sector. From a theoretical point of view this will be difficult to do, but there is an emerging body of somewhat anecdotal and case study evidence that might be brought to bear (Ouchi, 1984; Herman, 1981; Reich, 1983; Magaziner and Reich, 1982; Piore and Sabel, 1984).

Secondly, we need to understand how the structure of the firm influences performance. The history of the steel industry in the United States suggests that the very hierarchical, authoritarian structure of some firms was responsible for their being poorly co-ordinated, relying on antiquated systems of cost accounting, having inadequate knowledge of domestic markets, and having cost standards generally below those considered everyday practice in other industries. In contrast, the history of the computer industry suggests that the internal structure of IBM was the most important reason why it succeeded in the mainframe computer industry while Bendix, Philco, GE, RCA, Raytheon and numerous other firms with quite different structures but which attempted to compete in the mainframe computer industry were relatively unsuccessful. Indeed the histories of these two industries — as well as that of many others — suggest that the internal organizational structure of firms may be as important as their relationship to external forces in determining their market performance (Adams, 1971: 70–116; Katz and Phillips, 1982: 213). If so, we must focus attention on the internal structure of firms as well as on the governing mechanisms of entire sectors of the economy if we are to advance our understanding of how an economy performs.

Finally, we need to explore the policy implications of the kind of institutional analysis proposed here. In particular, debates about industrial policies, or how to develop government-business-labour relationships more appropriate to flexible adjustment to changing economic conditions, will remain diffuse and basically ideological until they are informed by an understanding of how different sectors of the economy are in fact 'governed' and how these governance arrangements are performing under current conditions. Our premise is that the governance structure of a sector or industry not only helps shape its economic performance, but that it also defines both the needs for and the constraints on government policies designed to improve industrial performance.

Notes

1. In the development of this four cell table, we are indebted to Jerald Hage for numerous stimulating conversations on the subject. See Hage and Clignet (1982).
2. For scholarship which confronts the issue of performance at the firm level, and which operates at the social psychological level, emphasizing informational perspectives, leadership characteristics, decision making processes, and methods of organizational learning, and conflict resolution, see Argyris and Schon, 1960; Fiedler 1967; March and Olsen, 1976; March and Simon, 1958; Sherif, 1962; and Weick, 1980. For studies that address performance by focusing on the structural characteristics of firms, see Chandler, 1962, 1977; Hage 1980, Mintzberg, 1979; and Lawrence and Lorsch, 1967. For an effort to integrate both perspectives, see Lawrence and Dyer, 1983.
3. This discussion of the dairy industry is based on the unpublished papers by Young et al. (1985) and Vander Schaaf (1984).
4. As a result of thousands of collective bargaining agreements between local craft unions and employers associations, there did emerge however in 1978 the National Construction Employers Council which was designed to parallel the AFL-CIO Building and Construction Trades Department for unions. As a result of anti-union or open-shop activities in the construction industry, there is also a national association of non-union contractors, the Associated Builders and Contractors, consisting of forty-five local or state chapters representing some 8000 construction firms.

References

Adams, Walter (1971). *The Structure of American Industry*. New York: The Macmillan Co.
Argyris, Chris and Donald A. Schon (1978). *Occupational Learning: A Theory of Action Perspective*. Reading, Mass: Addison Wesley.
Bickers, Kenneth (1984). 'U.S. Industrial Policy and the Institutional Organization of American Industries', Unpublished paper. Madison: University of Wisconsin.
Borrus, Michael, James E. Millstein and John Zysman (1983). 'Trade and Development in the Semiconductor Industry: Japanese Challenge and American Response', pp. 142-248 in John Zysman and Laura Tyson (eds), *American Industry in International Competition*. Ithaca: Cornell University Press.
Campbell, John, *Can We Plan? The Political Economy of Commercial Nuclear Energy Policy in the United States* (1984). Ph.D. Dissertation, University of Wisconsin in Madison, Department of Sociology.
Chandler, Alfred D. (1962). *Strategy and Structure*. New York: Doubleday.
Chandler, Alfred D. (1977). *The Visible Hand*. Cambridge, Mass.: Harvard University Press.
Chandler, Alfred D. and Herman Daems (eds) (1980). *Managerial Hierarchies: The*

Rise of the Modern Industrial Enterprise. Cambridge, Mass.: Harvard University Press.

Christiansen, Gregory B. and Robert A. Haveman (1982). 'Government Regulations and Their Impact on the Economy', pp. 112-23, in J. Rogers Hollingsworth (ed.) *Government and Economic Performance*. Beverly Hills: Sage Publications.

Derber, Milton (1984). 'Employers Associations in the United States', pp. 79-114 in John P. Windmuller and Alan Gladstone (eds), *Employers Associations and Industrial Relations: A Comparative Study*. Oxford: Clarendon Press.

Dyson, Kenneth and Stephen Wilks (eds) (1983). *Industrial Crisis*. Oxford: Martin Robertson.

Evenson, R.E. (1982). 'Agriculture', pp. 233-82 in Richard R. Nelson (ed.), *Government and Technical Progress*. New York: Pergamon Press.

Fiedler, Fred E. (1967). *A Theory of Leadership Effectiveness*. New York: McGraw-Hill.

Goldstine, Herman H. (1972). *The Computer from Pascal to Von Neumann*. Princeton: Princeton University Press.

Grabowski, Henry G. and John M. Vernon (1982). 'The Pharmaceutical Industry', pp. 283-360 in Richard R. Nelson (ed.), *Government and Technical Progress*. New York: Pergamon Press.

Hage, Jerald (1980). *Theories of Organizations: Forms, Process, and Transformation*. New York: John Wiley and Sons.

Hage, Jerald and Remi Clignet (1982). 'Coordination Styles and Economic Growth', pp. 72-92 in J. Rogers Hollingsworth (ed.) *Government and Economic Performance*. Beverly Hills: Sage Publications.

Herman, Edward S. (1981). *Corporate Control, Corporate Power*. New York: Cambridge University Press.

Hurd, Cuthbert (1980). 'Computer Development at IBM', in N. Metropolis, J. Howlett and Gian-Carlo Rota (eds) *A History of Computing in the Twentieth Century*. New York: Academic Press.

Katz, Barbara Goody and Almarin Phillips (1982). 'The Computer Industry', pp. 162-232 in Richard R. Nelson (ed.) *Government and Technical Progress*. New York: Pergamon Press.

Katzenstein, Peter (ed.) (1978). *Between Power and Plenty*. Madison: University of Wisconsin Press.

Kurth, James (1979). 'The Political Consequences of the Product Cycle: Industrial History and Political Outcomes', *International Organization*, 33: 1-34.

Lawrence, Paul R. and Davis Dyer (1983). *Renewing American Industry*. New York: The Free Press.

Lawrence, Paul R. and Jay W. Lorsch (1967). *Organization and Environment*. Boston: Harvard University Graduate School of Business Administration.

Levin, Richard C. (1982). 'The Semiconductor Industry', pp. 9-100 in Richard R. Nelson (ed.), *Government and Technical Progress*. New York: Pergamon Press.

Lowi, Theodore J. (1969). *The End of Liberalism*. New York: Norton.

Magaziner, Ira C., and Robert B. Reich (1982). *Minding America's Business*. New York: Harcourt, Brace, Jovanovich Publishers.

March, James and Herbert Simon (1958). *Organizations*. New York: John Wiley.

Mintzberg, Henry (1979). *The Structuring of Organizations*. New York: Prentice-Hall.

Mowery, David C. and Nathan Rosenberg (1982). 'The Commercial Aircraft Industry', pp. 101-61 in Richard R. Nelson (ed.) *Government and Technical Progress*. New York: Pergamon Press.

Nelson, Richard R. (ed.) (1982). *Government and Technical Progress: A Cross-Industry Analysis*. New York: Pergamon Press.

Nelson, Richard R., Merton J. Peck and Edward D. Kalachek (1967). *Technology, Economic Growth, and Public Policy*. Washington, DC: The Brookings Institute.
Ouchi, William G. (1977). 'Review of *Markets and Hierarchies* by Oliver E. Williamson', *Administrative Science Quarterly*, 22: 540-4.
Ouchi, William G. (1980). 'Markets, Bureaucracies, and Clans', *Administrative Science Quarterly*, 25: 129-41.
Ouchi, William G. (1984) *The M-Form Society*. Reading Massachusetts: Addison Wesley Publishing Co.
Piore, Michael J., and Charles F. Sabel (1984). *The Second Industrial Divide: Possibilities for Prosperity*. New York: Basic Books.
Phillips, Almarin (1975). *Technology and Market Structure: A Study of the Aircraft Industry*. Lexington: D.C. Heath.
Rae, J.B. (1968). *Climb to Greatness*. Cambridge, Mass.: MIT Press.
Reich, Robert B. (1983). *The Next American Frontier*. New York: Times Books.
Schmitter, Philippe C. and Donald Brand (1979). 'Organizing Capitalists in the United States: The Advantages and Disadvantages of Exceptionalism'. Unpublished paper presented before the American Political Science Association.
Schmitter, Philippe C. and Wolfgang Streeck (1981). 'The Organization of Business in Advanced Industrial Societies of Western Europe'. Berlin: International Institute of Management, Discussion Paper No. 81-13.
Sherif, Muzafer (1962). *Intergroup Relations and Leadership, Approaches and Research in Industrial, Ethnic, Cultural and Political Areas*. New York: John Wiley.
Streeck, Wolfgang and Philippe C. Schmitter (1984). 'Community, Market, State and Associations; The Prospective Contribution of Interest Governance to Social Order', Florence, Italy: The European University Institute. Working Paper 94.
Useem, Michael (1984). *The Inner Circle: Large Corporations and the Rise of Business Political Activity in the U.S. and U.K.* New York: Oxford University Press.
Vander Schaaf, James F. (1984). 'The National Milk Producers Federation: Building a Consensus and the Problem of Regionalism'. Unpubished paper. Madison: University of Wisconsin.
Wardell, W.M. (1979). 'The History of Drug Discovery, Development, Regulation', in R.I. Chien (ed.), *Issues in Pharmaceutical Economics*. Cambridge, Mass.: Lexington Books.
Wardell, W.M. and L. Lasagna (1975). *Regulation and Drug Development*. Cambridge, Mass.: Lexington Books.
Weick, Karl (1980). *The Theory of Social and Economic Organizations*. New York: Free Press.
Williamson, Oliver E. (1975). *Markets and Hierarchies*. New York: Free Press.
Williamson, Oliver E. (1981) 'The Economics of Organization: The Transaction Cost Approach', *Administrative Science Quarterly*, 26: 548-77.
Young, Brigitta, Leon Lindberg and J. Rogers Hollingsworth (1985). 'The Governance of the American Dairy Industry: From Regional Dominance to Regional Cleavage'. Unpublished paper presented before Conference on Regionalism, Business Interests and Public Policy.
Zysman, John (1983). *Governments, Markets, and Growth*. Ithaca: Cornell University Press.

Bibliography

Accounting Standards Committee (1978) *Setting Accounting Standards: A Consultative Document*. Accounting Standards Committee.

Accounting Standards Committee (1979) *Submissions on the Accounting Standards Committee's Consultative Document: Setting Accounting Standards* (2 vols.) London: Accounting Standards Committee of the Consultative Committee of Accountancy Bodies.

Accounting Standards Committee (1981) *Setting Accounting Standards*. London: Accounting Standards Committee of the Consultative Committee of Accountancy Bodies.

Accounting Standards Committee (1983) 'Review of the Standard Setting Process', *Accountancy*, July: 115 – 20.

Ackermann, C. (1981) 'Die Ausbildungsreglementierung für Lehrberufe, Falluntersuchungen über verbandliche Selbstregulierung und staatliche Steuerung in der Berufsausbildung'. Projektbericht Nr. 16 zum *Forschungsprojekt Parastaatliche Verwaltung: Die Erfüllung öffentlicher Aufgaben durch private und halbstaatliche Institutionen*, Institut für Orts, Regional- und Landesplanung der Eidgenössischen Technischen Hochschule Zürich, September 1981.

Adams, W. (1971) *The Structure of American Industry*. New York: The Macmillan Co.

Aitken, M. and J. Hage (1971) 'The Organic Organisation and Innovation', *Sociology*, 5(1): 63-82.

Aldrich, H. (1979) *Organizations and Environments*. Englewood Cliffs, N.J.: Prentice Hall.

Anderson, C.W. (1977) 'Political Design and the Representation of Interests', *Comparative Political Studies*, 10: 127 – 52. Also in Schmitter and Lehmbruch (eds) (1979).

Argyris, C. and D.A. Schon (1978) *Occupational Learning: A Theory of Action Perspective*. Reading, Mass.: Addison-Wesley.

Ashton, R.K. (1983) *U.K. Financial Accounting Standards*. Cambridge: Woodhead-Faulkner.

Astley, W.G., R. Axelsson, R.J. Butler, D.J. Hickson and D.C. Wilson (1982) 'Complexity and Cleavage: Dual Explanations of Strategic Decision Making', *Journal of Management Studies*, 19: 357 – 75.

Atkinson, M.M. and W.D. Coleman (1985) 'Corporatism and Industrial Policy' in Alan Cawson (ed.), *Organized Interests and the State: Studies in Meso-Corporatism*. Beverly Hills and London: Sage.

Bachrach, P. and M.S. Baratz (1970) *Power and Poverty: Theory and Practice*. Oxford: Oxford University Press.

Bauer, M., and E. Cohen (1983) *Qui governe les Groupes Industriels?* Paris: Seuil.

Baxter, W.T. (1981) 'Accounting Standards — Boon or Curse?', *Accounting and Business Research*, 12 (45): 3 – 10.

Beer, S.H. (1969) *Modern British Politics: A Study of Parties and Pressure Groups*. London: Faber (2nd edition).

Benson, J.K. (1975) 'The Interorganisational Network as a Political Economy', *Administrative Science Quarterly*, 20 (June): 229 – 49.

Berger, S. (ed.) (1981) *Organizing Interests in Western Europe: Pluralism, Corporatism and the Transformation of Politics*. Cambridge: Cambridge University Press.

Beudeker, G. (1963) 'Het Besluit Verpakte Geneesmiddelen', *Pharmaceutisch Weekblad*, 98: 814 – 26.

Beveridge, Sir W. (1942) *Social Insurance and Allied Services*. Report of the Departmental Committee later taken together with the Inter-departmental Committee on the Rehabilitation and Resettlement of Disabled Persons (the Tomlinson Report).

Bickers, K. (1984) 'U.S. Industrial Policy and the Institutional Organization of

American Industries'. Unpublished paper. Madison: University of Wisconsin.
Blau, P.M. (1955) *The Dynamics of Bureaucracy*. Chicago: University of Chicago Press.
Boddewyn, J.J. (1981a) 'Advertising Regulation, Self-Regulation and Self-Discipline Around the World', *Journal of International Marketing*, 1: 46 – 55.
Boddewyn, J.J. (1981b) 'The Global Spread of Advertising regulation', *MSU Business Topics*, Spring: 5 – 13.
Boddewyn, J.J. (1982) 'Advertising Regulation in the 1980s: The Underlying Global Forces', *Journal of Marketing*, Winter: 27 – 35.
Boddewyn, J.J L(1983a) 'Outside Participation in Advertising Self-Regulation: The Case of the Advertising Standards Authority (U.K.)', *Journal of Consumer Policy*, VI (1): 53 – 70.
Boddewyn, J.J. (1983b) *Outside Participation in Advertising Self-Regulation: Nature, Rationale and Modes*. Mimeograph. New York: Baruch College.
Boddewyn, J.J. (1983c) 'Belgian Advertising Self-Regulation and Consumer Organizations: Interaction and Conflict in the Context of the Jury d'Ethique Publicitaire (JEP)', *Journal of Consumer Policy*, VI (3): 303 – 23.
Boddewyn, J.J. (1984a) 'Outside Participation in Advertising Self-Regulation: The Case of the French Bureau de Vérification de la Publicité', *Journal of Consumer Policy*, VII(1): 45-64.
Boddewyn, J.J. (1984b) 'Outside Participation in Canadian Advertising Self-Regulation', *Canadian Journal of Administrative Sciences*, I(2): 215 – 31.
Boddewyn, J.J. (1984c) 'Developed Advertising Self-regulation in a Developing Country: The Case of Brazil's CONAR', XXXVIII (3), Winter: 15-93.
Boddewyn, J.J. (1985a) 'Advertising Self-Regulation: Private Government and Agent of Public Policy', *Journal of Public Policy and Marketing*, iv: 129–41.
Boddewyn, J.J. (1985b) 'The Swedish Consumer-Ombudsman System and Advertising Self-Regulation', *Journal of Consumer Affairs*, xix (1): 140–62.
Boddewyn, J.J. (1985c) 'Advertising Regulation: Fiddling with the FTC while the World Burns', *Business Horizons*, May-June: 32–40.
Booth, A. (1982) 'Corporatism, Capitalism and Depression in 20th Century Britain', *British Journal of Sociology*, 33 (2): 200 – 23.
Borrus, M., J.E. Millstein and J. Zysman (1983) 'Trade and Development in the Semiconductor Industry: Japanese Challenge and American Response', pp. 142 – 248 in J. Zysman and L. Tyson (eds), *American Industry in International Competition*. Ithaca: Cornell University Press.
Brasnett, M. (1969) *Voluntary Social Action: A History of the National Council of Social Service*. London: Bedford Square Press.
Bromwich, M. (1980) 'The Possibility of Partial Accounting Standards', *The Accounting Review*, LV (2): 288 – 300.
Bromwich, M. (1981) 'The Setting of Accounting Standards: The Contribution of Research' in M. Bromwich and A.G. Hopwood (eds), *Essays in British Accounting Research*. London: Pitman.
Bromwich, M. and A.G. Hopwood (1983) *Setting Accounting Standards: An International Perspective*. London: Pitman.
Brown, R. (1905) *A History of Accounting and Accountants*. Edinburgh: Blackwood.
Brussel, H. van (1979) 'De Invloed van het Georganiseerd Bedrijfsleven op de Uitvoering van de Sociale Versekering', *Social Maandblad Arbeid*, 34 (2): 241–7.
Burchell, S., C. Clubb, A. Hopwood, J. Hughes and J. Nahapiet (1980) 'The Role of Accounting in Organizations and Society', *Accounting Organizations and Society*, 5 (1): 5–27.
Burchell, S., D. Cooper and M. Sherer (1982) 'Conceptual Framework — One Step Forward, Two Back', *Accountancy*, May: 15.

Burns, T. and G. Stalker (1966) *The Management of Innovation.* London: Tavistock (first published 1961).
Butler, R.J. and D.C. Wilson (1985) *Markets and Voluntary Action as Alternatives to the Public Sector,* forthcoming.
Buxbaum, J.M. (1981) *The Corporate Politeia. A Conceptual Approach to Business, Government and Society.* Washington, DC: University Press of America Inc.
Campbell, J. (1984) *Can We Plan? The Political Economy of Commercial Nuclear Energy Policy in the United States.* Ph.D. Dissertation, Department of Sociology, University of Wisconsin, Madison.
Cawson, A. (1982) *Corporatism and Welfare.* London: Heinemann.
Cawson, A. (1984) *Macro, Meso and Micro-corporatism: Differing Levels of Analysis in the Theory of Neo-corporatism.* Working Paper, European University Institute, Florence, Italy.
Chandler, A.D. (1962) *Strategy and Structure.* New York: Doubleday.
Chandler, A.D. (1977) *The Visible Hand.* Cambridge, Mass.: Harvard University Press.
Chandler, A.D. and H. Daems (eds) (1980) *Managerial Hierarchies: The Rise of the Modern Industrial Enterprise.* Cambridge, Mass.: Harvard University Press.
Charities Digest (1984) *Annual Report of the Charities Aid Foundation.* Tonbridge, Kent: CAF Publications.
Chastney, J.G. (1975) *True and Fair View — History, Meaning and the Impact of the 4th Directive,* Institute of Chartered Accountants in England and Wales Research Committee Occasional Paper No. 6.
Cherrington, J. (1979) *On the Smell of an Oily Rag: My 50 Years of Farming.* London: Northwood.
Child, J. (1976) 'Organisations: A Choice for Man', pp. 234–57 in J. Child (ed.), *Man and Organisation.* London: Allen and Unwin.
Chirot, D. (1980) 'The Corporatist Model and Socialism', *Theory and Society,* 9 (2): 363–81.
Christiansen, G.B. and R.A. Haveman (1982) 'Government Regulations and Their Impact on the Economy', pp. 112–23, in J.R. Hollingsworth (ed.) *Government and Economic Performance.* Beverly Hills: Sage Publications.
Clegg, S., G. Dow and P. Boreham (eds) (1983) *The State, Class and the Recession.* London: Croom-Helm.
Clegg, S. and D. Dunkerley (eds) (1980a) *The Interntional Yearbook of Organization Studies.* London: Routledge and Kegan Paul.
Clegg, S. and D. Dunkerley (1980b) *Organisation, Class and Control.* London: Routledge and Kegan Paul.
Coleman, W.D. and H.J. Jacek (1983) 'The Roles and Activities of Business Interest Associations in Canada', *Canadian Journal of Political Science,* 16: 257–80.
Commissie Alternatieve Geneeswijzen (1981) *Alternatieve Geneeswijzen in Nederland.* 's-Gravenhage: Statsuitgeverij.
Consumentenbond (1983) 'Kruidenmiddelen', *Consumentengids,* 31 (1): 4–7.
Cooper, D.J. and M.J. Sherer (1984) 'The Value of Corporate Accounting Reports: Arguments for a Political Economy of Accounting', *Accounting, Organizations and Society,* 9 (2/4): 207–32.
Council of Europe (1972) *Resolution (72) 8 on Consumer Protection Against Misleading Advertising.* Strasbourg, France.
Crouch, C. (1979) 'The State, Capital and Liberal Democracy' in C. Crouch (ed.), *State and Economy in Contemporary Capitalism.* London: Croom Helm.
Crouch, C. (1981) *State, Market and Organization: A Classification of the Contri-*

bution of Neo-Corporatist Theory. Mimeo. Forthcoming, in an Italian translation, in Stato e Mercato.

Crouch, C. and A. Pizzorno (eds) (1978) *The Resurgence of Class Conflict in Western Europe since 1968*. 2 vols. London: Macmillan.

Czada, R. and W. Dittrich (1980) 'Politisierungsmuster zwischen Staatsintervention und gesellschaftlicher Selbstverwaltung', pp. 195 – 226 in V. Ronge (ed.), *Am Staat vorbei. Politik der Selbstregulierung von Kapital und Arbeit*. Frankfurt/M.-New York: Campus.

Dahl, R.A. (1982) *Dilemmas of Pluralist Democracy. Autonomy versus Control*. New Haven and London: Yale University Press.

Derber, M. (1984) 'Employers Associations in the United States', pp. 79 – 114 in J.P. Windmuller and A. Gladstone (eds), *Employers Associations and Industrial Relations: A Comparative Study*. Oxford: Clarendon Press.

De Wildt, G. (1984) 'De Waarde van een Gedragskode', *De Groene Amsterdammer*, 108(1): 9.

Dogterom, C.P. (1980) *Melk in Nederland, Grepen uit de Wordings Geschiedenis Van de Nederlandse Zuivel*. Den Haag: Kon.Nederlandse Zuivelbond FNZ.

Dyson K. and S. Wilks (eds) (1983) *Industrial Crisis*. Oxford: Martin Robertson.

Edey, H.C. (1977) 'Accounting Standards in the British Isles' in W.T. Baxter and S. Davidson (eds) *Studies in Accounting*. London: ICAEW (3rd edition).

Edwards, J.R. (1976) 'Accounting Profession and Disclosures in Published Reports, 1925-1935', *Accounting and Business Research*, Autumn. 289 – 303.

Eisenstadt, S.N. (1959) 'Bureaucracy, Bureaucratisation and Debureaucratisation', *Administrative Science Quarterly*, 4(3): 302 – 20.

European Advertising Tripartite (EAT) (1983) 'Self-Regulation and Codes of Practices', *Consumer Affairs* (London: J.W. Thompson), 61 (January – February) 13 – 18.

European Communities' Council of Ministers (1981) 'Council Resolution on a Second Programme (1981 – 1985) of the European Economic Community for a Consumer Protection and Information Policy', *Official Journal of the European Communities*, 3 June, C133/1 – 12 3.

European Consumer Law Group (ECLG) (1983) 'Non-legislative Means of Consumer Protection', *Journal of Consumer Policy*, VI(2): 209 – 24.

European Parliament (1980) 'Resolution Concerning an Action Programme of the European Community with Regard to Consumers', *Official Journal of the European Communities*, 10 November, C291/39 – 42.

Evenson, R.E. (1982) 'Agriculture', pp. 233 – 82 in R.R. Nelson (ed.), *Government and Technical Progress*. New York: Pergamon Press.

Farago, P., H. Ruf, F. Wieder (1984) 'Wirtschaftsverbände in der Schweizer Nahrungsmittelindustrie. Organisation und Aktivitäten von Verbänden der Milch, Fleisch und Obst/Gemüse verarbeitenden Industrien. Forschungsprojekt', *Die Organisation von Wirtschaftsinteressen in der Schweiz*, Bericht Nr. 1. Zürich: Soziologisches Institut der Universität Zürich. Typescript.

Ferraresi, F. (1983) 'The Institutional Transformations of the Post Laissez-faire State: Reflections on the Italian Case' in S. Clegg, G. Dow and P. Boreham (eds), *The State, Class and the Recession*. London: Croom-Helm.

Fiedler, F.E. (1967) *A Theory of Leadership Effectiveness*. New York: McGraw-Hill.

Freund, J. and F.J. Williams (1970) *Modern Business Statistics*. Revised by B. Perles and C. Sullivan. London: Pitman and Sons Ltd.

Garrett, A.A. (1961) *History of the Society of Incorporated Accountants 1885-1957*. Oxford: Oxford University Press.

Bibliography 259

Geluk, J.A. (1967) *Zuivelcoöperatie in Nederland. Ontstaan en Ontwikkeling tot omstreeks 1930.* Den Haag: Kon. Nederlandse Zuivelbond FNZ.
Gerboth, D.L. (1973) 'Research, Intuition and Politics in Accounting Inquiry', *The Accounting Review*, XLVIII(3): 475 – 82.
Giddings, P. (1974) *Marketing Boards and Ministers.* Farnborough: Saxon House.
Gilb, C.L. (1966) *Hidden Hierarchies. The Professions and Government.* New York and London: Harper and Row.
Goldstine, H.H. (1972) *The Computer from Pascal to Von Neumann.* Princeton: Princeton University Press.
Goldthorpe, J.H. (1985) 'The End of Convergence: Corporatist and Dualist Tendencies in Modern Western Societies' in J.H. Goldthorpe (ed.), *Order and Conflict in Contemporary Capitalism.* Oxford: Clarendon Press.
Gouldner, A. (1954) *Patterns of Industrial Bureaucracy.* New York: Free Press.
Grabowski, H.G. and J.M. Vernon (1982) 'The Pharmaceutical Industry', pp. 283 – 360 in R.R. Nelson (ed.), *Government and Technical Progress.* New York: Pergamon Press.
Grand Metropolitan (1983) *Annual Report.* London: Grand Metropolitan plc.
Grant, W. (1983a) 'Gotta Lotta Bottle: Corporatism, the Public and the Private and the Milk Marketing System in Britain'. Paper presented at the ECPR Joint Session, workshop on 'The Public and the Private', Freiburg, March 1983. *Sussex Working Papers on Corporatism*, No. 3, April 1983.
Grant, W. (1983b) 'The National Farmers Union: the Classic Case of Incorporation?', pp. 129 – 43 in D. Marsh (ed.), *Pressure Politics.* London: Junction Books.
Gupta, A.K. and L.J. Lad (1983) 'Industry Self-Regulation: An Economic, Organizational and Political Analysis', *Academy of Management Review*, VIII(3): 416-25.
Hage, J. (1980) *Theories of Organizations: Forms, Process, and Transformation.* New York: John Wiley and Sons.
Hage, J. and R. Clignet (1982) 'Coordination Styles and Economic Growth', pp. 72 – 92 in J.R. Hollingsworth (ed.), *Government and Economic Performance.* Beverly Hills: Sage Publications.
Hall, R.H. (1972) *Organizations: Structure and Process.* Englewood Cliffs, N.J.: Prentice Hall.
Hammergren, L. (1977) 'Corporatism in Latin American Politics', *Comparative Politics*, 9 (4): 443 – 61.
Hatch, S. and I. Mocroft (1979) 'The Relative Costs of Services Provided by Voluntary and Statutory Organizations.' *Public Administration*, 57 (Winter): 397 – 406.
Herder-Dorneich, P. (1973) 'Verbände im Wahlsystem-Verbandswahlen', pp. 163-188 in Ph. Herder-Dorneich, *Zur Verbandsökonomik. Ansätze zu einer ökonomischen Theorie de Verbände.* Berlin: Duncker und Humblot.
Herman, E.S. (1981) *Corporate Control, Corporate Power.* New York: Cambridge University Press.
Hickson, D.J., R.J. Butler, D. Cray, G.R. Mallory and D.C. Wilson (1985) *Top Decisions: Strategic Decision in Organizations.* Oxford: Blackwell and San Francisco: Jossey-Bass.
Hirschman, A.O. (1970) *Exit, Voice and Loyalty.* Cambridge, Mass.: Harvard University Press.
Hope, T. (1979) 'Accounting Policy: Theory of Pragmatism. Or Both?' in Accounting Standards Committe (1979), pp. 541 – 67.
Hope, T. and R. Gray (1982) 'Power and Policy Making: The Development of an R and

D Standard', *Journal of Business Finance and Accounting*, 9(4): 531 – 58.
Hopkins, L. (1980) *The Hundredth Year*, London: Macdonald and Evans.
Hopwood, A.G. (1974) *Accounting and Human Behaviour*, London: Haymarket.
Hopwood, A.G., S. Burchell and S. Clubb (1979) 'The Development of Accounting in the International Context' in A. Roberts (ed.), *An Historical and Contemporary Review of the Development of International Accounting*. Georgia State University.
Hopwood, A.G. (1983) "On Trying to Account for Accounting – Commentary upon W. Beaver's 'Research on Monitoring the Accounting Standard Setting Process" in M. Bromwich and A.G. Hopwood (eds), *Accounting Standards Setting; An International Perspective*. London: Pitman, 1983.
Horngreen, M. (1982) 'The Marketing of Accounting Standards', *The Journal of Accountancy*, October: 61 – 6.
Hughes, C.T. (1973) 'Corporatism and Development: The State and Interorganisational Relations', ISA 10th World Congress of Sociology, Mexico.
Hull, F. and J. Hage (1982) 'Organising for Innovation: Beyond Burns and Stalker's Organic Type', *Sociology* 16(4): 564 – 77.
Hurd, C. (1980) 'Computer Development at IBM', in N. Metropolis, J. Howlett and G. – C. Rota (eds), *A History of Computing in the Twentieth Century*. New York: Academic Press.
Institute of Chartered Accountants in England and Wales (1976) *The Corporate Report: An Academic View*, Research Committee Occasional Paper No. 8.
Institute of Chartered Accountants in England and Wales (1979) *Accounting Standards*.
Institute of Chartered Accountants in England and Wales (1982) *Accounting Standards*.
International Chamber of Commerce (1978) *Marketing: Discipline for Freedom*. Paris.
Jacobsson, B. (1983) 'Organized Interests and Political Control'. Paper presented at the Sixth EGOS Colloquium, Florence, 3 – 5 November 1983.
Jamous, H. and B. Peloille (1970) 'Changes in the French University-Hospital System' in J.A. Jackson (ed.), *Professions and Professionalization*. Cambridge University Press.
Jessop, B. (1979) 'Corporatism, Parliamentarism and Social Democracy' in P.C. Schmitter and G. Lehmbruch (eds), *Trends Towards Corporatist Intermediation*. London: Sage.
Johnson, N. (1981) *Voluntary Social Services*. Oxford: Blackwell and Robertson.
Johnson, T. (1980) 'Work and Power' in G. Esland and G. Salaman (eds), *The Politics of Work and Occupations*. Milton Keynes: The Open University Press.
Jones, E. (1981) *Accountancy and the British Economy 1840 – 1980: The Evolution of Ernst and Whinney*, London: Batsford.
Katz, B.G. and A. Phillips (1982) 'The Computer Industry', pp. 162 – 232 in R.R. Nelson (ed.), *Government and Technical Progress*. New York: Pergamon Press.
Katzenstein, P. (ed.) (1978) *Between Power and Plenty*. Madison: University of Wisconsin Press.
Kerr, C., J.T. Dunlop, F.H. Harbin and C. Myers (1971) *Industrialism and Industrial Man*. London: Penguin.
Korinek, K. (1976) 'Die Realisierung der Idee der Sozialpartnerschaft in der österreichischen Rechtsordnung', *Wirtschaftspolitische Blätter*, 23(4): 66 – 78.
Kostecki, M. (1981) 'Revolt of the Incapacitated', *5th EGOS Colloquium*, Glasgow.
Kurth, J. (1979) 'The Political Consequences of the Product Cycle: Industrial History and Political Outcomes', *International Organization*, 33: 1 – 34.

LaBarbera, P. (1980) 'Advertising Self-Regulation: An Evaluation', *MSU Business Topics*, Summer: 55 – 63.
Lafferty, M. (1979) 'How Good are the Standards We Now Have?' in R. Leach and E. Stamp (eds), *British-Accounting Standards: The First Ten Years*. Cambridge: Woodhead-Faulker.
Lakoff, S.A. and D. Rich (eds.) (1973) *Private Government*. Glenview, Illinois: Scott, Foresman and Company.
Lang, R.W. (1974) *The Politics of Drugs: A Comparative Pressure-Group Study of the Canadian Pharmaceutical Manufacturers Group and the Association of the British Pharmaceutical Industry*. Farnborough: Saxon House.
Lawrence, P.R. and J.W. Lorsch (1967) *Organization and Environment*. Cambridge, Mass.: Harvard University Press.
Lawrence, P.R. and D. Dyer (1983) *Renewing American Industry*. New York: The Free Press.
Leach R. and E. Stamp (1979) *British Accounting Standards: The First Ten Years*. Cambridge: Woodhead-Faulker.
Leat, D., G. Smolka and J. Unell (1981) *Voluntary and Statutory Collaboration: Rhetoric or Reality*? London: Bedford Square Press.
Lee, G.A. (1975) 'The Concept of Profit in British Accounting, 1760 – 1900', *Business History Review* XLIX (1): 6 – 36.
Lee, T.A. (1980) 'The Accounting Entity Concept, Accounting Standards and Inflation Accounting', *Accounting and Business Research*, Spring: 176 – 86.
Lehmbruch, G. (1977) 'Liberal Corporatism and Party Government', *Comparative Political Studies*, 10: 91 – 126. Also in Schmitter and Lehmbruch (eds) (1979).
Lehmbruch, G. (1982) 'Neo-Corporatism in Comparative Perspective' in G. Lehmbruch and P.C. Schmitter (eds) (1982).
Lehmbruch, G. and P.C. Schmitter (eds) (1982) *Patterns of Corporatist Policy-Making*. Beverly Hills and London: Sage Publications.
Levin, R.C. (1982) 'The Semiconductor Industry', pp. 9 – 100 in R.R. Nelson (ed.), *Government and Technical Progress*. New York: Pergamon Press.
Lowe, E.A. amd A.M. Tinker (1977) 'Siting the Accounting Problem: Towards an Intellectual Emancipation of Accounting', *Journal of Business Finance and Accounting*, 4(3): 263 – 76.
Lowi T. (1979) *The End of Liberalism*. New York: W.W. Norton (first publication 1969).
Luhmann, N. (1969) *Legitimation durch Verfahren*. Neuwied am Rhein und Berlin: Luchterhand.
Luhmann, N. (1981) *Politische Theorie im Wohlfahrtsstaat*. München: Piper.
Lukes, S. (1974) *Power: A Radical View*. London: Macmillan.
Macauley, S. (1983) *Private Government*. DPRP Working Paper, 1983 – 6, University of Wisconsin-Madison.
McConnell, G. (1966) *Private Power and American Democracy*. New York: Alfred C. Knopf.
Macve, R.H. (1981) *A Conceptual Framework for Financial Accounting and Reporting: The Possibilities for an Agreed Structure*, London: Institute of Chartered Accountants in England and Wales.
Magaziner, I.C. and R.B. Reich (1982) *Minding America's Business*. New York: Harcourt, Brace, Jovanovich.
March, J. and H. Simon (1958) *Organizations*. New York: John Wiley.

Marin, B. (1982) *Die Paritätische Kommission. Aufgeklärter Technokorporatismus in Österreich*. Wien: Internat. Publikationen.
Mintzberg, H. (1979) *The Structuring of Organizations*. New York: Prentice-Hall.
Mayntz, R. (1983) 'The Conditions of Effective Public Policy: A New Challenge for Policy Analysis', *Policy and Politics*, 11: 123 – 43.
Millerson, G. (1964) *The Qualifying Associations. A Study in Professionalization*, London: Routledge and Kegan Paul.
Ministerie van Landbouw en Visserij (1983) *Regelen met Betrekking tot Diergeneesmiddelen. Memorie van Toelichting* (Kamerstukken 17764). 's-Gravenhage: Staatsuitgeverij.
Moonitz, M. (1974) *Obtaining Agreement on Standards in the Accounting Profession*, American Accounting Association, Studies in Accounting Research No. 8.
Mowery, D.C. and N. Rosenberg (1982) 'The Commercial Aircraft Industry', pp. 101 – 61 in R.R. Nelson (ed.), *Government and Technical Progress*. New York: Pergamon Press.
Mrela, K. (1981) 'Alternative Organisations within an Institutional Structure of Policy Society', 5th EGOS Colloquium, Glasgow.
Mumford, M.J. (1978) 'Watts on "What's What"', *Certified Accountant*, December: 381 – 86.
Munneke, H.F., J.B.J.M.ten Berge, F.A.M. Stroink, P. Haighton and P.den Hoed (1983) *Organen en Rechtspersonen rondom de Centrale Overheid*. Den Haag: Statsuitgeverij.
National Council for Voluntary Organizations (1983) *Government Influence on Voluntary Organizations*. Working paper, London: Bedford Square Press.
National Council for Voluntary Organizations (1984) *Relations Between the Voluntary Sector and Government: A Code for Voluntary Organizations*. Working paper, London: Bedford Square Press.
Neelankavil, J.P. and A.B. Stridsberg (1979) *Advertising Self-Regulation: A Global Perspective*. New York: Hastings House.
NEFARMA (1977 – 79) *Annual Reports*. Utrecht.
Nelson, R.R. (ed.) (1982) *Government and Technical Progress. A Cross-Industry Analysis*. New York: Pergamon Press.
Nelson, R.R., M.J. Peck, E.D. Kalachek (1967) *Technology, Economic Growth, and Public Policy*. Washington, D.C.: The Brookings Institute.
Niekerk, G.L.P.van (ed.) (1978) *Wet op de Bedrijfsorganisatie*. Deventer: Kluwer.
Offe, C. (1975) 'Überlegungen und Hypothesen zum Problem politischer Legitimation'. Beitrag zum Duisburger Kongreß der DVPW (1975). Mimeo.
Offe, C. (1981) 'The Attribution of Public Status to Interest Groups. Observations on the West German Case', pp. 123 – 58 in S. Berger (ed.), *Organizing Interests in Western Europe*. Cambridge: Cambridge University Press.
Offe, C. (1983) 'Competitive Party Democracy and the Keynsian Welfare State; Some Reflections on Their Historical Limits' in S. Clegg, G. Dow and P. Boreham (eds), *The State, Class and the Recession*. London: Croom-Helm.
Olsen, J.P. (1981) 'Integrated Organizational Participation in Government', pp. 492 – 516 in P.C. Nystrom and W.H. Starbuck (eds), *Handbook of Organizational Design*, vol. 2. Oxford: Oxford University Press.
Olson, M. (1965) *The Logic of Collective Action*. Cambridge: Harvard University Press.
Olson, M. (1982) *The Rise and Decline of Nations. Economic Growth, Stagflation and Social Rigidities*. New Haven and London: Yale University Press.

Oppenheimer, M. (1973) 'The Proleatianization of the Professional' in P. Halmos (ed.), *Professionalization and Social Change*, Monograph 20, University of Keele.
Ouchi, W.G. (1977)'Review of *Markets and Hierarchies* by O.E. Williamson', *Administrative Science Quarterly*, 22: 540 – 4.
Ouchi, W.G. (1980) 'Markets, Bureaucracies, and Clans', *Administrative Science Quarterly*. 25: 129 – 41.
Ouchi, W.G. (1984) *The M-Form Society*. Reading, Massachusetts: Addison Wesley Publishing Co.
Panitch, L. (1979) 'The Development of Corporatism in Liberal Democracies', pp. 119 – 46 in P.C. Schmitter and G. Lehmbruch (eds) (1979).
Panitch, L. (1980) 'Recent Theorizations of Corporatism: Reflections on a Growth Industry', *British Journal of Sociology*, 31: 159 – 87.
Parker, L.D. (1976) *The Reporting of Company Financial Results to Employees*, ICAEW Research Committee Occasional Paper No. 12.
Perks, R.W. and L. Butler (1979) 'Accountancy Standards in Practice: The Experience of SSAP 2', *Accountancy and Business Research*, Winter: 25 – 33.
Perry, N. (1981) 'Information Brokerage and Organisational Dependence', *International Journal of Sociology and Social Policy*, 1 (3): 45 – 57.
Pharmaceutisch Weekblad (1977), 112.
Phillips, A. (1975) *Technology and Market Structure: A Study of the Aircraft Industry*. Lexington: D.C. Heath.
Pickering, J.F. and D.C. Cousins (1980) *The Economic Implications of Codes of Practice*. Manchester, England: University of Manchester Institute of Science and Technology, Department of Management Sciences.
Pike, F. and T. Stritch (1974) *The New Corporatism*. London: University of Notre Dame Press.
Piore, M.J. and C.F. Sabel (1984) *The Second Industrial Divide: Possibilities for Prosperity*. New York: Basic Books.
Pizzorno, A. (1978) 'Political Exchange and Collective Identity' in C. Crouch and A. Pizzorno (eds), vol. 2, 278 ff.
Pollard, S. (1965) *The Genesis of Modern Management*. Harmondsworth: Penguin.
Produktschap Zuivel (1980) *Jaarverslag 1980*. Rijswijk.
Pugh, D.J. and D.J. Hickson (1976) *Organisational Structure in its Context*. London: Saxon House.
Rae, J.B. (1968) *Climb to Greatness*. Cambridge, Mass.: MIT Press.
Reich, R.B. (1983) *The Next American Frontier*. New York: Times Books.
Reynders, L. and F. van Winden (1976), *De Farmaceutische Industrie in Nederland*. Amsterdam: SUA.
RGA (1974) *Nederlandse Code voor de Aanprijzing van Geneesmiddelen*. 's-Gravenhage: Staatsuitgeverij.
Ronge, V. (1980) 'Theoriestrategische Einführung: Quasi-Politik', pp. 11 – 29 in V. Ronge (ed.).
Roosenschoon, C.F. (1950) *Van Vader op Zoon. Gedenkboek uitgegeven ter Gelegenheid van het Vijftig Jarig Bestaan van de Algemene Nederlandse Zuivelbond*. Den Haag: Kon. Nederlandse Zuivelbond FNZ.
Roosenschoon, C.F. (1972) *Bakens in de Tijdstroom. Een Kenschets van de Bond van Coöperatieve Zuivelfabrieken in Friesland 1897 – 1972*. Leeuwarden: Bond van Coöperatieve Zuivelfabrieken in Friesland.
Ronge, V. (ed.) (1980) *Am Staat vorbei. Politik der Selbstregulierung von Kapital und Arbeit*. Frankfurt am Main: Campus.

Rooff, M. (1957) *Voluntary Societies and Social Policy*. London: Routledge and Kegan Paul.
Rothschild-Whitt, J. (1979) 'The Collectivist Organisation: An Alternative to Rational-Bureaucratic Models', *Administrative Science Quarterly*, 44 (August): 509–27.
Sagel, J. (1979) *Geneesmiddelenwetgeving*. Zwolle: Tjeenk Willink.
Schmitter, P.C. (1974) 'Still the Century of Corporatism?', *The Review of Politics*, 36: 85–131. Also in Schmitter and Lehmbruch (eds) (1979).
Schmitter, P.C. (1977) 'Modes of Interest Intermediation and Models of Societal Change in Western Europe', *Comparative Political Studies*, 10: 7–38. Also in Schmitter and Lehmbruch (eds) (1979).
Schmitter, P.C. (1982) 'Reflections on Where the Theory of Neo-Corporatism Has Gone and Where the Praxis of Neo-Corporatism May be Going' in G. Lehmbruch and P.C. Schmitter (eds).
Schmitter, P.C. (1983) 'Democratic Theory and Neo-Corporatist Practice'. *Working Paper* No. 74, Florence: European University Institute.
Schmitter, P.C. and D. Brand (1979) *Organizing Capitalists in the United States: The Advantages and Disadvantages of Exceptionalism*. Unpublished paper.
Schmitter, P.C. and G. Lehmbruch (eds) (1979) *Trends Towards Corporatist Intermediation*. New York and London: Sage Publications.
Schmitter, P.C. and W. Streeck (1981) 'The Organization of Business Interests. A Research Design to Study the Associative Action of Business in the Advanced Industrial Societies of Western Europe'. Discussion Paper IIM/LMP 81–13, Berlin: Wisenschaftszentrum.
Shackleton, K. (1977) 'Government Involvement in Developing Accounting Standards', *Management Accounting*, January and February (17–20); 73–6.
Sherif, M. (1962) *Intergroup Relations and Leadership, Approaches and Research in Industrial, Ethnic, Cultural and Political Areas*. New York: John Wiley.
Slimmings, W. (1979) 'The Scottish Contribution' in R. Leach and E. Stamp, *British Accounting Standards: The First Ten Years*. Cambridge: Woodhead-Faulker.
Solomons, D. (1978) 'The Politicization of Accounting', *The Journal of Accountancy*, November: 65–70.
Stacey, N. (1954) *English Accountancy: A Study in Social and Economic History: 1800–1954*, London: Gee.
Stamp, E. (1979) 'The Watts Report: An Uncertain Trumpet', *The Accountant's Magazine*, January: 10–661.
Stamp, E. (1980) *Corporate Reporting: Its Future Evolution*, The Canadian Institute of Chartered Accountants, Toronto.
Stamp, E. (1981a) 'Accounting Standards and the Conceptual Framework: A Plan for their Evolution', *The Accountant's Magazine*, July, 216–22.
Stamp, E. (1981b) 'A View From Academe' in R. Leach and E. Stamp, *British Accounting Standards: The First Ten Years*, Cambridge: Woodhead-Faulker.
Stamp, E. (1982) 'First Steps Towards a British Conceptual Framework', *Accountancy*, March, 123–30.
Stamp, E. and C. Marley (1970) *Accounting Principles and the City Code: The Case for Reform*, London: Butterworth.
Stichting Centraal Orgaan Zuivelcontrole (1983) *Statuten, Reglementen en Voorschriften*. IJmuiden: Kon. Vermande BV.
Streeck, W. (1972) 'Das Dilemma der Organisation. Tarifverbände zwischen Interessenvertretung und Stabilitätspolitik', pp. 130–67 in W. Meißner and

L. Unterseher (eds), *Verteilungskampf und Stabilitätspolitik*. Stuttgart-Berlin-Köln-Mainz: Kohlhammer.
Streeck, W. (1979) 'Gewerkschaftsorganisation und industrielle Beziehungen' in J. Matthes (ed.), *Sozialer Wandel in Westeuropa. Verhandlungen des 19. Deutschen Soziologentags*. Frankfurt am Main: Campus.
Streeck, W. (1982) 'Organizational Consequences of Corporatist Cooperation in West German Labor Unions', pp. 29 – 81 in G. Lehmbruch and P.C. Schmitter (eds).
Streeck, W. (1983a) 'Zwischen Markt und Staat. Interessenverbaende als Träger öffentlicher Politik', pp. 179 – 97 in F.W. Scharpf and M. Brockmann (eds), *Institutionelle Bedingungen der Arbeitsmarkt- und Beschäftigungspolitik*. Frankfurt am Main: Campus.
Streeck, W. (1983b) 'Die Reform der beruflichen Bildung in der westdeutschen Bauwirtschaft 1969 – 1982. Eine Fallstudie ueber Verbände als Träger öffentlicher Politik'. Discussion Paper IIM/LMP 83 – 23. Berlin: Wissenschaftszentrum.
Streeck, W., P. Seglow and P. Wallace (1981) 'Competition and Monopoly in Interest Representation', *Organization Studies*, 2: 307 – 30.
Teubner, G. (1978) *Organisationsdemokratie und Verbandsverfassung. Rechtsmodelle fuer politisch relevante Verbaende*. Tuebingen: Mohr.
Teubner, G. (1983) 'Substantive and Reflective Elements in Modern Law', *Law and Society Review*, 17: 239 – 85.
Thompson, D.L. (1983) 'Public-Private Policy: An Introduction', *Policy Studies Journal*, 11: 419 – 26.
Thompson, F. and L.R. Jones (1982) *Regulatory Policy and Practices: Regulating Better and Regulating Less*. New York: Praeger.
Thompson, J.D. (1967) *Organisations in Action*. New York: McGraw-Hill.
Thomson, P. (1983) 'Self-Regulation: Some Observations'. Mimeograph. London: Advertising Standards Authority.
Tinker, A.M. (1980) 'A Political Economy of Accounting', *Accounting, Organisations and Society*, 5 (1): 147 – 60.
Tinker, A.M. (1985) *Paper Prophets*. New York: Praeger.
Tinker, A.M., B.D. Merino and M.D. Niemark (1982) 'The Normative Origins of Positive Theories: Ideology and Accounting Thought', *Accounting Organisations and Society*, 7 (2): 167 – 200.
Tonkin, D. (1981) 'Politics and Accounting Standards', *Accountancy*, April: 133 – 4.
Traxler, F. (1981) 'Organisationsform des ÖGB und Wirtschaftspartnerschaft. Organisationsstrukturelle Bedingungen kooperativer Gewerkschaftspolitik', *Wirtschaft und Gesellschaft*, 7 (1): 29 – 52.
Traxler, F. (1982a) *Evolution gewerkschaftlicher Interessenvertretung. Entwicklungslogik und Organisationsdynamik gewerkschaftlichen Handelns am Beispiel Österreich*. Wien-Frankfurt/M.: Braumüller-Campus.
Traxler, F. (1982b) 'Zur Entwicklung kooperativer Arbeitsbeziehungen: Versuch einer Prozeßanalyse', *Zeitschrift für Soziologie*, 11 (4) 335 – 52.
Tweedie, D.P. (1983) 'The ASC in Chains: Whither Self-Regulation Now?', *Accountancy*, March: 112 – 20.
Udy, S. (1959) *Organisation of Work: A Comparative Analysis of Production Among Non-Industrial Peoples*. New Haven: HRAF Press.
United Nations, Economic and Social Council (1981 – 4) *Draft Guidelines for Consumer Protection*. New York.
Useem, M. (1984). *The Inner Circle: Large Corporations and the Rise of Business Political Activity in the UK and UK*. New York: Oxford University Press.
Van der Geest, S. (1984) 'Medicijngebruik in de Derde Wereld', *Intermediair*, 20 (5): 31 – 3.

Vander Schaaf, J.F. (1984) 'The National Milk Producers Federation: Building a Consensus and the Problem of Regionalism'. Unpublished paper. Madison: University of Wisconsin.
Van der Weele, M. (1981) 'De Bestuurlijke Organisatie van de Sociale Verzekeringen: Wetenschap of Belangenstrijd?', *Sociaal Maandblad Arbeid*, 36 (4): 323 – 32.
Van Hoepen, L. (ed.) (1948) *Van Veertig Zegenrijke Melkjaren 1908 – 1948*. Bussum: F.A.H. Kruyt.
Verkade, D.W.F. (1981) 'Geneesmiddelen en Merkenrecht', *Gezondheidsrecht*, 5: 133 – 55.
Voigt, R. (ed.) (1983) *Gegentendenzen zur Verrechtlichung*. Opladen: Westdeutscher Verlag.
Von Hayek, F.A. (1976 – 78) *Law, Legislation and Liberty. A New Statement of the Liberal Principles of Justice and Political Economy*. 3 vols. London: Routledge and Kegan Paul.
Walker, J. and R.H. Guest (1952) *The Man on the Assembly Line*. Cambridge, Mass.: Harvard University Press.
Wardell, W.M. (1979) 'The History of Drug Discovery, Development, and Regulation' in R.I. Chien (ed.), *Issues in Pharamaceutical Economics*. Cambridge, Mass.: Lexington Books.
Wardell, W.M. and L. Lasagna (1975) *Regulation and Drug Development*. Washington, DC: American Enterprise Institute.
Wassenberg, A. (1982) 'Neo-corporatism and the Quest for Control: The Cuckoo Game' in G. Lehmbruch and P.C. Schmitter (eds), *Patterns of Corporatist Policy Making*. London: Sage Modern Politics Series, vol. 7.
Watson, H.B. (1979) *Organizational Bases of Professional Status*. Doctoral Thesis, London School of Economics.
Watts, R.L. and J.L. Zimmermann (1978) 'Towards a Positive Theory of the Determination of Accounting Standards', *The Accounting Review*, LIII, 1: 112 – 34.
Watts, R.L. and J.L. Zimmermann (1979) 'The Demand for and Supply of Accounting Theories: the Market for Excuses', *The Accounting Review*, April: 273 – 305.
Watts, T. (1983) *The Role of the Accounting Standards Committee*. University College Cardiff Press.
Weetman, P. (1977) 'Accounting Standards: A Pause for Reflection', *Accounting and Business Research*, Summer: 168 – 76.
Weick, K. (1980) *The Theory of Social and Economic Organization*. New York: Free Press.
Weitbrecht, H. (1969) *Effektivität und Legitimität der Tarifautonomie*. Berlin: Duncker und Humblot.
Westwick, C.A. (1980) 'The Lessons to be Learned from the Development of Inflation Accounting in the U.K.', *Accounting and Business Research*, Autumn: 353 – 73.
Wiarda, H. (1974) *Politics and Social Change in Latin America*. Amherst: University of Massachusetts Press.
Wiarda, H. (1981) *Corporatism and National Development in Latin America*. Boulder, Colorado: Westview Press.
Williamson, O.E. (1975) *Markets and Hierarchies*. New York: Free Press.
Williamson, O.E. (1981) 'The Economics of Organization: The Transaction Cost Approach', *Administrative Science Quarterly*, 26: 548 – 77.
Willke, H. (1983) *Entzauberung des Staates: Ueberlegungen zu einer sozietalen Steuerungstheorie*. Koenigstein: Athenaeum.
Willmott, H.C. (1983) 'Organizing the Profession: A Sociological History of the

Segmented Development of the Accountancy Bodies in the U.K. 1880 – 1980', forthcoming in *Accounting, Organizations and Society*.
Wilson, D.C. (1984) 'Charity Law and the Politics of Regulation in the Voluntary Sector'. King's Counsel, vol. 34, forthcoming.
Wilson, D.C. and R.J. Butler (1983) 'Voluntary Organizations in Action; Strategic Choice in the Voluntary Sector.' Working paper no. 2, *Markets and Voluntary Action as Alternatives to the Public Sector*, University of Bradford Management Centre.
Wilson, D.C., R.J. Butler, D. Cray, D.J. Hickson and G.R. Mallory (1982) 'The Limits of Trade Union Power in Organizational Decision Making', *British Journal of Industrial Relations*, 20: 322 – 41.
Wilson, J.Q. (1974) 'The Politics of Regulation', pp. 135 – 68 in J.W. McKie (ed.), *Social Responsibility and the Business Predicament*. Washington.
Winkler, J. (1976) 'Corporatism', *European Journal of Sociology*, 17 (1): 100 – 36.
Winkler, J. (1977) 'The Corporatist Economy', pp. 43 – 58 in R. Scase (ed.), *Industrial Society: Class, Cleavage and Control*. London: Allen and Unwin.
Winter, M. (1983) *Corporatism in Agriculture — State Relations: The Role of the Milk Marketing Board*. Paper presented at the annual conference of the British Sociological Association, April 1983.
Wolfe, A. (1977) *The Limits of Legitimacy*. New York: Free Press.
Wolfenden, L. (1978) *The Future of Voluntary Organizations: Report of the Wolfenden Committee*. London: Croom-Helm.
Wolffers, I. (1983) *Medicijnen: Een Handleiding voor de Consument*. Amsterdam: Bert Bakker.
Wood, S. (1979) 'A Reappraisal of the Contingency Approach to Organisation', *Journal of Management Studies*, 16 (3): 334 – 54.
Woodward, J. (1958) *Management and Technology*. London: HMSO.
Woodward, J. (1965) *Industrial Organisation, Theory and Practice*. London: Oxford University Press.
WRR (Wetenschappelijke Raad voor het Regeringsbeleid) (1983) *Organen en Rechtspersonen rondom de Centrale Overheid*. 's-Gravenhage: Staatsuitgeverij.
Yamey, B.S. (1978) *Essays on The History of Accounting*. London: Arno.
Young, B. (1984) *The American Dairy Sector*. Unpublished paper. Madison: University of Wisconsin.
Zeff, S.A. (1971) *Forging Accounting Principles in Five Countries: A History and an Analysis of Trends*. University of Edinburgh.
Zeff, S.A. (1979) 'Setting Accounting Standards in the United Kingdom — An American View' in R. Leach and E. Stamp (eds), *British Accounting Standards: The First Ten Years*. Cambridge: Woodhead-Faulker.
Zey-Ferrell, M. (1981) 'Criticisms of the Dominant Perspectives on Organisations', *Sociological Quarterly*, 22 (2): 181 – 205.
Zuivelcontrole Instituut (1982) *Jaarverslag 1982*. Leusden.
Zysman, J. (1983) *Governments, Markets, and Growth*. Ithaca: Cornell University Press.

Index

Accountancy 48
Accountant, The 48
Accounting standard setting in UK 44–5, 48–50, 63–7: accounting as exemplar of associative model 65; background of self-regulation 45; establishment and segmentation of professional associations 47–8; influenced by pressure from industry 64; lack of mechanism to enforce standards 64–5; legal system and stimulus for self-regulation 46; nineteenth-century scandals and 46; organization and development of ASC 51–4; political perspective on accounting practice and 58–60; question of needs of society and 67; scandals of 1960s and 1970s and 63; technical perspective on accounting practice and 54–8; with reference to legitimation of authority 60–3
Accounting Standards Committee (ASC), UK 63, 66, 67: composition 51, 53; constitution and procedures 51–2; criticisms of 52, 58; on conceptual framework in accounting 56, 57, 64; on need for openness in standard setting 60–1; politics and 59–60; review of standard setting process 52–4; *Setting Accounting Standards* 46, 52, 53, 64; Statement of Standard Accounts Practice (SSAP) 52
Advertising self-regulation 31, 41–2: advertising industry's approach to 38–9; aspects of 35; private government or agent of government policy 33–4, 37–8; pure self-regulation 31–3, 34; role of advertising media 40–1; staff of self-regulating bodies 39–40; state involvement 40; strengths and weaknesses of regulation and self-regulation 36; types of controls 34
AEI-GEC takeover battle 49

Agricultural Marketing Act, 1931 183
Alcohol Education Centre 84
American economic governance 221: agriculture 229, 230, 231–2, 234; aircraft industry 242–3, 247; communications industry 244–5; construction industry 234; co-operatives 230; dairy industry 229–31; hierarchical activity 234, 235, 242–5 *passim*, 248, 251; large firms/high technology 225, 227, 228, 242–5, 246, 248, 249; large firms/low technology 225, 226–7, 235–8, 246, 249; lines of further research 251–2; literature on 222, 228–9; mainframe computer industry 243–4, 247, 251; manufacturing 234–5; nuclear power industry 245, 247; pharmaceutical industry 240–1, 247; role of agricultural research 232; role of associative behaviour 229, 231, 232, 234, 236, 238, 241, 242, 244, 245, 248–9; role of clans 229, 231, 232, 234, 236, 237, 239, 241–5 *passim*, 249–50; role of market 228, 229, 234, 237, 241, 244, 250; role of state 229–34 *passim*, 237–48 *passim*; semiconductor industry 239–40, 247; small firms/high technology 225, 227, 228, 238–42, 246, 248, 249, 250; small firms/low technology 225, 226, 227, 229–35, 246, 247, 249, 250; steel industry 251; typology of sectors of American economy 224–8
Amnesty International 81
Association of Certified Accountants (ACA) 50
Association of the British Pharmaceutical Industry (ABPI) 106: *ABPI News* 120; Board of Management 113; Code of Advertising Practice 113, 125; National Health Service Affairs Committee 115, 116; Negotiating

Committee 107, 109, 112, 114, 115, 122; PPRS Committee 122–3; role in PPRS 106, 109–26 *passim*
Associative model of social order 2–3, 4, 8–14, 65: basis 10; early advocates 8, 10; enabling conditions 10–11; interest stimulated by 14–15; lines of cleavage 14; medium of 11–12; motivational structure 12–13; properties 9, 12; public policy and 14–17
AT&T 244, 245
Austrian dairy industry: conditions of stability 154–63; decision-making process 158–60; economic-political goals 152; governing board (MWF) 152, 153, 156, 157, 160–6 *passim*; law governing (MOG) 151–2, 153, 154, 157, 158, 160, 161, 163, 164; number of firms in 165; 'Parity Commission for Wages and Price-Matters' 153, 157, 160, 163; political control of interest associations 153–4; Price Commission 157; private interest governance in 151–4; problem of overproduction 164; problem-solving capacity of system 163–7; professionalization of organizations running 160–1; Raiffeisen Co-operatives 155, 156; role of state in 161–3; turnover/cost relationship 165; wage and price fixing 157
Austrian organizations: Austrian Association of Chambers of Labour (ÖAKT) 153, 155–8 *passim*, 162, 166; Austrian Trade Union Federation (ÖGB) 153, 156, 157, 158, 160, 162, 166; Conference of the Presidents of Chambers of Agriculture (PWLWK) 152, 155–8 *passim*, 162; Conservative Party (ÖVP) 155; Federal Chamber of Trade and Industry (BWK) 152, 155–8 *passim*, 160, 162; ÖRV association 155; Social Democratic Party (SPÖ) 155; 'Social Partnership' system 160; Union of Manual Workers in the Food Industry 157; Union of Private White-Collar Workers 157

Beer, S.H.: theory of 'quasi-corporatism' 84
Belgian advertising regulation 38, 39
Bell Laboratories 239, 244
Beveridge Report, 1942 74
Bloom, John 49
Boddewyn, J.J. 31
Boeing aircraft company 243
British Advertising Standards Authority 32: advertising regulation 39
British Bangladesh Trust scandal 49
British Drug Houses 108
British milk marketing 182, 194–5: boards concerned with 182; conditions favouring corporatist policy-making 186–7; contribution of state 189–90; coping with instability 191–2; decontrol of liquid milk prices, 1984–5 193; how incorporation affects private governments 190–1; market structure 184–5; origins of scheme 183; problem of EEC cut back in milk production, 1984 194; questions and answers about 185, 195–6; reconciling representation with regulation 187–8; threat of UHT milk imports 193; threat to doorstep delivery 191; working of scheme 183–4; *see also* Milk Marketing Board for England and Wales
Burns, T. and Stalker, G. 88, 92, 103: *Management of Innovation, The* 96; political economy of 96–7; study of structural change in UK electronics industry 95–6, 97–102.
Butler, Richard, J. 72

Canada: advertising regulation 39, 40, 42; Consumer and Corporate Affairs Ministry 40
Cancer Research Campaign 84
Cawson, A. 77, 84: on voluntary co-operation in democracy 187–8
Chandler, A.D. 222, 235
Charity Commission 77: duties 79; influence 80, 81, 85; methods of control 82

Chartered Institute of Public Finance and Accounting (CIPFA) 50
Cherrington, John: on MMB 189–90
Child, J. 103
Ciba-Geigy Pharmaceuticals Ltd 122, 142
Ciba Laboratiries Ltd 112, 114
Committee of Enquiry into the Relationship of the Pharmaceutical Industry with the NHS (Sainsbury Committee), 1967 117, 119: Report 116
Committee of Public Accounts 106, 108, 111, 112, 116
Companies Act of 1862, UK 46
Consultancy Committee of Accounting Bodies (CCAB) 50, 51, 54, 65
Corporatism: collective private self-regulation under 213–14; 'societal' 197; 'state' 197; varieties of self-regulation 197–8
Corporatism in British voluntary sector 72–3, 84–6; influence of central government and Charity Commission 81–4. 85; relative influence of private associations and state agencies in decision-making 78–81; relative involvement of private associations and state agencies in decision-making 77–8 research into 72; sample and data on 75–7; self-regulation through associations 73-5
Council for the Security Industry 52
Council of Europe 37
Court Line Collapse 49

Dahl, R.A. 129
Dairy Trade Federaton (DTF) 186, 190–1: dispute with MMB, 1984, 192; income 190; Joint Committee with MMB 182, 185, 186, 189, 190, 191, 193
De-bureaucratization and private interest government 87, 103–4: associations' relations to state 93–4; attempt to shift from formal to substantive rationality 95; budgeting 88; changes in inter-organizational relations 89–92; devolution of decision-making 87; dissociation of levels 90–1; neo-corporatism and 92–4; off-loading of state activities 87–8; organic and mechanistic structure and 103; organizational structure changes 88–9, 94–6; political economy of Burns and Stalker and 96–7; reducing size of bureaucracy 88; studies concerning 97–102
Department of Health and Social Security (DHSS) 105, 119, 120, 121, 123, 124: negotiations concerning VPRS 117, 119, 121–2; Pharmaceutical Products Branch 123, 126
Department of Trade: concern for accounting standards 49, 63
Durkheim, Emile: concept of corporatism 8, 10
Dutch dairy industry 199: Butter Control Stations 207; Central Organ for Dairy Hygiene (COZ) 208; Central Organ for Milk Control (COM) 202, 203, 214; Cheese Control Stations 207; exports 199; importance to economy 199; Milk Control Stations 202–3; Milkpowder Control Station 207; preference for self-regulation 216, 217; private-assisted state regulation 206–13, 214; pure private regulation 200–1, 217; quality control of final products 206–8, 214, 215; quality control of raw materials 202–4, 215; Regional Organs for Milk Control (ROMs) 202, 203, 214; rise of public/private type of bureaucracy 219; social cohesion 216; social security regulations 209–12, 215, 216; STA (statutory trade association) 202, 203, 204–6, 209, 214, 215; state-assisted private regulation 202-6, 214, 217; strength of co-operatives 199, 216; success of corporatist self-regulation 218–19; supervision of works councils 212–13, 215, 216; tendency to merge in 199; see also Netherlands
Dutch Organization for Pure Scientific Research (ZWO) 220

Index   271

Dutch pharmaceutical industry 132–5: associated pattern 134–5; associations of animal drug manufacturers 135; BIPA importers' association 134, 137, 140; complexity of self-regulation 146–7; composition 132; drug imports 133; FIDIN manufacturers' association for animal drugs 135, 146; KOAG advertising regulatory body 139, 140; market for drugs 132, 133; NEFARMA association, *see* separate entry; NEROPHARM manufacturers' association 134, 137, 140; PHC regulatory cartel 134, 136, 137, 140, 141; regulation of advertisement 138–42, 143, 144; regulation of animal drugs 144–6; regulation of product quality 136–8, 143, 144; regulation of animal drugs 144–6; regulation of product quality 136–8, 143, 144; responsible government ministries 132, 140; RGA advertising regulatory body 140, 141

Economic governance 221–4; associational behaviour and 223; concept of clans 222–3; concept of community 222; governance defined 221–2; hierarchy and 222, 223; literature on 222; markets 222
Electronics industry, UK: failure of Scottish firms 97, 99–102, 103; study of structural change in 95–6, 97–102; success of English firms 97, 98–9
European Advertising Tripartite 32: on advertising control 33
European Communities 37
European Economic Community (EEC): Advisory Committee on Management of Milk and Dairy Products 209; Committee of Family Associations (COFACE) 32
European Parliament 37
European University Institute, Florence 220
Express Dairies 184, 192

Fairchild company 239
Farago, Peter 168
Farmers' Weekly 193
Federation of Alcoholic Rehabilitation Establishments 84
Federation of Milk Marketing Boards 191
Ferranti 100–3 *passim*
Financial Times 189
FMC meat processing company 194
Food and Drinks Industries' Council 190
Food Manufacturers' Federation 190
France: advertising regulation 38, 39, 40; Institut National de la Consommation 39

Geigy company 114
General Electric 245
General Microelectronics 239
Gerboth, D.L.: on politics of accounting rules 59, 61, 62, 63
Giddings, P.: on marketing boards 190
Glaxo Laboratories 108
Grand Metropolitan 184, 192
Grant, Wyn 126, 182
Greenpeace 81
Groser, Manfred 126
Guiri 32

Hage, J. and Clignet, R. 222
Health Act, 1977: government power to fix price of medicines under 121, 124
Health Services and Public Health Act, 1968 116
Hegel: idea of associative order 8
Hoffman-La Roche 120
Hollingsworth, J. Rogers 221
Home Office Voluntary Services Unit (VSU) 75
Hope, T.: on setting accounting standards 60, 61
Hope, T. and Gray, R.: on industry's pressure on ASC 64
Housing Act, 1974 75
Hughes, Michael 87

IBM 245: reasons for success 251

ICI 108
Imperial Cancer Research Fund 84
Inland Revenue 77: influence 80; 'policing' of charities 79, 81
Institute of Chartered Accountants in England and Wales (ICAEW) 46: *Corporate Report, The* 64, 67; creates Accounting Standards Steering Committee (ASSC) 50, 65; fails to integrate acountancy bodies 48; merges with SIA 47; reforms of accounting standards 49–50; *Statement of Intent on Accounting Standards in the 1970s* 49
Institute of Chartered Accountants in Ireland (ICAI) 50
Institute of Chartered Accountants of Scotland 48, 50: joins ASSC 50
Institute of Cost and Management Accountants (ICMA) 50
Intel 239
International Chamber of Commerce 33: International Code of Advertising Practice 37; on advertising regulation 37
International Federation of Pharmaceutical Manufacturers Associations (IFPMA) 134: 'Code of Pharmaceutical Marketing Practices' 142

Japan: clan-like business ties 236

Keynes, John Maynard: search for new social order 10
Kurth, J.: on state's role in USA 237

Lang, R.W.: on mutual dependency of ABPI and DHSS 118; on VPRS negotiations 115–16
Lawrence, P.R. and Dyer, D. 222
Leat, D., Smolka, G. and Unell, J.: on state influence on voluntary organizations 72
Lehmbruch, G.: view of British corporatism 74, 81
Levin, R.C. 239
Lindberg, Leon N. 221
Lockheed aircraft company 243

Lowi, T.J. 20: 'sponsored pluralism' concept 74

Macve, Prof. R.H.: investigates accounting framework 57
Mansholt, Sicco 205
Maxwell, Robert 49
May and Baker 108
Michels, Robert 3
Milk Marketing Board (MMB) for England and Wales 182, 195: butter, cheese and milkpowder manufacture 184; constitution 183–4; criticisms of 191, 194; Dairy Crest subsidiary 184, 195; democratic procedures 188; Disciplinary Committee 189; dispute with DTF, 1984 192; diversification by 194; Joint Committee with DTF 182, 185, 186, 189, 190, 191, 193; sale of milk to 184; success compared with other boards 186–7, 189, 190
Milk Producer 189, 192
Millerson, G.: on founding a professional association 47
Ministry of Agriculture: Consumer Committee 184, 189; fixing of milk prices 184–5; Milk Division 189
Ministry of Health: dispute with Pfizer Corporation 114; negotiations with pharmaceutical industry 108, 109, 112; role re supply of drugs etc. to NHS 107; *see also* Department of Health and Social Security
Ministry of Health and Social Services for Northern Ireland 105
Monopolies Commission: report on Roche Products' librium/valium case 120
Morrison, Mr: on accounting standards 48–9

National Association for the Care and Resettlement of Offenders 74
National Association of Citizens' Advice Bureaux 74
National Council of Social Service (NCSS) 73, 74
National Council for Voluntary Organizations (NCVO) 73, 75, 81, 82: state funding 83

National Council of Voluntary Youth Services 74
National Farmers' Union 188: Development Trust 194; Milk Marketing Scheme, 1933 183
National Health Service 84: attempts to limit drugs bill 107, 108; legal battle with Pfizer Corporation 113–14; Pharmaceutical Price Regulations Scheme (PPRS) and 105, 106, 115, 116, 119, 121, 124, 125
National Society for the Prevention of Cruelty to Children 81, 84
NEFARMA pharmaceutical association, Netherlands 134, 136, 142: 'Code of Behaviour' 140, 141–2; role 137–8
Netherlands: Act on Quality of Agricultural Produce, 1974 208; Act on the Export of Agricultural Produce, 1928 207, 208; Act on Works Councils, 1950 212; Butter Act, 1889 206; Councils of Labour 211; development of corporatism 218; FNZ co-operative national association 200; Food and Drugs Inspection Boards 203; Frisian Dairy Union 200–1, 215, 217; General Inspection Board 203–4; Ministry of Agriculture 203, 217; Quality of Agricultural Produce Act 203; 'Sector Associations' 209, 210; 'Sector Committees' 212; Social Economic Council 204, 212, 213; Social Security Organization Act, 1952 211; social security regulations 209–12, 216; supervision of works councils 212–13, 215, 216; *see also* Dutch dairy industry
Northern dairy company 184

Office of Fair Trading 32, 38, 40
Olson, M.: on state influence on voluntary bodies 85
Organon pharmaceutical company 142
Ouchi, W.G. 222: concept of clans 222–3
Oxfam 86

Pergamon-Leasco affair 49
Perry, N.: on mechanistic and organic management 96–7
Pfizer Corporation Ltd 112: legal battle with NHS 113–14
Pharmaceutical Price Regulations Scheme (PPRS) 105–6: background to 106–8; early oppositon to 111; method of operation 106; objectives 105; present version 121–3; relation to private interest government 123–6; voluntary nature to 1978 6; VPRS No. 1 108–11; VPRS No. 2 112–14; VPRS No. 3 115–16; VPRS No. 4 117–19; VPRS No. 5 119–21
Potato Board 187
Price Waterhouse 56
Private interest government 27–8 87, 150–1: aspects of quality regulation 131; concept of 16–17; conditions for in quality regulation 128–30; de-bureaucratization and, *see* separate entry; functional advantages 22–4; 'mixed mode' of policy-making under 25–7; organizational dynamics 17–21; organizations and political-organizational design 21; organizations and public status 19–20, 25–6; reasons for state facilitating private regulation 128; relation between organizations and interests 18–19; relation with community 27; relation with market model 26–7

Quadragesimo Anno, 1931 8
Queen in Council: petitioning the 47

Rerum Novarum, 1891 8
Roche Products Ltd 122: librium/valium case 120
Rolls Razor collapse 49
Royal National Institute for the Blind 81
Royal National Lifeboat Institution (RNLI) 82–3, 86

Sainsbury Committee, *see* Committee of

Enquiry into the Relationship of the Pharmaceutical Industry with the NHS
Saint-Simon, Comte de: idea of *associationnisme* 8
Sargent, Jane A. 105
Schmitter, Philippe, C. 1, 66, 81, 84, 221: defines types of corporatism 197, 213, 214
Schmitter, P.C. and Brand D.: on reasons why capitalists organize 249
Scottish Council 100, 101, 102
Scottish Dairy Trades Federation: disputes with Scottish MMB 192–3
Scottish Home and Health Department 105
Scottish Milk Marketing Board 182: disputes with Scottish DTF 192–3
Shaw, A.G. 126
Shelter 81
Shockley Transistor 239
Signetics 239
Social order: associative model, *see* separate entry; community model 1–8 *passim*, 11, 24, 66; market model 1–8 *passim*, 11, 23, 66; state model 1–8 *passim*, 11, 66
Society of Incorporated Accountants (SIA) 47: merges with ICAEW 47
Solomons, D.: anxiety about politicization of accountants 62; on technical perspective on accounting 54–5
Stamp, Edward: criticizes accounting standards 49; on politics on accounting standards 59–60
Stanford University, Cal. 239
Stock Exchange 52
Stonehouse, John 49
Streeck, Wolfgang 1, 66, 81, 126, 221
Streeck, W. and Schmitter, P.C. 222: concept of community 222
Sweden: advertising regulation 33, 40
Swiss dairy industry 168: Appenzeller cheese 175; Emmental cheese 168; cheese production 168–9; 'closed' regulation of cheese market 173–6; milk co-operatives 169–70; 'open' regulation of market for fresh milk products 176–7; organizations in 169–70; regulation of milk processing, *see* Swiss regulation of milk processing; structure 168–9; yoghurt 176
Swiss dairy organizations: Association of Box Cheese Manufacturers 169; Association of Ice Cream Manufacturers 169; Association of Milk Buyers 169, 173–4; Association of Soft Cheese Manufacturers 169, 175; BUTYRA (butter co-operative) 171, 173, 178; Central Association of Swiss Milk Producers (ZVSM) 169, 171, 173, 174, 175, 178; COOP consumer co-operative 170; Käseunion (Cheese Union) 171, 173–6 *passim*, 178; MIGROS consumer co-operative 170; 'Milk Group' of Association of the Swiss Food Processing Industry 169, 176; Regional Programme Commissions 171, 175; Special Commission on Milk 171, 178; Swiss Milk Commission 171
Swiss Federal Office of Agriculture 171, 173
Swiss regulation of milk processing 170–3, 177: authority to enforce 179–80; bodies running 171; corporatist arrangements 178, 180; cost effectiveness 178–9; heterogeneous structure of sector and 180–1; representation of interest organizations on semi-public boards 172

Teesdale, Mr: on VPRS in pharmaceutical industry 121–1
Thornton Baker 57
Times, The 49, 188
Touche Ross: on conceptual frameworks in accounting 57
Traxler, Franz 150
Treasury 108, 112

Unigate 184, 190, 194
United Nations 37: urges consumer protection 38, 42

Index   275

United States of America: American Farm Bureau Federation 232; Associated General Contractors Association 235; Business Council 236, 237; Capper-Volstead Act 230, 238; Committee on Economic Development 236; Community Credit Corporation 230, 231; Conference Board 236, 237; Council on Foreign Relations 236; Department of Agriculture 232, 238; Department of Commerce 238; Department of Defense 243; Department of the Army 243; Department of the Navy 243; Edison Electrical Institute 245; Electrical Power Research Institute 245; Financial Accounting Standards Board (FASB) 57; Food and Drug Administration 241, 242; NASA 239, 240; National Association of Home Builders 235; National Bureau of Standards 239, 243; National Cancer Institute Drug Development Program 241; National Farmers Union 232; National Science Foundation 239; Nuclear Power Forum 245; Orderly Marketing Agreements 233; State Agricultural Experiment Stations 232
University of California, Berkeley 239

Volkswagen Foundation 126
Vroom, Bert de 128

Waarden, Frans van 197
Walker, Peter 194
Wassenberg, A. 77, 84
Wellcome Foundation 108
Welsh Office 105
Western Electric 244
Western Union 244
Westinghouse Company 245
Williamson, O.E. 222
Willmott, Hugh 44
Wilson, David C. 72, 79
Wilson, J.Q.: on state intervention in quality regulation 131

Winter, M.: on milk collection 188; on MMB 190; on political significance of milk 195
Wolfe, A.: 'franchise state' concept 74–5
Women's Royal Voluntary Service 80
Wood, S.: criticizes Burns and Stalker 96
Wool Board 187
World Health Organization (WHO): code for pharmaceutical industry 142; Code of Marketing of Breastmilk Substitutes 33

Zysman, John: study of financial systems 229

Notes on contributors

J.J. Boddewyn is Professor of Marketing/International Business at the Baruch College of the City University of New York. His current research interests centre on the regulation and self-regulation of advertising around the world. He has also been working on international public affairs, business-government relations, foreign investment, and multinational service enterprises. He has a Ph.D. from the University of Washington (Seattle), and is a Fellow of the Academy of International Business.

Richard J. Butler is a Senior Lecturer in Organizational Analysis at the University of Bradford Management Centre, England. For a number of years he co-directed an extensive study of strategic decision-making in British organizations, the results of which are to be reported in a forthcoming book *Top Decisions* (Blackwell and Jossey-Bass, 1985). Other research includes projects on the strategy and structure of voluntary organizations, the strategy of firms in industries subject to de-regulation, and on processes of entrepreneurship.

Peter Farago is a researcher at the Sociological Institute of the University of Zürich. He has worked on social movements, public administration and interest organizations. He is co-editor of a forthcoming volume on *Wirtschaftsverbände in der Schweiz*.

Wyn Grant is Senior Lecturer in Politics and a member of the Institute for Employment Research at the University of Warwick. He is author of *The Political Economy of Industrial Policy* and *Independent Local Politics in England and Wales*, and co-author of *The CBI* and *The Politics of Economic Policymaking*.

J. Rogers Hollingsworth is Professor at the University of Wisconsin, Madison, holding positions in the Department of History, the Institute for Research on Poverty, and the LaFollette Institute for Public Policy. His publications in recent years have focused on American social policy and on the performance of the American economy.

Michael Hughes is Lecturer in the Department of Behaviour in Organizations and vice-chairman of the Board of Management and Organizational Sciences at Lancaster University. He holds a Visiting

Professorship in the Department of Management at Virginia Polytechnic Institute and State University. He has co-authored (with John Scott) a book on the anatomy of Scottish capital and has published on multinational corporations and corporate networks.

Leon N. Lindberg is Professor of Political Science at the University of Wisconsin, Madison. He has done research on the political economy of Western industrialized countries, in particular on the politics of inflation and economic growth. He is presently working at a project on 'Economists as Policy Intellectuals'.

Jane A. Sargent has recently submitted a Ph.D. thesis entitled 'The Pattern of British Interest Group Representation in The European Communities: Six Case Studies 1972–1982' to the University of London (London School of Economics and Political Science). Since May 1984 she has worked for the Retail Consortium, the peak association for the British retail trade, and is currently Executive Assistant to the Director General. In addition, she is working on several forthcoming publications arising from her Ph.D. research and from her participation in the international research project on business interest associations.

Philippe C. Schmitter is Professor of Political and Social Sciences at the European University Institute in Florence. Formerly he was at the University of Chicago and held a number of visiting appointments, among others at the International Institute of Management in Berlin.

Wolfgang Streeck is a Senior Fellow at the International Institute of Management in Berlin. He has worked and published on trade unions, business associations, political parties, industrial relations, manpower policy, and political theory.

Franz Traxler is *Wissenschaftlicher Assistent* at the Wirtschaftsuniversität, Vienna. He has done work in organizational sociology and industrial relations.

Bert de Vroom is a researcher at the Sociological Institute of the University of Leiden. He has done research on trade unions, consumer co-operatives and the steel and textile industry. For several years, he has been involved in the Dutch part of the international research project on business interest associations.

Frans van Waarden is currently working at the University of Leiden. He is responsible for the Dutch country study of the international research project on business interest associations. He has published on trade union policy, industrial democracy and corporatism and on the history of trade unions, the Dutch cotton industry and technology.

Hugh C. Willmott is a Lecturer in the Organisation, Personnel and Employment Division of the University of Aston in Birmingham, England. He has research interests in the areas of organization theory, management theory, labour process analysis, critical social theory and the philosophy of social science. He has conducted research into the welfare of the single homeless, the management of collective-democratic organization, and the organization and work of the professional–managerial class.

David C. Wilson is a Research Fellow in Organizational Analysis at the University of Bradford Management Centre, England. He has examined strategic decision-making in British organizations in an extensive study spanning the last ten years. Currently, he is co-director of a research project on the strategy and structure of voluntary organizations. He is also Editorial Assistant of the journal *Organization Studies*.